beyond

talk

Deaf Studies
Today! · 2012
www.deafstudies.org

Deaf Studies *Today!*

Beyond Talk

CONFERENCE PROCEEDINGS

UTAH VALLEY UNIVERSITY • OREM, UTAH
APRIL 11–14, 2012

Edited by Bryan K. Eldredge
and Doug Stringham

Deaf Studies *Today!*
A Professional Conference
at Utah Valley University
www.deafstudies.org

The biennial Deaf Studies *Today!* conference brings together the best and brightest minds in the interdisciplinary field of Deaf studies. Over three days, scholars from around the country (and beyond) present the latest research and thinking in the field in an environment conducive to the open exchange of ideas. Open to everyone interested in Deaf studies, including scholars, educators, students, Deaf people, and parents of deaf children, Deaf Studies *Today!* also aims to provide networking opportunities and promote Deaf-World interests.

Deaf Studies *Today!* includes presentations and workshops that cover a broad range of topics related to Deaf people, their language, culture, and associated issues. Presentations are based on original work and present current research/thinking relevant to the field of Deaf Studies, including but not limited to perspectives from anthropology, history, linguistics, interpretation and translation, education, psychology, sociology, public administration, political science, social work, philosophy, ethics, art, literature, American Sign Language instruction, and any number of other allied disciplines.

Proceedings of Deaf Studies *Today!* are published by the American Sign Language and Deaf Studies Program at Utah Valley University. Opinions expressed by the authors of these papers are their own and do not necessarily reflect those of the editors or of Utah Valley University. Authors are responsible for the accuracy of the references cited. While we have altered some terminology for consistency, use of the words '*Deaf*' or '*deaf*' in each paper also follows the authors' original manuscripts. American Sign Language-representative glosses are represented by small caps (e.g. DEAF, not 'deaf'). Deaf Studies *Today!* takes no responsibility for copyright infringements made by or in behalf of presenters or authors, and presenters agree to indemnify the publishers of Deaf Studies *Today!* against any illegal use of original artwork or creation.

The conference exists only because of the thousands of hours of work put forward by many different people. Most of those hours are volunteered by students and faculty at Utah Valley University. This work is dedicated to them.

2012 Proceedings Editors:

Bryan Eldredge, PH.D.
Chair, Deaf Studies *Today!* 2012
ASL & Deaf Studies at Utah Valley University

Doug Stringham, M.S.
Chair, Design & Publications
ASL & Deaf Studies at Utah Valley University

Table of Contents

Workshop Presenters

In addition to the presentation of academic papers, Deaf Studies *Today!* features workshops intended to inform and assist students and professionals in Deaf studies and those aimed at helping Deaf people. Workshops are generally hands-on in nature and take a how-to approach to subject matter. Workshop presenters do not submit papers for publication in the proceedings, but the conference organizers wish to recognize them for their contributions.

Beyond Words... Taking Action... Strategies for Deaf Studies Programs
JUDY FREEDMAN FASK & JOHN PIRONE

ASL Academic Village
MARY MCLERRAN

To Teach, or Not to Teach, That is the Question
KEITH GAMACHE, JR.

How to Study Abroad: Opportunities for Deaf/Signing Students
and Professionals in Italy
CHRISTINE BROWN

ASL Cinesthetic
MARIKA KOVACS-HOULIHAN

Minnesota Celebrates Our Deaf Heritage, Invest In our Future
DOUGLAS D. BAHL

Victim Advocacy: Using the EmPOWERment Model Through Language
STEPHANIE MATHIS

How to Link Complex English Constructs With
Complex ASL Construct and Vice Versa
CURT RADFORD, ED.D.

ASL and the US Census Bureau: What Happened With the 2010 Result?
What Can We Do?
BEN JARASHOW AND TRAVAS YOUNG

About Deaf Studies at Utah Valley University

In addition to being the home of Deaf Studies *Today!*, Utah Valley University (UVU) is home to a robust program in ASL & Deaf Studies.

Courses

Deaf Studies *Today!* is the creation of the American Sign Language and Deaf Studies Program at UVU in Orem, Utah. The UVU American Sign Language and Deaf Studies program is part of the Department of Languages. From its birth as a single beginning-level ASL class offered in the evening during the mid-1990s, the program has expanded to offer over fifty courses serving over 800 students each semester.

The program's course offerings range from beginning ASL courses to advanced classes in Deaf culture and history, Deaf literature, ASL grammar and linguistics, interpreting, Deaf-World discourse and much more.

Degrees

UVU offers five degree choices in Deaf Studies:

- Deaf Studies Major (B.A.)
  Emphasis 1: General Deaf Studies
  Emphasis 2: Interpreting
- ASL & Deaf Studies Education Major (B.A. — secondary education)
- A minor in Deaf Studies
- An ASL emphasis in Integrated Studies (B.A.)

Of course, many students majoring in other fields take ASL courses to fulfill the language requirements for B.A. degrees.

Information

More information about the UVU ASL & Deaf Studies Program is available at www.uvu.edu/asl.

About the 2012 Conference

The fifth Deaf Studies *Today!* Conference was held at Utah Valley University, Orem, Utah, April 11–14, 2012. Highlighting the conference were keynote addresses by distinguished scholars Patti Durr (Rochester Institute of Technology/National Technical Institute for the Deaf), Dr. Henry Klopping (California School for the Deaf, Fremont, retired), and Dr. Joseph J. Murray (Gallaudet University). The conference also featured the presentation of forty-five papers and workshops by sixty authors/presenters on topics ranging from signed language etymology to sociolinguistics to Deaf and ASL education and art.

Deaf Studies *Today!* was born out of a desire to bring scholars from the many disciplines comprising the field of Deaf Studies to a single academic conference. In addition to paper presentations, Deaf Studies *Today!* 2012 included a De'VIA panel and museum event, a Deaf "Night at the Movies" by David Pickett and Sean Christopher and a short ASL film festival, and panel discussions on deaf education, media perceptions of the Deaf-World by Mark Wood, and an ASL translation of the Bible by Linsay Darnall. The conference concluded with a special tribute to artist Chuck Baird prepared by Patti Durr and a live performance by Ben Jarashow.

Sponsors
Deaf Studies *Today!* expresses gratitude to Utah Valley University, The Office of the Academic Vice President, The School of Humanities, Arts, and Social Sciences, Interdisciplinary Studies, The Department of Languages and Conferences and Workshops who made this conference and these proceedings possible through their generous support.

Volunteers
Deaf Studies *Today!* would simply not exist were it not for the hundreds of hours of work volunteered by the students of Utah Valley University. They inspire us, and we give them our heartfelt thanks.

Stand and Be Counted Because You Count

PATTI DURR

Patricia Durr is an Associate Professor at RIT's National Technical Institute for the Deaf (NTID) in the Department of Cultural and Creative Studies. This address was given as a keynote address at Deaf Studies Today!*, April 2012.*

AS A MATTER OF INTRODUCTION, IT IS IMPORTANT TO NOTE THAT THIS keynote address was delivered in American Sign Language (ASL). Before embarking in the talk, I reminded the audience of how things "get lost in translation" as we move between two languages (ASL and spoken English) and diverse cultures. This is often unacknowledged, particularly when utilizing interpreters. This same reminder holds true when writing this paper, as the presentation was loaded with visual images and ASL video clips, which now have to be omitted or summarized into text English. It is my hope that the reader keeps in mind the ongoing translation negotiations while reading this paper. To see the power point slides for this presentation, please feel free to go to: https://handeyes.files.wordpress.com/2012/04/utah-2012-final.pdf.)

> "There are only two lasting bequests we can give our children: one is roots, and the other, wings." — Hodding S. Carter

Borrowing from a tradition I learned from Dr. Paddy Ladd, I decided to open the presentation with a "hats off" to a Deaf person who is no longer with us. I choose to honor Dr. Larry Fleischer, who is often referred to as the father of Deaf Studies, having carved out a space for the study of Deaf people at CSUN beginning in the late 1970s as a people instead of as "big ears and broken mouths." I open with a video clip of Dr. Fleischer telling us, in his own exquisite way and his flawless ASL, about the origins of Deaf Studies in academia. See https://www.youtube.com/watch?v=lgsR5jfS7F4

> So that 'cultural experience' which once was vague becomes illuminated. At CSUN we had a teacher-training program on how to teach Deaf children.

We taught them ASL, of course, but found it was not enough. We had to also teach them the culture. That was better but still not sufficient so we added and added and added and what ended up happening? We founded a BA in Deaf Studies because we ended up with so many courses it warranted a Bachelors degree. Now if we look at what our alumnus work experience was upon graduation then and now, we see quite a difference. Before they focused on their professional knowledge and by chance developed an interest in working with "the Deaf." They associated a bit with Deaf people, got their employment and were set in their ways for the rest of their career. Their attitude was pretty cemented. Now with that Deaf Studies degree at CSUN things have really changed. First they learned the language and the culture and learned of Deaf people "as a people" — a real bona fide "people" and then they considered what field they wanted to work in such as psychology or teaching or interpreting — who knows, they might even go off and work for a police department — its an unknown at the onset — but first off, they must come to know "the PEOPLE."

This clip tells us of the evolution of the field of deafness to the field of Deaf cultural studies and it parallels many of our own individual journeys to understanding ourselves as part of a Deaf whole. It also allows us to see how these roots gave way to our own wings.

DURR IN DIASPORA

I was solo mainstreamed in public school K–12 at a time before the Americans with Disabilities Act. In an elementary school class picture I can be seen seated front-and-center, as if placed there like a prop amongst all my hearing and speaking classmates. How many of us recall being physically moved from one place to another in elementary school as teachers fumbled, unable to communicate directions to us? Our state of agency was very low. Mine is all the more self-evident by my hands, shoved deep in my pockets, and my shy uncertain look at the camera. Do I smile now? Has the photographer already given the command to "say cheese?" Many of us can identify with that limbo state of not really knowing what is going on but going through the motions all the same, treading water in the mainstream.

My first grade report card consisted of mostly Is (for "Improving") or Ss (for "Satisfactory") except two Ns (for "Needs to Improve"). In what areas did I need to improve? In "Showing the ability to concentrate" and "Listens attentively." Ah, evidence of efforts to survive in the mainstream where *to hear* is all the rage. My third grade report card indicated that one of my teachers finally understood a wee bit of what it might be like to be partially Deaf in an all-hearing non-signing environment when she wrote my tenth week evaluation: "Patti does not always seem to concentrate well, but for her perhaps the strain of listening is very tiring. This may account for her attention wandering from time to time. She does seem concerned with getting her work completed."

| SOCIAL DEVELOPMENT AND WORK STUDY HABITS | | | | |

CODE

| S – SATISFACTORY |
| N – NEEDS TO IMPROVE |
| I – IMPROVING |

SOCIAL DEVELOPMENT	1	2	3	4
Works and plays well with others		S	S	S
Shows self control		S	S	S
Respects rights and property of others		S	S	S
Is courteous		S	S	S
Observes school regulations		S	S	S

WORK STUDY HABITS	1	2	3	4
Begins work promptly		S	S	S
Completes work on time		S	S	S
Uses leisure time well		S	S	S
Shows ability to concentrate		N	I	I
Is creative and resourceful		S	S	S
Listens attentively		N	N	I

My first grade report card

Most likely, I was trying to scavenger any visual information to clue me into what I was supposed to be doing when and how. Or, I was having interment moments where there was just too much guesswork and I went off to la la land. Eventually, I was drawn to trying to teach myself some ASL via a very old sign language book from the library. And while I was always a person of the eye, I came to become a person of the Hand too once I was no longer a solitaire and finally met other Deaf people in college. As Deaf leader and author J. Schuyler Long noted in his 1910 book *The Sign Language: A Manual of Signs*, "So long as there are two deaf people upon the face of the earth and they get together, so long will signs be in use."

So while Maslow's Hierarchy of Need chart examines physiological, safety, love/belonging, self-esteem and self-actualization needs, it neglects to note that *language* is a fundamental need and a cornerstone for the other hierarchies, just as oxygen and food are. It is most likely that Maslow did not note this because only in very rare and extreme cases are hearing children ever deprived of language, whereas, with Deaf children, it is often par for the course. (See also Petersen and Rems-Smario [2013] about the role of language in the self-actualization process.)

George W. Veditz knew, as did many others long before him, the importance of natural sign languages for the people of the HandEye.

The Sign Language: A Manual of Signs by J. Schuyler Long (1910)

Drs. Lane, Pillard, and Hedberg have sought to make it self-evident that Deaf people are "a people" through their research on Deaf genealogy and cultural and linguistic transmission.

It is through this examination of Deaf people as an ethnicity (via blood lines and fictive kinship), this challenging of audism (discrimination against Deaf people) and through the celebrating of Deaf gain (what Deaf people contribute to humanity) that we have come to understand "Deafhood." While Deafhood is a simple and organic construct, Dr. Paddy Ladd's introduction and conceptualization of the term have resulted in his becoming an emancipator in many ways. Deaf people as a people of the HandEye have begun to assert their somebodyness more and more:

- Dr. Paddy Ladd, a British Deaf scholar, coined the term "Deafhood"
- Ulf Hedberg, Deaf archivist, worked with Dr. Lane to prove Deaf ethnicity
- Dr. Richard Eckert, a Native American Deaf scholar has introduced "Deafnicity" and other sociological frameworks

- Dr. Tom Humphries, a Deaf scholar, coined the term "audism," the notion that to hear or behave as a hearing person is superior to being Deaf
- Drs. Joseph Murray and Dirksen Bauman, a Deaf and hearing team of scholars coined the term "Deaf Gain"

With the naming of these terms ("audism," "Deafhood," Deaf as ethnicity, "Deaf Gain," etc.) there has been a rise in our collective consciousness. The terms coined above illustrated beyond a shadow of a doubt, that Deaf people are not, in fact, dumb.

Several other authors and scholars have been working hard to advance the field of Deaf Cultural Studies, we would be remiss if we did not note the lack of women and low representation of people of color in the line up above. While the breakthroughs above are important, it is also vital that we widen the circle so that intersectionalities and underrepresented voices can be better considered, understood and valorized.

Telling our stories means owning our truth and this truth needs to be known. A clip from Dr. Joseph Valente's TEDxPSU talk illustrated how even Deaf children like himself and myself who had hearing privilege still long to fit in and strive for equality of condition. Deaf children in the deepest currents of the mainstream seek places and spaces for their Deafhood to shine. This is most successfully achieved via bi/multilingual environments.

Just as I had sought out an old dusty ASL book from my small hometown library, so too have many Deaf people sought ways to find their language and home community. This is true of the Deaf folks from the days of old when they learned sign as they were initiated into Deaf schools and is still true today. What George W. Veditz said over 100 years ago in 1910 still applies today, "We possess and jealously guard a language different and apart from any other in common use, a language which nevertheless is precisely what all wise Mother-nature designed for the people of the eye." One of the biggest markers of ethnic groups, in addition to norms of behavior, traditions, values, and material culture/possessions, is language. It is no coincidence that the very identifying cultural characteristic that Deaf people hold so dear (natural sign languages) is the thing that certain factions in the dominant culture has worked so hard to obliterate and ban (see Baynton [1996] *Forbidden Signs*).

Presently, the second wave of oralism is in full force and contributes to the endangered state of the Deaf signing ethnic group. Evidence of this is in the comeback of oral/aural only schools and programs. In addition, the Early Hearing and Detection Intervention (EHDI) system and the newborn hearing screening practices route newborns and infants into bilaterial cochlear implantation and auditory verbal therapy which bans ASL and the development of visual acuity). Further, genetics and stem cell research is being pushed upon Deaf subjects and families while parental rights are being trumpeted against bodily integrity and agency of Deaf children and individuals. Mainstream school programs are being pushed as the least restrictive environment when most Deaf survivors have testified it was the most restrictive. Many mainstreamed Deaf adolescents beg to attend a Deaf school when it is harder for parents to control and dictate their children. The increasing number of Deaf schools being closed across the United States and abroad is a clear consequence of the second wave of oralism.

In a video interview, Dr. Paddy Ladd warned about this ensuing tsunami of oralism and advised the building of a mountain, a mountain upon which Deaf children, youth, adults and elders could stand strong to survive and preserve our languages and cultures. A mountain built on the bedrock of truth telling via art and activism (see https://www.youtube.com/watch?t=48&v=Ov1QiMetrSQ).

> Once an older Hearing woman said to me long ago, after I had been trying to explain about Oralism and everything, "oh, the first thing oppression kills is creativity." And I was like, hmmm I wonder if this is true or not? I don't know, but I was struck by that statement and committed it to memory. We need to explore this notion, why would they kill creativity first? Well, creative people value themselves. If you don't have self-worth, you don't feel you have anything of value to share. You keep everything underground and hidden like the shared clandestine dormitory storytelling.

> When I lecture to my students (sorry a bit of BSL almost slipped out there) in class, I always tell them, "You have ten years to build a mountain. Build it tall before the waves of cochlear implants, Oralism, and mainstreaming crash upon us. If you take your time and are busy partying not building up the mountain, then the waves will wash away the little we have amassed. However, if you B U I L D a political discourse, through A-R-T and creative expression, you will be building an insurmountable mountaintop which the waves of oppression will not be able to dismantle. We will survive." (Christie & Durr, 2011)

The chief way oppressive systems keep a people down is via the three Es: *education*, *eugenics*, and *economics* (which includes employment). Given the fact that oppressive groups have long controlled Deaf education, sciences relating to Deaf people, and economies affecting Deaf people, it is amazing that we are still standing, and our language has survived. How do oppressive systems justify the keeping of a people down?

- Through bigotry (labeling ASL people as unsuccessful, unintelligible, clannish, behind, illiterate, unemployable, shiftless, etc. while labeling

those who can speak and hear as superior, successful, desirable, etc.)
- Through falsehoods (proclaiming ASL makes a person illiterate and un-American)
- Through fear mongering (painting Deaf people as crazy extremists)

The true extremists are the English-*only* advocates, those who believe by any mean means necessary to deny ASL to Deaf people, including:
- Solitary confinement on children and adults
- Shaming and mocking
- Repeated aggressive surgery with lukewarm results
- Aggressive "therapies" (AVT and LSL)
- Invented signed systems
- Praise and reward for the "success" of parents, schools, and implants

Several important documents have come out recently calling attention to the harms of aggressive implanting and the denial of natural sign language:
- Language acquisition for deaf children: Reducing the harms of zero tolerance to the use of alternative approaches by Humphries et al and
- The ICED 2010 Accord for the Future,
- The World Federation of the Deaf Human Rights,
- World Health Organization Report on Disabilities, and
- The UN Convention on the Rights of Persons with Disabilities

Levels of equality (Baker, et al, 2004)	Models of 'deafness' (Corker 1998, Ladd 2003, Lane 2005, etc.)	General characteristic reasons for such disadvantaged situations	General characteristic solutions/reasons to address situations
Basic equality	Medical	Minority languages blamed for poverty/ disadvantaged. Individuals, not socieities are blamed for problems	Banish/ameliorate/ replace minority languages with majority languages in order to increase likelihood of accecssing majority societies
Liberal egalitarians	Social	Signed languages are unfairly treated should be supported as much as possible. Treated as compensatory tools	Signed languages are tolerated rather than celebrated

Equality of condition	Deafhood	Minority languages are unfairly situated by structural factors and societies	Societal or structural issues must be addressed to ensure the equal treatment of minority languages

Equality of Condition via Deafhood Framework; John Bosco Conama (2011)

While these efforts are good and needed, it is hoped that an Equality of Condition framework will be employed to ensure true justice and protection for Deaf signing children, adults, and their families. Above is an outline of John Bosco Conama's Equality of Condition via Deafhood Framework, which requires structural changes instead of welfare or social services band-aid fixes. Conama has also been emphasizing the adverse impact of affective inequality in education. Kathleen Lynch, a scholar of affective equality, notes "Being deprived of the capacity to develop supportive affective relations, or of the experience of engaging in them when one has the capacity, is therefore a serious human deprivation and injustice; it is a form of affective inequality." In order for affective equality to be present three key components must be central: love, care and solidarity.

Many Deaf View/Image Art (De'VIA) artworks illustrate the harms that have been perpetrated against Deaf infants, children, youth and adults; see Betty G. Miller's "Ameslan Prohibited," Chuck Baird's "Mechanical Ear," Susan Dupor's "Family Dog" and Nancy Rourke's "Mask of Benevolence" and "Struggled Puppet," David Call's "The Missing Jigsaw Pieces" and Ellen Mansfield's "I will never forget" just to name a few.

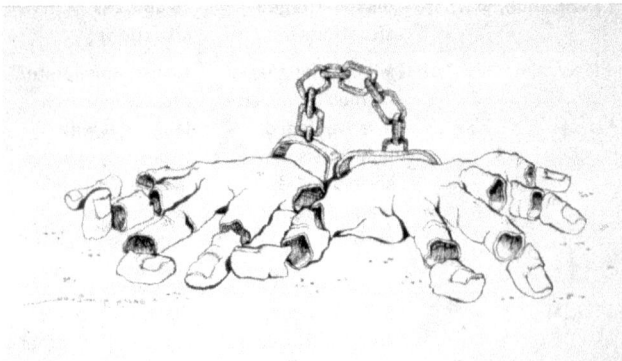

"Ameslan Prohibited" by Betty G. Miller

Deaf education and Deaf upbringing has been plagued by a lack of love, care, and solidarity, largely due to the banishing of natural sign languages from the living rooms and classrooms of Deaf people's lives. Educators sanctioned this by passing the ICED Milan 1880 resolutions. Deaf survivors have described the abuse experienced by this banishment: rapped rulers against wee fingers; locked young children in school closets; forced hands into scolding hot water; insistence upon children wearing devices that cause harm or discomfort; treatment of Deaf children as family pets or class room oddities; and, preferential treatment of Deaf students who had better speaking/listening skills or a greater command of English than their peers.

In addition to trying to suppress Deaf children and adults via the denial of sign language and assimilationist educational practices, the dominant culture works to starve off the people so that they dwindle and disappear. This is often done via eugenic practices. Alexander Graham Bell, who gained prestige from the telephone, used his power and influence to push for Deaf people *not* to marry other Deaf people for fear of propagating a "Deaf race."

Today, this has manifested as genetic tracking, surveillance, and counseling. Recently, a stem cell research project solicited "subjects for experimentation: Deaf newborns and infants, six weeks to eighteen months old. Infants as young as five months old are being implanted despite the fact that the FDA approves of the surgery for twelve-month-old children or older. The EHDI pipeline is geared toward oral/aural interventions when it really should and could be an affective equality system whereby they screen for "early healthy Deaf identity." The closing of Deaf schools is a chief way of starving off Deaf communities and natural sign languages. As Veditz astutely noted in 1910, "Where ever the deaf have received an education the method by which it is imparted is the burning question of the day with them, for the deaf art what their schooling make them more than any other class of humans. They are facing not a theory by a condition, for they are first, last and all the time the people of the eye."

So while the current technique is to take the Deaf infant and child *out* of any Deaf signing environment, Deaf people are still facing a human condition: they still naturally and organically gravitate to acquiring information via the eyes and the hands. This has been proven when Deaf adults, who have cochlear implants, sue colleges to have CART and other visual based access to instruction. Their bilateral implants are unable to give them full equality of condition and affective equality.

Deaf schools have recently closed in Newfoundland, Nebraska, New Hampshire, South Dakota, Wyoming, and Vermont. While many more Deaf schools are under threat of being closed, very few of the existing Deaf schools have bilingual programs (ASL & English), and many are impoverished in terms of the language environment. Schools that provide instruction in ASL as the primary language with English as a second language often follow a Deafhood pedagogical approach (see Dr. Paddy Ladd's Deafhood Pedagogies) and are founded on an Equality of Condition and Affective Eqaulty approach.

With this second wave of oralism, humanity is under assault and our language ecology is threatened. It is estimated two languages disappear *every* month. Figures on endangered languages do not even acknowledge all the signed languages that have been killed off and/or are under threat.

The theme of the Deaf Studies *Today!* 2012 conference is "Beyond Talk" and so we must ask ourselves what we do with this knowledge, with the overwhelming evidence that there is an organized, systematic, relentless effort to ban natural sign languages from the hands, eyes, and minds of Deaf children around the globe. A shift from basic and liberal egalitarianism to equality of condition; real systematic and structural changes are needed and long overdue and Deaf Cultural Studies must play a key role in this transformation for the sake of "a People."

As Harlan Lane noted "What can people of good will do?...If you are the oppressed minatory, you have a special responsibility not only to learn and teach but also to act on behalf of reform. The strength of the oppressed is in their collectivity." Deaf Cultural Studies plays a critical role in examining the collective nature of the people of the Hand Eye. NTID's Deaf Cultural Studies program statement says that

> students will develop critical consciousness of power-relationships and social justice as well as an understanding of individual and social identity with specific reference to the Deaf experience. Focusing on the Deaf experience, students will study how meaning is created and shared via the power of cultural institutions and values and how institutions and values impact the formation of identities, social roles, and expectations.

With knowledge comes power and responsibility. Where injustice and inequalities are known or emerge, students, faculty, programs and community members must work to resist and reform. Alice Walker's novel reveals that resistance is the secret to possessing joy and so to we see with the study of "a people" requires reflection and *action*. The studying of American Sign Language, Deaf culture, and "the *people*" calls upon us to go "beyond talk" and take a stand. (See also numerous De'VIA artworks where the hand stand is prominently displayed, David Call's "United We Stand," Nancy Rourke's "Stand for Justice and Deafhood Stand Up.")

Affective education and equality of condition call upon us to employ love, care, and solidarity within our communities and when approaching the oppressors. In addition to doing this we must always examine our own privileges and prejudices and work diligently to remove them. With our passion to bring about positive social change, we must always remember our compassion. In "A Letter from a Birmingham Jail," Martin Luther King, Jr. wrote about how he initially was upset to be called an extremist and then he decided to be an extremist of love and that too is what we are called to do if we ever want to see the dream realized "when some day Deaf children are not judged by their dB or speech but by the content of their character."

We need to employ these tools of soul force/soul truth when advocating for social justice against the various quagmires and alphabet soup systems (EHDI, CDC, NIH, NIDCD, NCHAM, JCIH, ASHA, AGBAD, etc.) that perpetuate the prejudice that it is better to be hearing than to be Deaf.

It is through doing — going beyond talk — that we move Deaf cultural studies from theory to praxis. As Thomas Jefferson said "Do you want to know who you are? Don't ask. Act! Action will delineate and define you." And while he did not fully work for the betterment, equality and justice of all people, being a slave owner who kept his own biracial children in bondage, he did pen the words in the Declaration of Independence that this country is constantly trying to translate from paper to practice, "We hold these truths to be self-evident, that all men are created equal, that they are endowed by their Creator with certain unalienable Rights, that among these are Life, Liberty and the pursuit of Happiness." Deaf folks of all races, creeds, genders, and abilities are created equal, they are just not treated as such.

Mohandas Gandhi's Soul Force/Truth Force of peaceful resistance and direct action, nonviolent noncooperation, and civil disobedience are achieved through the key components of affective education, love, care and solidarity. Gandhi went beyond talk: "The difference between what we do and what we are capable of doing would suffice to solve most of the world's problems." (Yet, too many of us do not do and let fear and indecision prevent us for being positive change agents.)

"A small body of determined spirits fired by an unquenchable faith in their mission can alter the course of history." (This we know to be true for we have seen it so time and time again, especially now in the digital age.) "A coward is incapable of exhibiting love; it is the prerogative of the brave." (Love is very powerful and not for the faint of heart.) Gandhi not only said these things, he lived these things. He went beyond talk and successfully led his nation to independence.

Martin Luther King, Jr. a disciple of Gandhi's Soul Force/Truth Force also lived beyond talk and successfully led his nation to end segregation: "I believe that unarmed truth and unconditional love will have the final word in reality. That is why right, temporarily defeated, is stronger than evil triumphant." (This has been proven time and time again, especially in cases where injustice takes a stronghold.) "The ultimate measure of a man is not where he stands in moments of comfort and convenience, but where he stands at times of challenge and controversy." (Too many of us choose to be bystanders, standing by during a time when were are desperately needed to stand up and stand in.) "A man dies when he refuses to stand up for that which is right. A man dies when he refuses to stand up for justice. A man dies when he refuses to take a stand for that which is true."

This is what living beyond talk means. It means that we awake and we act. That we employ soul force/truth force, not just to bring about justice and equality but also to breath life back into our own souls as there has been too many deaths of the spirit.

Living and working beyond talk calls upon us to live out the courage of our convictions as Rosa Parks did (we have seen the mug shot of Rosa holding up her arrest number #7053), as Tommie Smith and John Carlos did in the 1968 Olympics (we have seen images of gloved solidarity fists and bare feet), as feminists did during the Women's rights movement (we have seen pictures burning bras), as LGBTQ did as they marched for marriage equality (we have seen images of Gay pride parades), as Native Americans did when they protested the murder of John T. Williams (A First Nation partially-Deaf woodcarver who was killed by a rookie cop in Seattle, Washington), as the 99% did in the Occupy Wall Street Movement (see pictures of Dorli Rainey, an eighty-four-year-old woman who was pepper sprayed by the police), and as Deaf people did during the Deaf President Now, the Unity for Gallaudet and the Audism Free America protests (we all know images of DPN, UFG, and AFA events). See also the #blacklivesmatter movement, which emerged after this 2012 presentation was given, in response to the horrific murders of Black people by police (see Ferguson and Baltimore and more). And STAND.

Thankfully the Deaf-World has had more and more lights, more and more individuals and groups going beyond talk. We thank Jill Radford, a principal at Utah's Jean Massieu School who stepped down from her post to take a stand against Oralism. We thank the Ohlone College Deaf Studies Department for their letter to NTID stating they could no longer do business with the school if they did not remove the offensive and unjust plaque honoring Alexander Graham Bell. We thank the Orange and Brown Coalition for employing soul force and truth force and to get the A.G. Bell plaque down and dorm name changed. We thank the Deaf Bilingual Coalition for organizing A.G. Bell protests. We thank Audism Free America (AFA) for hosting protests, rallies, demonstrations, vigils, sit-ins and engaging in direct peaceful confrontation against the 2nd wave of Oralism and audism. We thank the De'VIA artists for shedding light on the truth via their art truth telling and ARTivism (taking art out on the ground via activism). These *actions* and many more have gone beyond talk and have ensured that we do not just teach and learn a language (ASL) and a culture as academic pursuits but that we actually engage in social justice for "a people."

While there are many more good deeds that are not listed here, there are many many many more missed opportunities. Too many times we do NOT act. We do not go beyond talk. What stops us? Fear, hopelessness, learned helplessness, lack of faith and love, lack of exposure, individualism over collectivism, and hatred.

These obstacles are real but they are not insurmountable. Others have faced far worse and still stood and still came from love. They mustered up love, caring, and solidarity and employed soul force/truth force and brought about *real* and much needed social change. It was not an exercise in academic rhetoric, it was and is very real and very needed. The key to overcoming our most debilitating fears is hope, faith, and love. We put this into action for our profession, for our people, and for all of posterity.

NAD President George W. Veditz said, "And right here let me say that the organized deaf do not understand their might. It is in their power, if united to dictate to the schools what methods of educations should be pursued therein. Their cause is so palpably just that public, legislators and parents must in the end side with them."

Love, caring, and solidarity — the corner stone of affective education — can bring about equality of condition via the employment of soul force/truth force for the cause is so palpably just.

As we opened with Dr. Larry Fleischer, we close with him sharing a tiny clip from George Veditz' beloved 1913 *Preservation of Sign Language* film and his own astute observations on the key component of Veditz' hope (https://www.youtube.com/watch?v=8NRz99Ko_bI. Veditz challenged that "I hope we all will cherish and defend our beautiful sign language..." Some of you have seen Veditz's film before. What is most important here is that sign DEFEND.

Veditz (1913) signing DEFEND

Fleischer (1993) signing DEFEND

As we see in Nancy Rourke's "We Came, We Saw, We Conquered" painting where she used imagery from Goya's "The Third of May 1808" and Mary Thorney's "Milan 1880" to create a new work showing how the ICED 2010 had overturned the ICED Milan 1880 due to the solidarity and collective *act*ion of Deaf people and allies.

We Came, We Saw, We Conquered by Nancy Rourke

The hidden message shows how a love for natural sign languages all over the globe, Deaf culture, and Deaf people as a PEOPLE prevailed.

We Came, We Saw, We Conquered by Nancy Rourke (with hidden message)

This new paradigm came about from Deaf people developing a collective consciousness and moving beyond talk to praxis. This is one of the fundamental purposes of Deaf Cultural Studies and that which gives us roots and wings. Stand and be counted because you count!

REFERENCES

Christie, K. & Durr, P. (2011). The HeART of Deaf Culture: Literary and Artistic Expressions of Deafhood. https://heartofdeafculture.wordpress.com.

Conama, J. B. (2011). Equality of Condition and Deafhood. https://www.youtube.com/watch?v=Kgf-IoxOQQM

Fleischer, L. (1993). ASL Lecture Series. https://www.youtube.com/watch?v=8NRz99Ko_bI and https://www.youtube.com/watch?v=lgsR5jfS7F4.

Petersen, L. & Rems-Smario, J. (2015). Maslow's Hierarchy: The Important Role of Language in Achieving Self-Actualization," THRIVE, 2(1), p. 20–21. https://issuu.com/csdthrive/docs/baby_thrive_2014_print_2

Veditz, G. W. (1913). *The Preservation of Sign Language*, National Association of the Deaf. Film.

Veditz, G. W. The President's Message, Proceedings of the Ninth Convention of the National Association and the Third World's Congress of the Deaf. Colorado Springs, CO. August 6–13 1910. Los Angeles, CA: The Philocophus Press, 1912, (p. 29)].

Deaf/Queer Experience as a Manifestation of Deafhood

CHRISTINE B BROWN

"Deafness is a desire for communication, and gayness is a communication for desire; they are the opposite sides of the same coin for love." Raymond Luczak (Luczak, 2007)

NEVER HAVE I COME ACROSS TWO COMPLETELY UNIQUE AND DIVERSE identities also sharing such strong overlapping and intersecting experiences. Starting at a point of coincidence and evolving into a fascinating exploration of identity development and intersections, themes in deaf/queer identity development — processes of self-realization, struggles, understanding, and acceptance — come to light. Further, the ongoing "processes of becoming" enables deaf/queer individuals to establish a greater self-understanding from which they can then look outwards, recognizing similarities with others who are also on their own varying processes of becoming and hopefully striving to become the best individuals they can be.

If such processes of self-understanding and realization continue within individuals and even throughout communities, societies would simultaneously stand to benefit from a collective not only aiming to better themselves, but better understand others as well. This process enables possibilities to develop community and societal foundations based on educated respect for one another — realizing our similarities despite our differences — through exchanges stemming from a grounded place of self-understanding. Though these notions may appear to be essentialist, experiences of deaf and queer individuals in their processes of becoming are grounded in incredibly intense experiences, struggles, and triumphs. Such individual and collective developments and processes are profound, and in no way verge on essentialism, but rather, they are places of truth for each individual. Deaf/queer individuals, along with other minorities, are not often given an alternative to self-analysis and reflection since being "different" from the majority can initiate the process of self-realization due to embodied experiences of the obstacles and oppressions society places upon them.

Differences of individuals is certainly not limited to just deaf/queer, however, as the groundbreaking, first ever World Report on Disability points out. In a joint production by the World Health Organization (WHO) and the World Bank, they write that "more than a billion people in the world today experience disability" (World Health Organization, 2011). The range of experiences and diversity within disability is vast due to individual circumstances, but common themes are apparent, such as, "poorer health, lower education achievements, fewer economic opportunities and higher rates of poverty than people without disabilities" (World Health Organization, 2011). Further, these similar trends are often a direct result to obstacles faced daily by individuals within societies that don't grant adequate services or access.

Now put aside, for a moment, the "more than a billion people" who experience disability, and think about other differences within American and other international societies around the world, such as race, socio-economic status, gender, and religion. It doesn't take long until virtually everyone in the world eventually falls into some category of "difference." Deaf/queer individuals themselves are unique not only because of the incredible diversity already present within such an identity experience, but also because of their surprisingly intricate processes of becoming.

Hence, by closely exploring deaf/queer individuals, we can begin to better understand the process of identity development, self-awareness, and ultimately self-acceptance. Such knowledge and processes are crucial aspects not only for bettering oneself, but also society. However, understanding and acceptance of self and others must come from within — an established place of truth (is this also an established term or just a phrase?) — a foundation of understanding within oneself so that we might then be able to look out and have understanding towards others.

Again, though this process may appear essentialist, it is rather logical if approached from an angle that processes of introspection leading to self-understanding helps in formulating a grounded foundation of knowledge which we might further utilize in contextualizing, thus better understanding and relating to, the experiences of others. I invite readers to engage critically in the identity development and processes of becoming exhibited (This sounds like additional specific jargon or phrasing like 'process of becoming' and 'established place of truth.' If so, please clarify.) within deaf/queer experiences and apply such aspects of the process to whatever facets of identity, understanding, and stages of personal reflection one finds oneself at a point in time.

The overall purpose of this framework is to explore the unique identity, development, and shared experiences of deaf/queer individuals in order to see whether such processes might shed light on individual development as applied directly to the concept of Deafhood. Some questions will be helpful to keep in mind while viewing the argument through this framework. What does a better understanding of deaf/queer processes of identity development and experiences illuminate with regards to being a first generation identity? This addresses diversity and the unique identity development, or processes of becoming, of deaf/queer individuals. Are any fundamental, underlying commonalities or themes, within deaf/queer (identity?) despite their over-whelming diversity?

This is addressed through an overview of parallel themes presented in a chart developed for the first-self identified Deaf/Queer academic publica-tion written by MJ Beinvenu and expanded with themes I've developed from personal experience, research, and observations. What the specific intersec-tion of deaf and queer through deaf/queer illuminates? Inclusion? Diversity? Communication? And do these intersections parallel other experiences? All of these questions are examined through a deaf/queer lens as applied to the concept of Deafhood.

Because of the specific identity of deaf and queer, this framework is perhaps geared most readily towards the fields of Deaf Studies, Disability Studies, Queer Studies, or Gender Studies. In fact, due to the limited pub-lications concerning specifically deaf/queer identities and individuals, this framework must be approached from those individual respective fields to construct a better understanding of how the individual experiences of deaf and queer converge into a single, shared experience: deaf/queer. However, approaching this concept through an interdisciplinary perspective might be beneficial as well, utilizing this exploration of identity development within such a diverse and unique cultural community who simultaneously portray strong thematic characteristics throughout various stages of becoming. This introduction sets the framework of the extraordinary uniqueness of initial identity development, something I refer to as 'first-generation identities,' followed by a definition of deaf/queer as well as an explanation of the theoret-ical concept of Deafhood. In doing that, a model becomes apparent in which we might move "Beyond Talk," towards informed possibilities for action.

In order to develop a strong understanding, clear terminology is key. Usage of queer indicates any sexual identity or preference that differs from a heterosexual identity or preference. Thus, queer is inclusive of gay, lesbian, bisexual, transgender and intersex identities — anyone who does not partake or identify with the heterosexual lifestyle or experience. Further, queer is not only about identity, but also desire and preference, physical, mental, or emotional. At its root, it's about connection and love. Similar to the use of deaf, I purposely use queer throughout this paper, unless an individual chooses to self-identify as something else. I don't use gay, lesbian, or other generic labels because such individual identities do not take into account the vast range of experiences present within the queer community. Further, since used as an all-encompassing term, it is not to disregard political, cultural, or personal identities or experiences, but rather provide a platform or space for including those aspects in such discourse instead of limiting them through specific categories of identification.

Being deaf or hard of hearing is not limited to either a medical or cultural experience since there is great diversity of identity and experience amongst deaf, as well as queer, individuals. Hence, I do not make such distinctions or differentiations, but instead use deaf as an all-inclusive term. Similarly, queer is an inclusive term indicating an individual with a preference or lifestyle that differs from the heterosexual preference or lifestyle. Deaf/queer (what? Identity? Perspective?) is the touchstone for deaf/queer theory. It is the intersection of deaf and queer identities within an individual. Similar to other identities, no two individuals are alike, but in this framework, the processes of identification, realization, and becoming exhibited within deaf/queer individuals are demonstrated through recurring themes shared amongst an incredibly diverse range of individuals and backgrounds, coming together based on strong emotive similarities of experiences.

FIRST-GENERATION IDENTITIES

Deaf/queer individuals face obstacles daily in many societies, but despite the incredible diversity within these two experiences, they collectively come together, forming a community comprised of an overwhelming majority of first-generation identities. This is because most queer individuals have heterosexual parents, and most deaf individuals have hearing parents, thus, shared identity, experience, and culture, are things most deaf/queer individuals seek from outside their nuclear families. By looking closely at publications, research, and autobiographies of deaf/queer individuals, themes begin to emerge regarding how deaf/queer individuals develop an understanding of self that, in some ways, are "against all odds." The United States has historically had a homophobic and patronizing environment that still prevails in various degrees towards deaf/queer individuals. Being gay, lesbian, bisexual, transgendered — queer — often goes against societal, familial, religious, and even legal aspects of our societal institutions. In fact, as noted by the American Psychiatric Association, it wasn't until 1973 that homosexuality was removed from the DSM-II as part of a classification of mental disorders.

Often overlooked though, is that its removal, at the time, was simply a compromise, as the wording of homosexuality was replaced with "Sexual Orientation Disturbance" (Spitzer, 1981) This societal environment directly impacts queer youth, as they are two to three times more likely to attempt suicide than other young people, comprising up to 30% of completed youth suicides annually. Looking at this from a gendered perspective, 25% of lesbians and 20% of gay men have actually attempted suicide. If these statistics from the Lambda, an organization that "promotes research into lesbian and gay issues and lifestyles for the purpose of public education," (Gibson, 2009) was not compelling enough, gay males are six times more likely to make a suicide attempt than heterosexual males, and lesbians are more than twice as likely to try committing suicide than the heterosexual women in the study. Gay youth face extreme physical and verbal abuse, rejection and isolation from family and peers, but the main point is that these issues impact youth insofar that they attempt, and unfortunately many succeed, in committing suicide, in rates well above their heterosexual peers.

Hence, discussions regarding identity development and the need for support from peers, family, friends, and society within that process, is one not to be taken lightly. Though the above information may put a damper on perceptions of issues regarding deaf/queer, it is important to keep in mind that such discussions of identity development, intersections and so forth, do go beyond such discourses and into matters, literally, of life and death as well. Deaf individuals are often immediately confronted by the medical profession as well, trying to "change" them to be more like hearing individuals. Further, deaf individuals are often the only deaf person in their family or town. Such isolation and negativity creates a dynamic for many to "sink or swim," and though there are not enough studies to draw a parallel here to queer suicide rates, *Annals of General Psychiatry* literature review of suicide in deaf populations, (Windfuhr & Turner, 2007) demonstrates similar common issues of rejection and isolation from family and peers among deaf individuals.

The resulting disproportionate level of suicide documented regarding queer youth is a result of the hostility present within their lives and is just one example of the importance and impact a society perpetuating support and positive reinforcement as well as educated respect could have on its youth. Key to deaf/queer individuals ability to prevail, whether through sheer will, determination, or familial support is the opportunity for individual exploration of self and identity. Until one is able to come to a place of understanding and self-acceptance — through a process of becoming — it is nearly impossible to live a fulfilling life with positivity, celebrating and affirming the value within our unique individuality.

Again, since deaf/queer individuals are predominantly first-generation, finding support from others in order to develop self-acceptance and understanding can be, for some, an insurmountable task. Perhaps this fuels the overwhelming drive to be with others in solidarity who understand, or struggle themselves, to find a place of acceptance. But once that connection is made to become part of and participate in a larger community through events or transnational geographical spaces that bring deaf and queer individuals together, passionate communities form, filling the air with such positive energy and celebration as experienced from yearly Pride events and Deaf conferences and social gatherings.

These environments may be temporary spaces occurring transnationally, or exist in more permanent locations such as San Francisco, Northampton, Massachusetts, or Gallaudet University, and the Rochester Institute of Technology. These spaces are historically established areas deaf/queer individuals seek out to live, work, receive an education, and socialize. Such places have brought first-generation individuals together from all corners of the world, from every diverse background imaginable, forming communities through a sense of being amongst others who are able to understand what it is to be deaf and what it is to be queer in some of the most profound manners of human connections, communication and love.

WHAT IS DEAF/QUEER?

Before understanding deaf/queer, deaf and queer must be understood individually. However, there is no single way of being or experiencing, and going into depth regarding either identity is not realistic for the purposes of this paper. Individuals have differing experiences — histories, backgrounds, environments — which impact identity development. These factors include family, friends, schools, languages, various media, religions, technologies, medical professions that make impressions on an individual's sense of self and identity. However, in attempting to understand the essence of what deaf means, two differing frameworks are immediately presented. The first consists of viewing deafness as something needing to be fixed: a pathological view. This takes place through various means to alleviate deafness with speech therapy, assistive listening devices, hearing aids, or even surgery, as is the case with cochlear implants (CIs).

This view aims to fit deaf individuals within hearing society. The other view involves sign language, culture, and history, viewing deafness with pride amongst a community of deaf individuals. Sometimes these differing views conflict in deaf educational philosophies and in how student's learning needs are accommodated in a hearing environment. The main distinction to note within the context of first-generation identity, as mentioned previously, is that most deaf individuals are born to hearing parents, and thus do not share the same identity with them, and are born into a different identity experience. According to the 2006-2007 Gallaudet Research Institute Annual Survey of Deaf and Hard of Hearing Children and Youth, 83.4 percent of deaf or hard of hearing children are born to hearing parents, and 77.4 percent are the only child in their family who are deaf or hard of hearing. This is significant because it shows that most deaf children are "first-generation," and often isolated from the beginning. While the causes of being deaf can range from hereditary, illness or complications at a young age, or birth, 57.0 percent of the time, the cause is not known. Yet medical and technological fields continue to search for cures. Granted, one can become deaf or hard of hearing at any point after birth as well.

Queer, on the other hand, is not usually identifiable until a child is at least a few years old, and since it concerns individual personal preference, is completely dependent upon individual processes of self-realization and identification. Societies attempt to label and identify someone regardless of such individual processes, but personal preference is still just that: personal. There is also ongoing debate regarding nature vs. nurture in terms of whether it is a choice to be queer, or if it's a result of environment. However, if and when one does come to self-identify as queer, there is a vibrant queer — gay, lesbian, bisexual, transgender, intersex — community one can become a part of, should one choose to be open about and pursue their sexual preferences and desires. Similarly, since the majority of children are conceived through traditional means of procreation, queer individuals also do not share an identity or experience with their parents, thus comprising a predominantly first-generation collective of individuals as well.

This initial stage of identity development, looking outside the nuclear family in order to find others with similar identities and experiences, community, and culture, leads to the intersection of deaf/queer found within individuals who identify as both deaf and queer. Such an identity is fascinating in its complexity, processes, and nuances of identity development as demonstrated within recurring themes among diverse deaf/queer individuals. Such diversity in itself lends to an entirely different area worthy of study and focus, especially in terms of how it can lead to the exploration of intersections with other identities and experiences. However, this paper focuses primarily on the creation of a deaf/queer framework as applied to Paddy Ladd's theory and concept of Deafhood. Before contextualizing deaf/queer within theory, let's contextualize and ground both deaf and queer in terms of their historical initial movements as collectives.

DEAF PRESIDENT NOW (DPN) AND STONEWALL:
PARALLELS WITHIN HISTORICAL MOVEMENTS

Prior to the 1969 summer Stonewall riots that took place outside of the Stonewall Inn and its historically queer bar in Greenwich Village, a gay neighborhood in downtown New York City, there was no clear gay rights movement. The Stonewall riots initiated a turning point, the moment the queer community said "enough is enough" to government-sponsored oppression targeting queer individuals and the queer community. Though it is unclear exactly who started the riots, what is unquestionable is that the movement triggered progress towards equal rights and recognition of queer individuals. Each year the queer community grows in numbers and strength as increasing numbers of legislative actions working towards equality are proposed each year, and the numbers of out and proud queer individuals, along with their allies, grows at each annual national and international gay pride festival. Of course, there have been some variation over the years and moments of great triumphs as well as setbacks, but overall, the gay rights movement has increased in visibility and positively expanded its influence on individuals, legislation, and society.

Similarly, at the Deaf President Now (DPN) protests at Gallaudet University in 1988, the Washington, D.C. campus was shut down for a week while students and faculty relentlessly made four clear demands to the school's Board of Trustees. On the second day of protests, Monday, March 7, students agreed to open campus again in the event that these four demands were met:

1.   Zinser's resignation and the selection of a deaf president;
2.   Spilman's resignation from the board;
3.   An increase in deaf representation on the board to 51 percent;
4.   No reprisals against the protesters (Gannon, 1989)

Perhaps the election of a hearing, unqualified candidate was the Rosa Parks' moment the deaf community needed to garner a response the media and public would support; regardless, the campus and deaf community had also reached a point of "enough is enough." Where the queer community reached that same point that fateful summer night in 1969 and decided to resist police harassment and brutality, fighting back, the deaf community reached that point when a hearing president who was learning ASL was chosen over two fully qualified deaf candidates, Gallaudet alumni themselves.

The campus and deaf community fought back in a manner perhaps as sudden as the Stonewall riots, seeking recognition and empowerment through self-representation at their own campus. Ultimately, the demands were met and the rally successful, having garnered a huge amount of media attention and public support practically overnight.

Like the gay rights movement, there have been moments of success and setbacks, but most changes have happened through legislation such as the passing of the Americans with Disability Act (ADA) in 1991, or Section 504 of the Rehabilitation Act of 1973, or more specifically, the Individuals with Disabilities Education Act (IDEA) in 1989 and 2004. Overall though, it almost appears as though the deaf rights movement was successful in that initial movement, it has lacked much progression since. There was a second wave of protests at Gallaudet University in 2006, the various reasons it took place still being contested today, but discussions surrounding identity politics aside, similar to the first protest, the 2006 protest led to increased visibility and arguably increased deaf empowerment.

However, events since the 1969 and 1988 movements have taken quite different paths within the respective communities in regards to their political, societal, institutional, and interpersonal resistance. Similar to parallels of individual identity formation of deaf and queer persons, their political movements share many similar aspects in their respective development. Such parallels include attempting to overcome oppressions. The initial moments of both these historical events and movements are worth further exploration at another time. For the purposes of this paper, such initial historical developments are beneficial to keep in mind with regards to applying a deaf/queer framework in that both movements stemmed from individuals reaching pivotal moments that led to collective action.

Further, historical events of communities provide a background in terms of how societal and community events can impact individuals when exploring their own identity and experiences within such an identity experience. Hence, we begin to see how the initial identity development of the deaf and queer movements parallels and impacts the initial identity developments of individuals. Having a brief historical contextualization of each initial movement, let's look at how such processes play out within an identity, experience, and theory within a deaf/queer framework.

DEAF/QUEER FRAMEWORK DEFINED

In March 2011, I had the pleasure of meeting Paddy Ladd and partaking in his workshop on Deafhood at the University of Bristol Centre for Deaf Studies. Much of Ladd's focus was on colonialism and Deafhood in that it allows analysis of different types of oppression and a framework to compare deaf oppression — that of audism — with others who are similarly oppressed. Ladd argues that deaf were colonized through Oralism, mainstreaming, and Cochlear Implants (CIs), all aspects still prevailing today, yet deaf have persevered. Moving forward though, Ladd looks towards the benefits Deafhood has to offer, writing that "Deaf people [are] the world's first truly global citizens, and thus a model for society — Global Unity!" Ladd urges deaf individuals to "reach for an inner, larger Deafhood self" in order to "find a better vision of how to behave towards each other" in a manner that "can actually benefit all Deaf people." This is something he notes as 'Deaf Reconstruction' (emphasis original) (Ladd, 2008).

However, not only is equality fundamental in that no one is 'More Deaf' than someone else, "Deafhood is a lifelong process... search" within each individual. Ladd, in discussing "International Deafhood," writes that deaf are interconnected with "an entire planet of Deaf people, who you can communicate with" through "International Signing" and usage of ones' "true Deaf skills, of visual thinking" and "Deaf Space." This application of Deafhood in order to see a "larger vision... positive aspects of *all* cultures" while forging alliances with others sharing intersections with deaf, is a fundamental aspect of Ladd's current Deafhood framework (Ladd, 2008).

Meeting Paddy Ladd and having the opportunity to briefly discuss my own deaf/queer framework with him was inspiring. In terms of intersections, there were many between my own framework and Ladd's. In presenting my thesis to the Bristol University Centre of Deaf Studies in a combination of newly acquired British Sign Language, International Sign, and of course some American Sign Language when needed, signing abstract concepts in a manner that would be universally understood proved revolutionary. I could have just signed DEAF, but that wasn't what I wanted to convey, since the experience of being deaf is so much more, as Ladd suggests, is rooted in something deeper, universal.

So in order to find that meaning, one must look within, reflecting on their own experiences, identity, everything they've acquired up until that moment, digging towards their core and unpeeling the layers until able to arrive at the bare essence, underlying truth of that experience and pull it up and out from within. At this point, the response to "What is deaf?" is unique to that individual, yet understood by all others who share a similar process of experience and realization that comes from within. There is no singular name for this sign or singular name for identifying such a moment in time, as it's an ongoing process, true to each individual, thus cannot be essentialist. In a way, this notion of understanding in relation to experience and identity, though universal, is like the North Pole in that there is no true "center," or North as the North Pole itself is constantly moving.

This signed explanation is one with potentially fascinating intersections in that one could name another minority experience such as female or queer, then go through the same steps of looking back and accumulating past experiences, then looking "in," searching, reflecting, then arriving at an overall sense or understanding of said experience. By pulling meaning out from within, having "arrived" at some aspect concrete enough to hold, look at, and understand, even if literal words themselves fail to label and identify, the meaning is still there, having processed it, holding, seeing the result of such critical engagement.

The interesting thing though, is that this signed process makes sense to many, and is signed in the same way, reaching a point of understanding and identification, regardless of which specific experience one is discussing. Thus, the intersection lies in that shared process and common result, allowing possibilities of coalitions or alliances with those sharing such intersections of realizations concerning what each experience means to them and their overall sense of self in relation to it. Hence, a deaf/queer framework is one that utilizes an understanding of the process of individual acceptance, having critically reflected upon how past events have formed and impacted individual experiences, and how such experiences or events helped shape the individual in that moment with regards to meaning and identity concerning specific aspects such as deaf or queer, but also applicable to any other identity as well.

With use and application of a d/q framework, through encouraging a process of engaged reflection, individuals become not only more self-aware, but more readily able to understand others and differences, as well as similarities, of experiences as well. However, while d/q processes of becoming help give a concrete application for the concept and theory of Deafhood, a better understanding and overview of Paddy Ladd's theory helps clarify and contextualize a d/q framework similar to a symbiotic relationship.

OVERVIEW OF DEAFHOOD

Paddy Ladd expressed in his PowerPoint presentation on March 1st, 2011, that "Deafhood is actually a search to understand ourselves!" (Ladd, 2011) However, he suggests that such understanding must first come from having understood our past — history — in order to better contextualize our current experiences within society. He demonstrates this through understanding Deaf history. Applying this notion to d/q, by having awareness of our past environment, and everything leading up until now, we are better able to navigate the impact such events and history have on us as individuals and as a collective. Within the context of Deaf history, Ladd notes that one prominent concept is that of colonialism as a form of oppression. With such oppressions, Ladd offers a definition that Deafhood is "the total sum of all positive meanings of 'Deaf,' past, present and future" and that "all the largest meanings of what Deaf people have been, are, and can be." (Ladd, 2011)

Perhaps most notably, Ladd suggests that it is a process, writing that Deaf individuals can overcome our oppressions by reaching "for an inner, larger Deafhood self" in order to "find a better vision of how to behave towards each other." This process, Ladd rightly recognizes, is one "that can actually benefit all Deaf people." To this I would make an extension, suggesting that it doesn't just stop with Deaf people but can benefit all of society as well if similar processes, such as experienced within d/q processes of becoming, or any process involving self-reflection and understanding, are engaged.

The process itself is not a one-time act, but rather an ongoing journey or "lifelong process. Lifelong search" that must be maintained. This process is one that can continuously be pursued since we can always be better, learn more, and become more educated. Ladd suggests that this can take place through "deepening our Deafhood." However, this only makes his concept that much more abstract since no concrete example is offered, other than applying the concept to an international level for "Deaf Global Citizenship."

In short, Deafhood, as Ladd notes, is understanding one's past, how it impacts the present, and then engaging in a process of looking within in order to actively pursue becoming better individuals.

DEAF/QUEER EXPERIENCE AS AN EXPANSION OR MANIFESTATION OF DEAFHOOD

So what exactly then is a deaf/queer framework within all this? This key theme is simple in essence: Deafhood is a process of becoming, and this process can be seen most clearly in the Deaf becoming and the queer becoming. Thus, Deaf/queer is similar to Ladd's notion of finding a deeper sense of self and understanding in terms of how we see our similarities — intersections — and using those intersections to form alliances with others in order to achieve our shared goals of equality.

In order to understand or have meaning associated with experience or identity, an individual must first take a moment to stop and thoughtfully look back, reflecting on past experiences leading up until now as they pertain to a certain experience, such as deaf/queer. After having accumulated a summary of all past experiences up until that moment, one must then look within and reflect on how such experiences impacted them. That often entails digging and sorting through layers of self-perceptions, as well as those accumulated consciously or subconsciously from others. By looking within, one can eventually sift through and arrive at the root — the meaning of deaf, queer, woman, and so forth — as it pertains to them. That one word now truly has meaning since it was formulated through experience, reflected upon, and rooted, grounded from within. Throughout this process one then arrives at a better understanding of oneself.

However, since we are never static within our lives, meaning and understanding can change, hence the importance of recognizing that this process is ongoing. However, once it has been explored, it perhaps becomes easier since a foundation of self-awareness and understanding begins to develop since, arguably, one doesn't have to re-establish everything from scratch each time, having already reflected on all past experiences in order to arrive at the present, so it's kind of similar to maintaining a bike after having already assembled the parts. Sure, it is quite possible that an event or experience can completely wipe out our understanding of who we are, but that's also just a part of life.

A deaf/queer framework also incorporates inclusion within its foundation. We as a society, and as individuals with our moments of intersections with others, are incredibly diverse and different in our own ways. Thus, it is crucial that we not only see our differences in a positive light through educated respect, but also that we actively foster the concept of equality by being fully inclusive and accessible to all. Grounding principles of inclusion of diversity and communication access are derived specifically from both the deaf and queer communities, but applicable to society as a whole, since issues of diversity and communication are prevalent in most, if not all, exchanges. Thus, deaf/queer processes of becoming is a concrete example or manifestation of Ladd's academic and theoretical concept of Deafhood.

CHARTS OF DEAF AND QUEER IDENTITY PARALLELS

MJ Bienvenu and Kendra Smith produced a chart in 1999 (table 1), that is included in MJ Bienvenu's 2008 article, "Queer as Deaf: Intersections," to explore such historical parallels between the deaf and queer communities and experience (Bienvenu, 2008). They are included in their entirety below to exemplify the strong parallels in identity development and experience. Note the themes that emerge from the charts, such as parents, societal perceptions, culture, and so forth.

These charts offer some nice points for reflection, but a few sections could use clarification or expansion. For example, with age of onset, there are many individuals who become deaf as a child, or later in life. Also, the category of culture is rather vague in stating "Old envy young" and "Young

Queer	Deaf
Parents	
• Few parents of Gay/Lesbian are queer • Many parents don't accept • Psychiatrist • Seek cure	• Only 5–10% of Deaf have Deaf parents • Many parents don't accept • Therapist • Seek cure
Education	
• Denial	• Denial
Society	
• Normalization • Homophobia • Epithets • Misconceptions (sex, sex, sex) • Homosexuality • Acceptance/tolerance • Resistance to public identity based on community membership • Denial of self-labeling • Lesbian/Gay Studies	• Hearingization • Audism • Epithets • Misconceptions ('can't' syndrome) • Deafness • Acceptance/tolerance • Resistance to existence of Deaf culture • Denial of self-labeling • Deaf Studies
Culture	
• Denial/silence • Coming out repeatedly • Misrepresentation (Andrew Cunanan) • "Passing" • Stereotypes (tomboys, sissies)	• Denial/silence • Acknowledging repeatedly • Misrepresentation (Heather Whitestone) • Speech = more desirable • Stereotypes (wild, emotional)
Identity	
• Denial	• Denial
Language	
• Often the language of the majority	• ASL, BSL, etc.
Congress	
• Barney Frank, S. Gunderson, G. Studds	• No Deaf representatives
Media	
• Recognition	• Not much after DPN, unless attention is on gaining hearing (cochlear implants)
Age of onset	
• Genetic; coming out age	• At birth
Culture	
• Old envy young	• Young envy old

Table 1: "Queer as Deaf: Intersections," by MJ Bienvenu, in *Open Your Eyes: Deaf Studies Talking*, 264–273 (Minneapolis: University of Missesota Press, 2008). Based on "Queer/Deaf similarities, created by Kendra Smith and MJ Bienvenu as a class handout, Gallaudet University, 1999.

Queer	Deaf
Identity	
• Both find, develop, and share identity with others outside nuclear family • Both literally ostracized from families and friends (queeer: disowned; Deaf: in manner of communication) • Both medicalized, but queer removed from DSM, deaf still medicalized • Both constantly developing and shifting — identity not *fixed*, static • Some queer able to "pass" in society as heterosexual • Some hard of hearing, deaf able to "pass" as hearing (or deaf in the case of CODAs)	
Religion	
• Viewed as sin by many	• Viewed as imperfection to become "whole" in heaven
Legal	
• Historically criminalized • Victims of police brutality • Killed — victims of hate crimes • Placed into asylums	• Involuntary sterilization • Denied services or access • Not viewed as fully capable • Placed into institutions
Rights/Privileges	
• Refused national constitutional right to marry (yet fear of passing on 'gene' through intermarriage not seen as threat with gays) • Taxes and inheritance still problematic	• Overcame marriage debates • Overcame driving rights debate
Education Content	
• Nature/nurture; evolutionism/ creationism • Sex education include queer topics? • History includes Stonewall?	• Linguistic access/oralism • Taught accurately in ASL; understood? • History include deaf? DPN?
Historical Treatment	
• Criminalized and abused	• Patronized and pitied

Table 2: Author's additions to the Smith & Bienvenu (1999) framework

envy old." Perhaps one can make a guess that with 'queer,' it is referring to sexual desire, and with 'deaf,' referring to a period of time past generations took part in, sometimes referred to as "the Golden Age." Overall, I would expand these parallels and comparisons further, as explored in my own chart presented below to more fully explore these first-generation identities and experiences.

Overall, themes that emerge seem most strongly to center around issues of acceptance, membership, belonging within family, peers, society, institutions such as religion, politics, and so forth. Further exploration and research is vital to continue such discussions and explorations, but at the moment,

some of the emerging themes appear to come after a period of self-awareness and self-acceptance. And after having gone through that, a greater
awareness towards others and openness towards others appears to be possible as well. All of these aspects and themes come through within identity
development and experiences. This specific intersection of d/q leads then, to
a d/q framework through the processes of becoming, thus providing a foundation for contextualizing what Deafhood is.

By utilizing these experiences and identity development that is inher-
ent within many deaf/queer individuals because, often, they are not given a
choice but are forced to go through processes of becoming in order to survive in our society, a model becomes clear as to what that process can look
like through the strong existence of parallel themes and experiences that we
can then use as a model or foundation to move "Beyond Talk."

POSSIBILITIES OF FIRST-GENERATION IDENTITIES

> As African Americans and feminists took the lead in the past to help the
> larger society to theorize subjecthood in the 1970s and 1980s, so can the
> Deaf, the disabled, and queer folk help postmodern society to imagine what
> subjectivity looks like in a postidentity period. This process is necessarily
> collective and situational.... [T]hose discussions... will benefit from an
> awareness of the regnant issues and ideas that are disturbing and intriguing
> all identity groups not only in the United States but throughout the world.
> (Davis, 2008)

As postulated by Lennard Davis, deaf, queer, as well as disabled, are in a
unique position to make significant contributions not only to their own
respective fields, but also to society and the world at large. One of the main
reasons being because of the flexibility that comes with having such individual diversity within a shared collective coming together with a clean slate,
without having 'inherited' their identity or experience from parents and
families. Realizing and exploring the intersections taking place within these
three identities throughout local and global societies can greatly benefit us
all with regards to individual and collective understanding because despite
such diversity, communities have formed based on intersections: realizing,
and ideally respecting, commonalities of experience.

It is crucial that exploration of these experiences and intersections are
approached through a process that values the participation of all individuals through a means of equal access to communication as well as respect
for and inclusion of diversity. With such a foundation, and a lens focusing on our collective intersections, by realizing and attempting to capitalize on such a unique disposition, minorities, having come together through

societal oppressions, can perhaps, numerically, and strategically, have the upper hand. That is because deaf, queer, and disabled individuals are prevalent within all factions of society due to an overwhelmingly 'first-generation' occurrence, resulting in an increased understanding of self by having experienced oppressions and developed a clearer understanding of self as a result of those struggles of resistance. Some might even have noticed the complex network of overlapping identities and experiences.

Further, having such vast differences of background and experience makes it challenging for society to continue to maintain control — lasso us all with one rope. Thus, with a shift in perspective and strategy, those oppressed can become empowered and perhaps lead the way for society as a whole to attempt to move past the oppositional and divisive histories of racial, minority, identity, linguistic, and nationalistic politics that prevent us from realizing our innate similarities. We can strive to become more self-aware, better communicators, all while learning from and respecting differences. Academically, we should strive to capitalize on our intersections within various academic fields as well as in our personal experiences and relations in order to begin a collective discourse as to how we can utilize those commonalities and intersections to work towards our common goals — that of a more equal society.

But first, let's return to discussing Davis' mention of three specific identities in order to "help postmodern society… imagine what subjectivity looks like in a postidentity period": Deaf, disabled, and queer. These three experiences are not random, but rather strategic in that they share a connection through their uniquely similar process of identity development. As several scholars have noted within various fields, these identities and experiences are overwhelmingly, what I consider, a 'first-generation' experience, or in the case of Frank Bechters' wording more specifically regarding the signing Deaf community, a "community of 'converts'" (Bechter, 2008). Most deaf, disabled, or queer individuals do not have parents who are also deaf, disabled, or queer. Lennard Davis proposes referring to this category of experience as "one-generation" identities, instead of using "outdated, outmoded, and potentially dangerous categories of ethnicity, minority status, nationhood (including "world" and "culture")" in an effort to "redefine the nature of social identity." Davis notes that there is no benefit in forcing ones' foot into a glass slipper. Instead we should focus on making "a new shoe that actually fits" (Davis, 2008). Though I like the collectivity of "one-generation," it also implies the possibility of there being a single way to exist as a generation, and also, that it is a single occurrence, to take place, then ceases to continue once the generation passes on. Hence, my personal preference is to regard deaf and queer as 'first-generation,' since it suggests more momentum and the ability to continue, but by all means, let's make a new shoe.

Davis continues this exploration, writing about "one-generation" identities as consisting of "people with disabilities, Deaf people, gay people, and Codas" arguing that they "can say 'we represent the way out of the identity politics dead end.'" He continues by writing "social groups… are not defined solely by bodily capabilities," and that, presumably as a result of "one-generational" identities, "[w]e are not a group that has been defined in advance by an oppressor, but [instead] we choose to unite ourselves together for new purposes." This flexibility to unite on ones' own volition is a crucial point as most deaf, disabled or queer individuals do not inherit a definition of said experience from their parents, thus can't be readily claimed by an oppressor. One could argue though, that society attempts to control deaf and queer through legislation impacting language, education, and rights as citizens.

However, Davis continues to assert that with the freedom "one-generation" identities provide, "[w]e are, precisely, not an ethnic group or a minority but something new and different emerging from the smoke of identity politics and rising like a phoenix of the postmodern age." He is right in recognizing that our difference in identity formation perhaps leads to opportunity, and that out of this comes the overall realization that with such open territory to claim concerning identity, "[t]he key to both [disability and queer theory] is that identity is part of a continuum." With such a range of experience, the possibilities of intersections are great. Further, such identity "is malleable and not grounded in the traditional medicalized or essentialized views of the body."

WHERE TO GO FROM HERE?

This paper not only aims to provide a better understanding of first-generation identities and what such points of intersections yield, but also explore how such processes of becoming lead to better self understanding, thus the possibility and contextualization of what pursuing Ladd's concept of Deafhood might look like. Hence, the overall purpose in exploring the unique identity development and shared experiences of deaf/queer individuals in order to see whether such processes might shed light on individual development as applied directly to the concept of Deafhood, was addressed in several ways.

An initial question asked whether understanding deaf/queer processes of identity development better illuminated first-generation identities. This involved the diversity, unique identity development, and processes of becoming amongst d/q individuals, and was explored throughout this paper and demonstrated through similarities in identity development.

The second question explored if there were any fundamental, underlying commonalities, or themes within deaf/queer, despite their overwhelming diversity. Themes such as family, religion, initial moments of recognition, struggles, and so forth, usually followed by how such struggles were overcome, are common amongst d/q individuals. In researching and exploring deaf/queer narratives, struggles are almost always overcome following reaching a low point, desperation, a moment where there literally was nowhere else to turn but inwards, and attempt to begin the process of self-acceptance. It was from that initial moment of self-acceptance that individuals are able to begin building and reaching out into other aspects of their lives such as family and friends.

The third question sought to answer what the specific intersection of deaf and queer through d/q illuminated. As the discussion opening this concluding discussion suggests, the intersection of two first-generation identities through d/q sheds light on their possibilities. By highlighting points that not only should be explored further, such as how individuals overcome individual struggles, which then provides potential groundwork for countering systemic and societal oppressions, forging ahead into paths of resistance, it becomes clear that there is much to learn from the intersections that appear within these incredibly diverse populations. Exploring such intersections leads not only to a better understanding of first-generation experiences and the diversity within overlapping identities, but also gives a glimpse as to their possibilities if further explored. More specifically, the intersections of deaf and queer highlighted processes involving acceptance, self-awareness, and developing awareness of others and openness towards others as a result of have experienced first hand such processes.

If only one point is taken from this paper though, it should be that I don't believe there is a "nirvana" with regards to Deafhood and identity development. If anything that moment of realization is realizing that we are on a constant journey and process of becoming. However, one theme does appear to come through in all this, and that is the initial moment of self-acceptance, in that it tends to come after great despair, after having broken down, and broken through all previous systems, and perceptions of self, and down to the bare essence of who the individual is and what they face. From there begins a process of rebuilding, of understanding, from a foundation of honesty and truth that comes from within.

CONTRIBUTION TO DEAF STUDIES AND DEAFHOOD

While the scope of all these questions suggests the need for further research in greater depth, it appears such endeavors would yield results valuable to multiple fields, and especially to any interested in interdisciplinary studies, or interpersonal or individual relations. Obviously, the most apparent findings within this paper is how d/q processes of becoming — exploring deaf/queer identity development — is not only a lens into better understanding the concept of Deafhood, but that such processes themselves are a manifestation of Deafhood. Being one of the most prominent theories within Deaf Studies, yet also possibly one of the most divisive with regards to varying interpretations as to what Deafhood actually means, this paper perhaps might provide contextualization and clarification towards what the process Ladd refers to within his academic and theoretical discussion looks like in practice as exemplified through d/q individuals.

FURTHER EXPLORATION

Having noted the historical parallels between the deaf and queer movements, it appears further exploration of such movements might also prove to be highly insightful into identity, experience, as well as community and cultural underlying beliefs. Further, specific strategies that emerge through moments of resistance might prove beneficial towards these movements ongoing efforts, as well as for other movements who perhaps increasingly realize the need for inclusiveness of individuals and diversity in order for their movement to not only be representational, but successful.

While initial processes of identity development have been explored in a manner leading up to processes of becoming, similar to the concept and process of Deafhood, further exploration regarding what one actually does having achieved such an understanding, foundation, point of acceptance, would be an important study to undertake as well. Are there common themes post deaf/queer initial identity development? What do deaf/queer individuals end up doing with such an understanding of self and others? Does going through such processes of becoming actually lend to a greater sense of Deafhood in a manner that Paddy Ladd suggests, of becoming the best deaf individual one can become or in a manner of becoming the best individual one can become with regards to any identity or experience? And does this process offer a foundation for others outside deaf/queer to apply to their own experiences? If so, how are processes of becoming being pursued? How are they utilized? Perhaps the only way to answer any of these questions is through determining whether individuals, and society as a whole, are willing to hold themselves to higher standards than they currently do: to strive to make an ideal their reality and to become better than they otherwise might be.

THEMES AND IDEAS THAT AROSE

As noted, deaf individuals are remarkably diverse when it comes to identity since deaf individuals are also part of other social categories and experiences, much like queer individuals, therefore they are already poised to form alliances with other constructed identities or experiences. For example, one can be both Black and Deaf, or Jewish and Deaf, meaning, such individuals can be a connecting bridge between the two cultures or identities. Why not then, with 'representatives' from every single aspect of society, use that to our advantage? The natural diversity amongst deaf and queer allows for a platform to create collaborative action, working together to gain external support, which once one realizes that minorities in this country are larger in numbers than the majority, we can then creatively work towards any cause we believe worthy of standing behind and actively create positive change towards equality, inclusiveness, and communication access.

REFERENCES

Bechter, F. (2008). "The Deaf Convert Culture and Its Lessons for Deaf Theory." In *Open Your Eyes: Deaf Studies Talking.* Minneapolis: University of Minnesota Press, 2008.

Davis, L. J. (2008) "Postdeafness." In *Open Your Eyes.* Minneapolis: University of Minnesota Press, 2008.

Gannon, J. R. (1989). *The Week the World Heard Gallaudet.* Washington, DC: Gallaudet University Press.

Gibson, P. (2009). Gay Male and Lesbian Suicide, http://www.lambda.org/youth_suicide.htm (accessed October 2010).

Ladd, P. (2011). *Deafhood: An introduction.* March 2011. Bristol: University of Bristol Centre for Deaf Studies.

Ladd, P. (2008). *Deafhood: An introduction.* October 2008. Bristol: University of Bristol Centre for Deaf Studies. Luczak, R. (2007) *Eyes of desire II: A Deaf GLBT reader.* Minneapolis: Handtype Press.

Spitzer, R. L. (1981). "The diagnostic status of homosexuality in DSM-III: a reformulation of the issues," 138: 210-215, *The American Journal of Psychiatry,* 1981, http://ajp.psychiatryonline.org/cgi/content/abstract/138/2/210 (accessed June 26, 2011).

Windfuhr, K. & Turner, N. K. O. (2007). *Suicide in deaf populations: a literature review,* 6:26, October 8, 2007, http://www.annals-general-psychiatry.com/content/6/1/26 (accessed June 26, 2011).

World Health Organization, World report on disability, 2011, http://www.who.int/disabilities/world_report/2011/en/index.html (accessed June 10, 2011).

Is There Such a Thing as American Sign Language Literacy?

ANDREW BYRNE, PH.D.

WHILE THERE IS WIDESPREAD ACCEPTANCE OF ASL AS A LANGUAGE, there has not been the same level of discussion as to what constitutes ASL *literacy*. Since ASL has no widely accepted written form, could it still be viewed as having literacy? Currently, the field of ASL and Deaf Studies is engaged in a lively debate with two opposing views. The first view was espoused by the Deaf sociolinguist Dr. Stephen Nover (2004a, 2004b) who has led a major reform movement in ASL/English bilingual education for Deaf students (see Nover, Christensen, & Cheng, 1998). Nover's claim is that "ASL has no written form and therefore no literacy" (Czubek, 2006, p. 374).

An opposing viewpoint was proposed by Todd Czubek, a former teacher and coordinator in schools for the Deaf and now a Ph.D. candidate in the Applied Linguistics program at Boston University. Czubek (2006) wrote an essay using quotes from poems, philosophers, theories, and stories from his Deaf grandmother to present the opposing view that ASL, indeed, has a literacy. He claimed, "I believe that there is such a thing as ASL literacy" (p. 374). He presents his point of view and claims that instead of limiting ourselves to just labels such as literacy, we should go beyond by focusing on "whether or not we will accept parochial attitudes and exclusive taxonomies that perpetuate a bias all things not written" (p. 374). While Czubek defends the notion of ASL literacy with philosophical stances and entertaining stories, he does not fully develop the notion of ASL literacy in a scholarly fashion that could be useful to ASL and Deaf Studies specialists and educators as this paper will attempt to do.

Nover and Czubek are on opposite sides of the spectrum in their points of view. Indeed, opposing viewpoints or using the metaphor "wars" are not uncommon in any new developing discipline. Cases in point are the communication wars in Deaf Education (Ladd, 2008), the Reading Wars (Adams, 1990), and the Linguistic Wars (Harris, 1993). The field of ASL and Deaf Studies is no different. A serious discussion of ASL literacy debate should bring both viewpoints to the table for discussion. The conceptualizations of literacy and ASL literacy will be presented with four reasons to support the fact that there is such a thing as ASL literacy.

CONCEPTUALIZATION OF LITERACY

The connection between language and literacy is important because they complement each other and are essential to every aspect of an individual's life. Before making an attempt to comprehend what literacy is and the problem of defining literacy, the distinction of orality and literacy needs to be understood first.

Between 1100 and 700 BCE, the Greek society was completely oral (Havelock, 1976, 1986). "Classics of ancient Greek literature must have been passed on orally for a long time before being written down" (Frishberg, 1988, p. 151). This indicates that "…written forms of language are not required for a community to possess a well-formed aesthetic in poetry, narrative, humor, and rhetoric" (p. 150). The Greek alphabet was invented around 800 BCE. Its original purpose was to mark ownership (Powell, 2002). "This society became literate only by slow degrees" (Havelock, 1986, p. 29). Three hundred years after the invention of the alphabet, the society had a considerable body of literature written but "ancient Greece was in many ways an oral society in which the written word took second place to the spoken" (Thomas, 1992, p. 3). As time progressed, the Greeks became so accustomed to the written form that they had lost their grip on preserving their oral traditions. The oral poems composed by Homer and Hesiod were written down which subsequently led to the beginning of the history of the European literature (Havelock, 1976, 1986). Many people do not realize that the development of Greek literature actually came from an even older tradition of oral storytelling.

Tannen (1982b) clearly provides the distinction of orality and literacy, which draws from the scholarly research of Havelock (1963), Lord (1960), Olson (1977), and Ong (1967). The distinction is as follows:

Orality	Literacy
• "Formulaic expressions (sayings, clichés, proverbs, and so on) are the repository of received wisdom" (p. 1).	• "Knowledge is seen as facts and insights preserved in written records (p. 1).
• "Thought is 'exquisitely elaborated' through a stitching together of formulaic language…" (p. 2).	• "Thought is analytic, sequential, linear" (p. 2).
• "Truth…resides in common-sense reference to experience" (p. 2).	• "[Truth] resides in logical or coherent argument" (p. 2).
• In speaking, "the meaning is in the context" (p. 2).	• In writing, "the meaning is in the text" (p. 2).

Interestingly, at the same time, Tannen (1982b) challenges the distinction of orality and literacy, which is also known as the oral-literate divide. Her research demonstrates that "the speaker [who] is…more 'oral' are nonetheless highly literate people" (p. 13). Therefore, the divide should be replaced with a continuum. She notes,

> "[B]oth oral and literate strategies [related to conversational style and fluency] can be seen in spoken discourse. Understanding this, let us not think of orality and literacy as an absolute split, and let us not fall into the trap of thinking of literacy, or written discourse, as decontextualized. Finally, the examples presented of conversational style make it clear that it is possible to be both highly oral and highly literate. Thus, let us not be lured into calling some folks oral and others literate" (1982a, pp. 47–48).

Furthermore, Edwards and Sienkewicz (1990) point out that orality and literacy should not be considered as a divide but a continuum. An excellent example is the sermon of the Afro-American preacher. "On the one hand the preacher is steeped in the literate culture of the book, of the Bible; on the other hand the medium of the preacher's message is purely oral" (p. 7). The preacher is in both oral and literate worlds almost simultaneously. This example is no different from a Deaf individual who uses ASL as "oral" and English as literate. To conclude the relationship of orality and literacy, Finnegan (1988) writes:

> Orality and literacy are not two separate and independent things; nor (to put it more concretely) are oral and written modes two mutually exclusive and opposed processes for representing and communicating information. On the contrary, they take diverse forms in differing cultures and periods, are used differently in different social contexts and, insofar as they can be distinguished at all as separate modes rather than a continuum, they mutually interact and affect each other, and the relations between them are problematic rather than self-evident (p. 175).

Opening a dictionary of English word origins, one will usually discover that the term *literacy* is based on literate, which arose in the fifteenth century from the Latin word *litteratus*, meaning "one who knows the letters" (Chantrell, 2002; Harper, 2001). Also, it can mean "the man of letters" or "a reader of letters" (Havelock, 1976). Literacy by itself was formed for the first time in English in the 1880s (Brockmeier & Olson, 2009). Because of the origin of literacy, to the eyes of anyone, it is generally and automatically referred to anything that is printed. However, Samantha Schad, an Oxford University Press etymologist specializing in Latin and Greek, argues:

> It is a widely held misconception that establishing the original meaning of a word in some way helps to highlight the true meaning of the word. In fact, as you are no doubt aware, words change their meaning through time, and the current accepted meaning of a word may be very different from its original meaning. *The Oxford English Dictionary*, which illustrates the use and meanings of every word throughout its history within English, shows this very clearly. The etymology or derivation of a word may well help to account for its original meaning, and indeed the earliest sense of a word often sheds light on its etymology, but a word as used in contemporary English has often departed a long way from its original or 'etymological' sense (S. Schad, personal communication, August 13, 2010).

A dictionary of English word origins usually ends with Latin, however, the term *literacy* actually can be traced to Greek:

- Derived from the English word *literate*
- Derived from the Latin word *litteratus* (learned, cultured, erudite; marked, branded, tattooed w)
- Derived from the Humanistic Latin word *litteræ* (letter; letter, epistle)
- Derived from the Etruscan word *littera*
- Derived from the Greek word *diphthera* (διφθέρα; skin, leather, hide)

If we wish to connect literacy to "skin, leather, or hide," it might be a good stopping point because we could argue that we should not use the etymology of *literacy* as a sole basis. When asked to share her perspective on the etymology of literacy and to clarify what the Greek derivation of leather, hide, skin actually represents, Schad explains:

> As for the etymology of Latin littera, this is in fact uncertain and disputed. The word used to be associated with Latin linere, 'to smear,' as Roman schoolchildren wrote on wax tablets (with a stylus), and smeared over the wax to erase the letters. But this view is now generally rejected. Derivation from Greek διφθέρα [diphthera] is another hypothesis that has been proposed. There are two problems with this: the form of the word and the meaning of the word. In ancient Greek, διφθέρα means 'piece of leather, prepared hide (of an animal), something made of leather.' The evidence that it might

mean 'letter' is very late and very slight. Then we would have to explain how Greek διφθέρα turned into Latin *littera*. Some words were borrowed into Latin from Greek through Etruscan, a language spoken in ancient Italy, but there is very little evidence for Etruscan, so it is often difficult to prove that this is what happened (S. Schad, personal communication, August 13, 2010).

One might use Schad's point as a basis to counter the general belief that the origin of *literacy* is solely connected to those who know the letters. We are currently uncertain how Greek *diphthera* turned into Latin *littera* because, like Schad pointed out, "a word as used in contemporary English has often departed a long way from its original or 'etymological' sense."

Roberts (1995) explains that, "[t]he problem of defining literacy has bewitched scholars, policy makers and practitioners since the early 1940s. The range of definitions of 'literacy' and 'illiteracy' advanced in the past half-century is remarkable, yet there remains little agreement among 'experts' over what these terms mean" (p. 412). He adds, "[T]he sheer number and variety of definitions is staggering in magnitude and, from one perspective, thoroughly confusing: literacy, it seems, can mean whatever people want it to mean" (p. 419). According to Street (2008), "the answers to the question 'what is literacy?' have been sometimes surprising. It turns out that literacy means different things to different people across different periods of time and in different places" (p. xiii). Interestingly, Olson (1987) argues that the reason for the unclear definition of literacy is due to an absence of theory. "[W]hat is lacking is not a definition but a theory. [I]t is not clear how the related notions fit into a theory. Lacking the theory, writers and laymen alike seize on some property — ability to read and write one's name…and the like — as a definition for literacy" (p. 7).

Nowadays, it is generally known that literacy itself means the ability to read and write (e.g., Gee, 1991; Lane, Hoffmeister, & Bahan, 1996; Langer, 1991; Luria, 2006; Narasimhan, 2004; Olson & Torrance, 2009; Pattison, 1982; Trezek, Wang, & Paul, 2010). However, the United Nations Educational, Scientific, and Cultural Organization (2003) states that "literacy is about more than reading and writing, it is about how we communicate in society. It is about social practices and relationships, about knowledge, language and culture" (p. 1). In addition, Luria (2006) writes, "Literacy [is] more broadly defined not only as the ability to speak, read, and write, but also to do math, use the computer, and possess knowledge of one's place or situation within the local and larger society" (p. 233). Layton and Miller (2004) write, "[L]iteracy is not restricted to the mechanics of reading and writing but that being literate involves taking part in oral discussions where the focus is literature" (p. 56). Another broader definition comes from Foley (1994): "[T]he term 'literacy' will be used broadly to refer to the mastery of language, in both its spoken (or augmented) and written forms, which enables an individual to use language fluently for a variety of purposes" (p. 184). Langer (1991) takes a step further by defining literacy as not just the acts of reading and writing but also culturally appropriate ways of literate thinking. Literacy can be defined as "the ability to think and reason like a literate person, within a particular society" (p. 11). The ASL community in most parts of Canada and the United States can be considered as a particular society within the global community of thousands of societies.

Where the definition of literacy was once restricted to the ability to read and write, literacy is now more broadly defined as the ability to use varied skills of language including listening, speaking, reading, writing, and thinking. The most comprehensive and current definition of literacy may be that

> Literacy is defined as the ability to use language and images in rich and varied forms to read, write, listen, view, represent, and think critically about ideas. It involves the capacity to access, manage, and evaluate information; to think imaginatively and analytically; and to communicate thoughts and ideas effectively. Literacy includes critical thinking and reasoning to solve problems and make decisions related to issues of fairness, equity, and social justice. Literacy connects individuals and communities and is an essential tool for personal growth and active participation in a cohesive, democratic society (Ontario Ministry of Education [OME], 2008, p. 6).

Due to rapidly changing definitions, the term literacy, as a single phenomenon, may be obsolete today. Roberts (1995) states that "[t]he term 'literacy' is thus always a kind of misnomer: an inadequate way of describing the myriad specific literacies. There is no core definition of literacy to which we can turn as a benchmark for testing the validity of particular definitions; particulars are all we have. Strictly speaking, for these thinkers, there is no such thing as a definition of literacy, only definitions of this literacy or that literacy" (pp. 422–423). According to Vincent (2003), "literacy has become too promiscuous. The word itself, the fragment of language, is daily extending its application. We have more and more literacies" (p. 341). Street (1999) stresses that there are many literacies within any culture. Each has its own code and validity (as cited in Crossley & Watson, 2003). Perceived as a possibly appropriate term for the 21st century, the acceptance of literacies as a term is growing. Currently, drawing from a variety of sources such as Abilock (2011), Grover (2002), Harste (2003), Kellner (2000), and Kenosha Literacy Council (2011), different kinds of literacy may be

Emotional	Technological	Health	Information
Scientific	Adolescent	Early	Media
Preschool	Oral	Vernacular	Cultural
Financial	Family	Computer	Mathematical
Critical	Visual	Functional	Liberatory
Adult	Digital	Workplace	Humanistic
Xerox	Religious	Automotive	Amish
Linguistic	Academic	Universal	Script
Global	Historical	Geographic	Legal
Prose	Document	Quantitative	Statistical

Regardless of some critics thinking that the term literacy, as a single phenomenon, may be outdated today, this term continues to be used everywhere within the business, educational, legal, medical, and other sectors. All of the aforementioned definitions of literacy are applicable to both spoken and written languages. In addition, there are a growing number of publications that use the term "oral literacy" (see Balnaves, 2007; Hamer, 2005; Sayer, 1980; Spies-Butcher, 2007; Trezek, Wang, & Paul, 2010). In spite of some critics who perceive "oral literacy" as a contradiction in terms, a growing number of people are accepting it because literacy is not only limited to written (printed) form but also to spoken (oral).

CONCEPTUALIZATION OF ASL LITERACY

Compared to the published discussions on the relationship between ASL and English, and especially how ASL can be used to support the development of English literacy (see Bailes, 2001; Goldin-Meadows & Mayberry, 2001; Hoffmeister, 2000; Lane et al., 1996; Neuroth-Gimbrone & Logiodice, 1992; Padden & Ramsey, 2000; Strong & Prinz, 1997, 1998, 2000; Supalla & Cripps, 2008; Wilbur, 2000), the published discussions on ASL literacy by itself and the relationship between ASL literacy and ASL literature (see Ashton, Cagle, Kurz, Newell, Peterson, & Zinza, 2011, Christie & Wilkins, 1997; Czubek, 2006; Gibson, 2000; Hoffmeister, 2000; Kuntze, 2008; Lane et al., 1996; Paul, 2006; & Snoddon, 2010) are sparse.

Thus, more attention should be spent on ASL literacy and the relationship between ASL literacy and ASL literature. Needless to say, developing strong English literacy skills is vital for success in using English as a second language for Deaf students. However, developing strong ASL literacy skills first is fundamental. Lane, et al. (1996) concisely explains, "Achieving English literacy is vital to the success of the Deaf child as he or she grows up in our hearing society. However, to be fully successful, Deaf children will need to be able to function in the DEAF-WORLD as well" (p. 305).

At the present time, the definition of ASL literacy has not yet been established and widely accepted. Since ASL has no widely accepted written form, could it still be viewed as having literacy? Critics consider ASL to have no literacy because literacy by itself refers to spoken languages that have written forms. On the contrary, critics believe that signed languages with no written forms such as ASL do have literacy. The following table, then, includes contexted arguments, comparisons, and contrasts of various contemporary definitions of ASL literacy.

Sources	Definitions of ASL Literacy
Ashton, Cagle, Kurz, Newell, Peterson, & Zinza (2011)	No distinct definition provided but the authors write, "Where once the definition of literacy was confined to the ability to read and write, literacy today is more broadly defined as the ability to function in a culture. Like many world languages ASL has no written form. Therefore standards in other languages for reading and writing do not necessarily apply in the same way to the study of ASL. The lack of a written form does not preclude literary uses of ASL. Similar to oral traditions in spoken languages, there is a long standing use of ASL for storytelling, poetry, drama, humor and folklore. There are emerging schools of thought that point to similarities between the skills needed in writing and those needed to compose recorded ASL products, such as videotexts, sign mail, and films" (pp. 8–9).
Christie & Wilkins (1997)	Based on the three positions of literacy identified by Paulo Freire and Donaldo Macedo (see McLaren, 1991), in an effort to define ASL literacy, Christie and Wilkins describe each position of literacy: 1) ASL Functional Literacy: "…basic language skills that enable a person to use ASL to communicate effectively in the DEAF-WORLD" (p. 57) 2) ASL Cultural Literacy: "…the values, heritage, and shared experiences necessary to understand and interpret the relationships of ASL literary works to our lives as Deaf people" (p. 57) 3) ASL Critical Literacy: "…the use of literature as a means of empowerment and an ideological awareness of the DEAF-WORLD in relation to other worlds" (pp. 57-58)
Czubek (2006)	No distinct definition provided but Czubek writes, "'So, let us explore ASL and ASL literacy because as creative beings…we shall not cease exploration and at the very end of all our exploring will be to arrive at where we have started and to know the place for the first time.' — T.S. Eliot, *Little Gidding*" (p. 380).

Gibson (2000)	ASL literacy is defined as "a measure of [1] the ability to understand and express [ASL] eloquently; [2] acquisition of knowledge of content areas including Deaf history, ASL literature, different Deaf cultures, Deaf traditions, Deaf politics, controversial or current issues (Deaf Education, ASL Literacy, Deaf Community and Underemployment) and trends; [3] having extensive knowledge, and experience associated with Deaf culture; and [4] to feel empowered to connect with the world, take control of one's own life, and contribute to the Deaf community as well as to a changing society" (p. 10).
Hoffmeister (2000)	No distinct definition provided but Hoffmeister writes, "Literacy, as defined here, includes not only reading skills but also skills required to become a literate user of American Sign Language (ASL). Literacy skills in ASL have only recently begun to be identified" (p. 143).
Kuntze (2008)	No distinct definition provided but Kuntze discusses the following main topics: Analogic and digital symbols in human communication, inference-making skills, visual literacy, ASL literacy, text and literacy, and on being literate. Under the topic of ASL literacy, he discusses the use of analogic representations in ASL utterances.
Lane, Hoffmeister, & Bahan (1996)	No distinct definition provided but the authors write, "The stories told in Deaf clubs, in residential schools, by Deaf parents to their Deaf and hearing children, are all part of the literature of Deaf culture, learned, remembered and passed on from generation to generation. We consider this a part of ASL literacy, for we subscribe to the view that expands the notion of literacy beyond reading print and refocuses it on the language registers that must be mastered. These include the formal storytelling register, with its coherent, complex, decontextualized language, which exists as assuredly in ASL as it does in English" (p. 304).
	The authors add, "ASL literacy is similar in some ways to the literacy of many cultures where print is not available to carry messages from one generation to the next. Stories are developed which have particular structures, specific themes, and an established set of goals. The common structures make it easy for the members of the culture to recognize a story for the cultural artifact that it is, to identify with the elements of the story, and to remember it. The ability to understand and recognize the structure and theme of these stories is part of ASL literacy knowledge" (p. 304).

Paul (2006)	No distinct definition provided but, drawing from the work of Tyner (1998), different forms of literacies are divided into tool literacies and literacies of representation. While tool literacies refer to technological tools in society such as computer literacy, literacies of representation refer to the need of analyzing information and understanding how meaning is constructed. Some examples of literacies of representation include oral literacy, print literacy, and sign literacy (e.g., ASL literacy).
	Paul has proposed to reconceptualize literacy as a form of "captured" verbal information. "Script (or print) literacy refers to the capture of verbal language or information through print or written symbols, that is, via written language. Performance literacy refers to the capture of spoken or signed information only through the use of audio books or video books (in one sense, this is similar to ASL literacy, i.e., on videos). Caption literacy is the combination of script and performance literacy with a video background. Within Tyner's (1998) framework, script literacy, performance literacy, and caption literacy refer to different literacies of representation" (p. 383).
Snoddon (2010)	No distinct definition provided but, drawing from the work of Gee (2008), Snoddon views ASL literacy as "a social practice that must be acquired through social and cultural participation" (pp. 198-199).

For a contemporary definition of ASL literacy, Gibson may possibly prove the most suitable. However, definitions by Gibson (2000), Lane et al. (1996), Langer (1991), and the Ontario Ministry of Education (2008) could be intertwined to create a more comprehensive definition of ASL literacy:

> ASL literacy is defined as the ability to use ASL for deciphering, organiz-
> ing, and communicating information, ideas, and thoughts effectively and
> eloquently. It involves the capability to decode, cogitate, reason, assess,
> and evaluate ASL informational texts and literary works at the social and
> academic levels. An individual has the ability to construct and present ASL
> literary works imaginatively and eloquently. ASL literacy includes the ability
> to acquire extensive knowledge and experience associated with ASL cul-
> ture, ASL history, ASL literature, ASL/English bilingual education, signed
> language cultures, and other relevant issues. It provides an individual the
> ability to effectively lead one's life, to actively contribute to the ASL com-
> munity, and to successfully meet the expectations and challenges of global
> signed language communities and global communities at large.

There are four reasons to support the fact that there is such a thing as ASL literacy. First of all, even though the publications on ASL literacy are currently sparse, the works by Ashton, Cagle, Kurz, Newell, Peterson, and Zinza, Christie and Wilkins, Czubek, Gibson, Hoffmeister, Kuntze, Lane et al., Paul, and Snoddon should be viewed as fueling the discussion to begin defining and more fully developing the notion of ASL literacy in a scholarly fashion that could be useful to the fields of ASL and Deaf Studies.

A contemporary development that has not yet been published points to the importance of ASL literacy. In 1993, with the passage of Bill 4, ASL and Lingues des Signes Quebecois (LSQ) were authorized as languages of instruction for Deaf students in Ontario. When compared to norms of first language children, the expectations of Deaf children's average ASL literacy skills were lower (Gibson, 2006). In response to this, the establishment of an ASL curriculum began in 1999 under the direction of Heather Gibson. Similar to English or French-speaking Canadian students taking formal courses in English and/or French, Deaf students in Ontario are now being offered "(a) the formal study of their own language (that is, of the grammatical structure, vocabulary, and pragmatics of ASL, including its discourse, conversational structures, and rules of use, and the stylistic and register forms found in the literature and text of the language and (b) extensive exposure to ASL and ASL literature, texts, and media arts at the academic level" (Gibson, 2006, p. 101). Currently, the general and specific expectations for nursery to grade 8 have been developed and are being field tested (H. Gibson, personal communication, December 27, 2009).

Exclusively fieldtested on Deaf students of Deaf ASL-using parents, field testing consists of videotaping learning activities according to the ASL curriculum, field notes taken during the instruction of Deaf students, and classroom observers who participate in various learning activities as presented by the ASL curriculum. The main purpose of this curriculum is to measure Deaf students' progress of the development and demonstration of their ASL and ASL literacy skills (Gibson, 2006). Two separate assessment tools are used to measure progress: ASL Development Checklist for students up to five years old and ASL Proficiency Assessment (ASL-PA) for students from six to twelve years old (H. Gibson, personal communication, May 18, 2010).

For the first time in almost two hundred years since the establishment of the first permanent and publicly supported American school for Deaf students in 1817 in North America (Carbin, 1996), the Ontario ASL curriculum used at an academic level is the only one in existence anywhere in North America. Also, for the first time, Deaf students are given opportunities to study their own language and experience sophisticated ASL literary works throughout their schooling. ASL curriculum is still in the draft form and the final version will be submitted soon.

Secondly, the previous section on Understanding Literacy discusses the etymological fallacy of literacy. This discussion should be easily applicable to ASL because the etymology should not be considered as a sole basis. In other words, it is a weak argument for not recognizing the term, ASL literacy.

The next reason is that more and more publications now use the term *oral literacy*. While both Hamer (2005) and Balnaves (2007) view oral literacy as a powerful tool for oral storytelling, Sayer (1980) defines oral literacy as the ability to express thoughts verbally and critically. He feels that, compared to the importance of teaching reading and writing, speaking as a skill should be given equal priority. According to Spies-Butcher (2007), "the skills of oral literacy clearly go beyond those learned in debating and public speaking. Oral literacy is about a broader notion of communication. Nonetheless, these skills are an important component of our ability to communicate, and particularly our ability to gain recognition and respect for our ideas and opinions. These skills are particularly important because they are central to much of the way in which our society publicly deliberates, and because these skills are often used as an informal mechanism for stratification and establishing (or more likely reinforcing) social hierarchies" (p. 269). In parallel with the wider use of the term, oral literacy, the proposal for using the term, signed literacy (e.g., ASL), should be considered.

Lastly, explaining how to apply the three positions of literacy to ASL and indicating the importance of the relationship between language such as ASL and literacy, Gibson (2000) provides a convincing example of a Deaf teacher who taught a lesson of an ASL poem, #S-N-O-W in her nursery and junior kindergarten classroom.

> This poem opens with students lying on the floor, with their hands using the open 5 handshape (indicating that it is snowing) in the air. Then they fingerspell the letters slowly one by one (#S-N-O-W) starting from the top towards the floor, using different directions, handshapes, movements and actions of the snow in ASL. When they fingerspell using the "W" handshape, they throw their hands right into their faces. This indicates that the snow flops right into their faces. Those students who did this activity demonstrated proficiency and eloquence in using their language creatively beyond **functional literacy skills in ASL**.
>
> Not only did those students fingerspell the word #S-N-O-W, but they also did so in artistic ways of using different movements, directions, handshapes and actions of the snow. This poem uses particular art forms found in the Deaf cultural context. The students apply cultural literacy in their poem. This poem reflects the symbolism of Deaf Spirit, as it is arranged in a visual form that follows ASL principles.
>
> In terms of ASL critical literacy, we can see that there is a particular pattern of movement and action in the poem. If we ask students to analyze what movement this poem, #S-N-O-W particularly reflects, it will exhibit that the movement for four different handshapes is the same. It follows the principles and structures of an ASL poem (pp. 10–11).

We should consider Gibson's example as evidence that the positions of literacy identified by Freire and Macedo should now encompass not only oral and written languages but also signed languages such as ASL. Also, Gibson's example is powerful enough to indicate that there is such a thing as ASL literacy. Just like any other language in the world, there is more than sufficient evidence that ASL is a language with "its grammar, its literature and poetry, its evolution, its cognitive processing and how the brain works to accomplish it, its acquisition as a first language by children with deaf parents, its registers and dialects, and so on" (Lane, 1992, p. 46). ASL also permits its users to communicate and think thoughts and ideas effectively, critically, imaginatively, and analytically.

Ppublications by Ashton, Cagle, Kurz, Newell, Peterson, and Zinza, Christie and Wilkins, Czubek, Gibson, Hoffmeister, Kuntze, Lane et al., Paul, and Snoddon can be viewed as a growing interest in defining and describing the notion of ASL literacy. It has been well known that ASL has no written form. This is not a major concern because two-thirds of the spoken languages in the world have no written forms today (OzIdeas, 2008). As a matter of fact, since the beginning of human history, out of probably tens of thousands of languages, only approximately 106 have ever been converted to the written form (Ong, 1982, 2009). Because of the firm recognition of ASL as a natural and legitimate language, it must be considered as having literacy because of the inseparable connection between language and literacy. If not for language, there would be no literacy. Therefore, literacy should not only be limited to written and spoken forms but also to signed (i.e., ASL literacy). In sum, literacy is an all-encompassing term for every human language, whether it is spoken, written, or signed. Yes, there is such a big thing as ASL literacy!

REFERENCES

Abilock, D. (2011). 21st century literacies. Retrieved from http://www.noodletools.com/debbie/literacies/

Adams, M. (1990). *Beginning to read: Thinking and learning about print.* Cambridge, MA: MIT Press.

Ashton, G., Cagle, K., Kurz, K. B., Newell, W., Peterson, R., & Zinza, J. E. (2011, March). *Standards for learning American Sign Language: A project of the American Sign Language Teachers Association.* Retrieved from http://www.interpretereducation.org/wp-content/uploads/2011/06/ASL-Standards-March-2011-draft-pub.pdf

Bailes, C. N. (2001). Integrative ASL-English language arts: Bridging paths to literacy. *Sign Language Studies,* 1(2), 147-174.

Balnaves, K. (2007, July). Narrative, games and the oral literacy revolution. Paper presented at the AATE & ALEA National Conference on Critical Capital: Teaching & Learning, Canberra, AU. Retrieved from http://www.englishliteracyconference.com.au/files/.../Kim%20Balnaves.pdf

Brockmeier, J., & Olson, D. R. (2009). The literacy episteme: From Innis to Derrida. In D. R. Olson & N. Torrance (Eds.), *The Cambridge handbook of literacy* (pp. 3–21). New York, NY: Cambridge University Press.

Carbin, C. F. (1996). *Deaf heritage in Canada: A distinctive, diverse, and enduring culture.* Toronto, ON: McGraw-Hill Ryerson Limited.

Chantrell, G. (Ed.). (2002). *The Oxford dictionary of word histories.* New York, NY: Oxford University Press.

Christie, K., & Wilkins, D. M. (1997). A feast for the eyes: ASL literacy and ASL literature. *Journal of Deaf Studies and Deaf Education, 2*(1), 57–59.

Crossley, M., & Watson, K. (2003). *Comparative and international research in education: Globalisation, context and difference.* New York, NY: RoutledgeFalmer.

Czubek, T. A. (2006). Blue listerine, parochialism, and ASL literacy. *Journal of Deaf Studies and Deaf Education, 11*(3), 373–381.

Edwards, V., & Sienkewicz, T. J. (1990). *Oral cultures past and present: Rappin' and Homer.* Cambridge, MA: Basil Blackwell, Inc.

Finnegan, R. (1988). *Literacy and orality: Studies in the technology of communication.* Oxford, UK: Blackwell Publishing.

Foley, B. E. (1994). The development of literacy in individuals with severe congenital speech and motor impairments. In K. G. Butler (Ed.), *Severe communication disorders: Intervention strategies* (pp. 183–199). Gaithersburg, MD: Aspen.

Frishberg, N. (1988). Signers of tales: The case for literary status of an unwritten language. *Sign Language Studies, 59,* 149–170.

Gee, J. P. (1991). What is literacy? In C. Mitchell & K. Weiler (Eds.), *Rewriting literacy: Culture and the discourse of the other* (pp. 3–11). New York, NY: Bergin & Garvey.

Gibson, H. (2000, March). American Sign Language curriculum: A GOLDEN KEY! *OCSD Bulletin, 6*(3), 9–11.

Gibson, H. (2006). American Sign Language curriculum for first-language ASL students. In H. Goodstein (Ed.), *The Deaf Way II reader* (pp. 100–106). Washington, DC: Gallaudet University Press.

Goldin-Meadows, S., & Mayberry, R. I. (2001). How do profoundly deaf children learn to read? *Learning Disabilities, Research, and Practice* (Special issue: Emergent and early literacy: Current status and research directions), 16, 221–228.

Grover, J. (2002). Kinds of literacy. Retrieved from http://c2.com/cgi/wiki?KindsOfLiteracy

Hamer, J. (2005). Exploring literacy with infants from a sociocultural perspective. *New Zealand Journal of Teachers' Work, 2*(2), 70–75.

Harper, D. (2001). Online etymology dictionary: Literacy. Retrieved from http://www.etymonline.com/index.php?search=literacy&searchmode=none

Harper, D. (2001). Online etymology dictionary: Literate. Retrieved from http://www.etymonline.com/index.php?term=literate

Harper, D. (2001). Online etymology dictionary: Literature. Retrieved from http://www.etymonline.com/index.php?search=literature&searchmode=none

Harris, R. A. (1993). *The linguistic wars.* New York, NY: Oxford University Press.

Harste, J. C. (2003). What do we mean by literacy now? *Voices from the Middle,* 10(3), 8-12.

Havelock, E. A. (1963). *Preface to Plato.* Cambridge, MA: Harvard University Press.

Havelock, E. A. (1976). *Origins of Western literacy.* Toronto, ON: The Ontario Institute for Studies in Education.

Havelock, E. A. (1986). *The muse learns to write: Reflections on orality and literacy from antiquity to the present.* New Haven, CT: Yale University Press.

Hoffmeister, R. J. (2000). A piece of the puzzle: ASL and reading comprehension in deaf children. In C. Chamberlain, J. Morford, & R. Mayberry (Eds.), *Language acquisition by eye* (pp. 143–163). Mahwah, NJ: Lawrence Erlbaum Associates, Inc.

Kellner, D. (2000). New technologies/new literacies: Reconstructing education for the new millennium. *Teaching Education, 11*(3), 245–265.

Kenosha Literacy Council. (2011). *Types of literacy.* Retrieved from http://www.kenoshalit.org/WhatIsLiteracy/types.php

Kuntze, M. (2008). Turning literacy inside out. In H-D. L. Bauman (Ed.), *Open your eyes: Deaf studies talking* (pp. 146–157). Minneapolis, MN: University of Minnesota Press.

Ladd, P. (2008). Colonialism and resistance: A brief history of deafhood. In H-D. L. Bauman (Ed.), *Open your eyes: Deaf studies talking* (pp. 42–59). Minneapolis, MN: University of Minnesota Press.

Lane, H. (1992). *The mask of benevolence: Disabling the deaf community.* New York, NY: Alfred A. Knopf.

Lane, H., Hoffmeister, R., & Bahan, B. (1996). *A journey into the DEAF-WORLD.* San Diego, CA: DawnSignPress.

Langer, J. A. (1991). Literacy and schooling: A sociocognitive perspective. In E. H. Hiebert (Ed.), *Literacy for a diverse society: Perspectives, practices, and policies* (pp. 9–27). New York, NY: Teachers College Press.

Layton, L., & Miller, C. (2004). Interpretations of literacy. *Cambridge Journal of Education, 34*(1), 51-63.

Lord, A. (1960). *The singer of tales.* Cambridge, MA: Harvard University Press.

Luria, H. (2006). Literacy and education in a globalized world. In H. Luria, D. M. Seymour, & T. Smoke (Eds.), *Language and linguistics in context: Readings and applications for teachers* (pp. 233–242). Mahwah, NJ: Lawrence Erlbaum Associates.

Narasimhan, R. (2004). *Characterizing literacy: A study of Western and Indian literacy experiences.* Thousand Oaks, CA: SAGE Publications.

Neuroth-Gimbrone, C., & Logiodice, C. (1992). A cooperative bilingual language program for deaf adolescents. *Sign Language Studies, 74,* 79-91.

Nover, S. M. (2004a). A theoretical framework for language planning in ASL/English bilingual education. Manuscript in preparation.

Nover, S. M. (2004b, October 22). The road to success: ASL is the key! Presentation at the ASL Specialist Conference, St. Paul College, St. Paul, MN.

Nover, S. M., Christensen, K. M., & Cheng, L. L. (1998). Development of ASL and English competence for learners who are deaf. *Topics in Language Disorders, 18*(4), 61-72.

Olson, D. R. (1977). From utterance to text: The bias of language in speech and writing. *Harvard Educational Review, 47,* 257–281.

Olson, D. R. (1987). An introduction to understanding literacy. *Interchange, 18*(1/2), 1-8.

Olson, D. R., & Torrance, N. (Eds.). (2009). *The Cambridge handbook of literacy.* New York, NY: Cambridge University Press.

Ong, W. J. (1967). *The presence of the word.* New Haven, CT: Yale University Press.

Ong, W. J. (1982). *Orality and literacy: The technologizing of the word.* New York, NY: Methuen & Co. Ltd.

Ong, W. J. (2009). The orality of language. In S. D. Blum (Ed.), *Making sense of language: Readings in culture and communication* (pp. 45–51). New York, NY: Oxford University Press.

Ontario Ministry of Education. (2008). Reach every student: Energizing Ontario education. Retrieved from http://www.edu.gov.on.ca/eng/document/energize/

OzIdeas. (2008). Writing system alternatives: Introduction to a book on writing systems of the world. Retrieved from http://home.vicnet.net.au/~ozideas/writintro.htm

Padden, C., & Ramsey, C. (2000). American Sign Language and reading ability in deaf children. In C. Chamberlain, J. Morford, & R. Mayberry (Eds.), *Language acquisition by eye* (pp. 165–189). Hillsdale, NJ: Lawrence Erlbaum Associates.

Pattison, R. (1982). *On literacy: The politics of the word from Homer to the age of rock.* New York, NY: Oxford University Press.

Paul, P. V. (2006). New literacies, multiple literacies, unlimited literacies: What now, what next, where to? A response to blue listerine, parochialism and ASL literacy. *Journal of Deaf Studies and Deaf Education,* 11(3), 382–387.

Powell, B. B. (2002). *Writing and the origins of Greek literature.* New York, NY: Cambridge University Press.

Roberts, P. (1995). Defining literacy: Paradise, nightmare or red herring? *British Journal of Educational Studies,* 43(4), 412–432.

Sayer, J. E. (1980). Speaking out for oral literacy. *Curriculum Review,* 19(2), 147.

Snoddon, K. (2010). Technology as a learning tool for ASL literacy. *Sign Language Studies,* 10(2), 197–213.

Spies-Butcher, B. (2007, September). Debating and public speaking as oral literacy: Promoting democratic education. Paper presented at the Future Directions in Literacy: International Conversations Conference, Sydney, AU. Retrieved from http://ses.library.usyd.edu.au/bitstream/2123/.../FutureDirections_Ch15.pdf

Strong, M., & Prinz, P. M. (1997). A study of the relationship between American Sign Language and English literacy. *Journal of Deaf Studies and Deaf Education,* 2(1), 37–46.

Strong, M., & Prinz, P. M. (1998). ASL proficiency and English literacy within a bilingual deaf education model of education. *Topics in Language Disorders,* 18(4), 47–60.

Strong, M., & Prinz, P. M. (2000). Is American Sign Language skill related to English literacy? In C. Chamberlain, J. P. Morford, & R. I. Mayberry (Eds.), *Language acquisition by eye* (pp. 131–141). Mahwah, NJ: Lawrence Erlbaum Associates.

Supalla, S., & Cripps, J. (2008). Linguistic accessibility and deaf children. In B. Spolsky & F. M. Hult (Eds.), *The handbook of educational linguistics* (pp. 174–191). Malden, MA: Blackwell.

Tannen, D. (1982a). The myth of orality and literacy. In W. Frawley (Ed.), *Linguistics and literacy* (pp. 37–50). New York, NY: Plenum.

Tannen, D. (1982b). The oral/literate continuum in discourse. In D. Tannen (Ed.), *Spoken and written language: Exploring orality and literacy* (pp. 1–16). Norwood, NJ: Ablex Publishing Corporation.

Thomas, R. (1992). *Literacy and orality in ancient Greece.* New York, NY: Cambridge University Press.

Trezek, B. J., Wang, Y., & Paul, P. V. (2010). *Reading and deafness: Theory, research, and practice.* Clifton Park, NY: Delmar Cengage Learning.

United Nations Educational, Scientific and Cultural Organization. (2003). Literacy, a UNESCO perspective. Retrieved from unesdoc.unesco.org/images/0013/001318/131817e0.pdf

Vincent, D. (2003). Literacy literacy. *Interchange,* 34(2/3), 341–357.

Webster, A. K. (2006). Keeping the word: On orality and literacy (with a sideways glance at Navajo). *Oral Tradition,* 21(2), 295–324.

Wilbur, R. B. (2000). The use of ASL to support the development of English and literacy. *Journal of Deaf Studies and Deaf Education,* 5(1), 81–104.

Introducing Haiku Poems: Utilizing the Same ASL Handshapes for Pedagogical Purposes

MERRILEE GIETZ

THIS STUDY PROPOSES THE USE OF AMERICAN SIGN LANGUAGE (ASL) to introduce English haikus. By capitalizing on common underlying proficiencies, the proposed language handling technique can be used to develop critical thinking skills among bimodal bilinguals. This poetry style was chosen because of its references to nature and ease in accessing students' communication modality and visualization skills (Hauser & Marschark, 2008). While abundant curriculum materials have been developed for second language (L2) learners, limited resources are available for deaf first language (L1) learners (Allen, 2008).

LITERACY

Literacy traditionally means that someone is able to read and write, but a different perspective defines literacy in terms of sign languages and written languages (Crubek, 2006). This perspective of ASL literacy includes functional, critical, and cultural elements. The functional element is when a person is capable of using ASL as his or her first language in effectively communicating with other native ASL users. The critical element is when a person reflects knowledge in important human relationships in society. The cultural element is when a person enhances her/his comprehension of ASL literacy through shared values and shared experiences (Christie & Wilkins, 1997).

MODALITIES

Historic assumptions towards deaf children have prevented full access to the visual modality for bimodal bilingual children (Hauser & Marschark, 2008), who are capable of using a spoken language and a signed language (Emmorey & McCullough, 2009). Theoretically, "the visual modality is specialized for processing information presented simultaneously across space, whereas the auditory modality is specialized for processing information presented sequentially across time" (Hall & Bavelier, 2011, p. 465). Insignificant research exists that focuses on deaf children's visual learning, and the limited studies that do exist suggest that providing access to two modalities, audio-lingual and visual, results in better comprehension, learning, and memory (Hauser & Marschark, 2008). Deaf signers have a great advantage in the use of spatial memory, which would support a learning strategy for visual attention by signers in the classroom (Hauser & Marschark, 2008). This avenue may be ideally explored for ASL phonological teaching strategies such as haikus.

PHONOLOGY

English phonology is the smallest contrastive unit of language that refers to sounds. Conversely, ASL phonology has five parameters: handshape, location, orientation, palm orientation, and non-manual signals while English phonology has three parameters: place of articulation (location), manner of articulation (how), which has two types of articulation: voiceless and voiced (Isenhath, 1990; Valli, Lucas, Mulrooney & Villanueva, 2011). Additionally, English has a linear structure while ASL has a spatial structure that produces language in space and in the chest area. Furthermore, ASL phonology includes cheremes (hand formations) while English phonemes are in the form of sounds. (Emmorey, 2002; Fischer, 2000).

English poetry works incorporate phonological tools that can be used to teach deaf students how to read in English (Sutton-Spence, 2001).

PHONETIC RHYMES AND RHYTHMS IN ASL AND ENGLISH

Phonocentrism in any language is the central focus of the audio-lingual modality of speech and hearing (Bauman, Nelson & Rose, 2006). Rhyme helps hearing students remember new words (Allen, 2008). Additionally, rhyme is a sound pattern forming phonetic structure (Bauman et al., 2006; Blondel & Miller, 2001), while rhythm is the ordinary movement (beat) that creates the meter poem (Russo, Giuranna, & Pizzuto, 2001). ASL rhymes can be used as a visual learning tool to help Deaf ASL users learn and remember new words. Snodden, Cripps and Small (2004) stated, "Rhymes are ASL poems that have repeated handshapes, movements, location or repetition of how the palm faces. Rhythms involve the pacing of the recurring motions in ASL poems that form a pattern in time. ASL rap can be a combination of rhymes and rhythms" (p. 19). In poetry, ASL meter is an important key of using high, low or stable beats such as seeing parametric movements of visualization so the eyes sense "dancing" (Valli et al., 2011).

In ASL poetry, the phonological features of rhyme are expressed in the recurring parameters of handshape, location, palm orientation, movement, and non-manual signals; this is akin to sound patterns being continually repeated in English poetry (Bauman, 2006; Brondel & Miller, 2001; Peters, 2000; Russo et al., 2001). Sign language poets use both hands to create an alternating balance in sign production utilizing the same parameters of handshape, movement, and/or orientation frequently and in proportion (Russo et al., 2001). However, English poetry lines are phonetic to the point of phonocentrism, while ASL has a more spatial composition in its image poetry. This exploration is focused on lines of poetry in ASL (Bauman, 2006).

ASL poet and linguist Clayton Valli indicated that linear poetic rhyme is based on phonetics, and ASL poetry exhibits spatial poetic rhyme also based on phonetics (Bauman, 2006). Philosopher Derrida stressed that any linear phonetic rhymes must be standardized; however, this implies suppression of poets not able to express their other languages (Bauman, 2006). ASL offers a discourse of visualization that uses rhythms and repetition, a part of an important part of the impact for visual strategies to tap into ASL learners' sign language. By utilizing this visual discourse, bimodal bilinguals gain conceptual understanding of rhyme and rhythm and can successfully transfer this knowledge to English acquisition (Valli et al., 2011).

CONNECTION BETWEEN ASL AND ENGLISH LITERACY WORKS

Klima & Bellugi (1979) suggested that poetic ASL works could be utilized using English through haikus since learners could be taught to visualize concepts in their native language. The phonological similarities help L1 learners visualize printed text. ASL poet Dorothy Miles utilized this strategy to describe animals in her work (Sutton-Spence & Napoli, 2010). In another example, Valli used the poem, "Hands" (see DVD review in Lindgren, DeLuca, and Napoli, 2008) and "Dandelions" (see DVD review in Valli et al., 2011) to describe his perception of nature. Additionally, he illustrated the beauty of nature through visualization. "The ASL poet Clayton…points out that a great part of the world does not hear; he lists rocks, water, trees, mountains, clouds — natural entities that surround us" (Sutton-Spence & Napoli, 2010, pp. 447-448). These four words — rock, water, tree and mountain — were produced by manipulation of the 5 handshape to form images of nature using ASL. L1 Deaf ASL students use visual modality by observing nature around them; they do not hear sounds. As a result, the haikus offer a tool to complement their visual access.

HAIKUS

An ASL phonological strategy for teaching deaf students is introducing them to haikus, popular in Japan for their strong connection with nature (Reichhold, 2008; Yasuda, 2001). Renowned Japanese poets Basho, Buson, Issa, Kume, and other haiku disciplines created haikus more than 500 years ago (Miyamori, 2002; Reichhold, 2008; Hass, 1994; Yasuda, 2001). Haikus use a person's expression and thoughts on form and content, experience and length, incorporating aesthetic attitude and experience perceiving objects in nature. Haikus also use three elements: where, what, and when. Take for example the following haiku:

Where	On the withered bough
What	A crow alone is perching;
When	Autumn evening now.

(Yasuda, 2001, p. 53)

Elementary and middle school Deaf students utilized the ASL 5 handshapes in signing haikus written by famous Japanese poets. Using this procedure, ASL and English literature blended together so the students could recognize both languages. They immediately played with ASL words after reading the haikus. The students excitedly offered answers of printed-English meanings after they independently figured out, to their amazement and satisfaction, what the haikus meant.

Students utilized the ASL 5 handshape for the following haiku samples (Reichhold, 2008):

I walk across sand
And find myself blistering
In the hot, hot heat

Breathing gills
On the bed of river—
Water warming.
Spring winds

Hoping the flowers burst
Out in laughter

The sun covered
By clouds for a while
Migrating birds

COMPREHENSION

Comprehension input, along with contrastive dialogue, allows deaf children to recognize each language (English and ASL) and use competence in translating between the two languages (Allen, 2008). Deaf students are capable of using metalinguistic skills to codeswitch between in ASL and English. This helps them be distinctly aware of the important differences between ASL and English (Paul, 2009).

Guided codeswitching and other sophisticated language handling techniques facilitate deaf children's language development and linguistic transfers between ASL and English (Andrews & Rusher, 2010). These techniques lead them to identify the distinction of sounds and print in phonological processing, even between linguistically distant languages such as ASL and English (Andrews & Rusher, 2010). ASL has distinctly freer syntax and English has a more linear structure (Emmorey, Borinstein, Thompson, & Gollan, 2008). There have been suggestions that a better method is needed for using bilingual techniques to expand ASL vocabulary by using similar ASL handshapes: "For instance, teaching ASL vocabulary such as MOTHER, FATHER, FINE, DEER were utilized the 5 handshape on the context of a conversation or while reading text" (Simms, Andrews, & Smith, 2005, p. 43). This technique can lead to connections between printed English and fingerspelling (Simms et al., 2005).

Iconicity also assists deaf readers in relating to signs and their meanings. An iconic sign looks like what it represents. For example, the signs for EAT and TREE look like what they represent: the act of eating and the shape of a tree (Lederberg & Spencer, 2008). Deaf and hard of hearing children may have difficulty with indirect word learning because of dependence on visual information, but handle direct word learning well (Lederberg & Spencer, 2008). This is especially true when teachers employ adequate language handling techniques.

PERCEPTION

Deaf people have a unique ability to develop perception of sign language while hearing people develop the ability to perceive speech (Emmorey, 2007). Word recognition occurs when a signer produces a sign and its meaning is perceived. One study indicated that native ASL users noticed the movement and location of ASL words while they did not pay attention to the patterns of handshapes (Emmorey, 2007). Other studies showed that native signers did not perceive handshapes and the place of articulation distinctively (Morford, Grieve-Smith, MacFarlane, Staley, & Waters, 2008). Deaf ASL users strongly detected sign movement and location in ASL perception, but they replied on movement based on their linguistic knowledge (Hidebrandt & Corina, 2002)

Focusing on the single parameter of handshape, results showed that lexical recognition was effective (ten Holt, van Doorn, de Ridder, Reinders, & Hendriks, 2009). This maintained a focus on the single parameter of handshape as a straightforward means of improving knowledge of sign perception in future studies (ten Holt, et al., 2009). The evidence supported similarities to ASL phonology that utilized place of articulation of handshapes so this hypothesis suggested that ASL had a signed data system of working memory (Emmorey, 2000).

The ASL movement parameter has a strong temporal system in phonology, but more time is required to produce each sign (Emmorey, 2007). According to Emmory and Wilson (2004), spatial coding is relatively strong in a visual language, but temporal coding tends to be weak. The challenge in designing an experiment was to employ the same modality of ASL and English in spoken languages, even though ASL is a spatial language while English is not. Deaf people have smaller amounts of working memory for short time spans compared to hearing people, but ASL and English bilingual users who were hearing and grew up with deaf parents successfully distinguished signs and English in working memory (Emmorey & Wilson, 2004). These findings could potentially support further investigations on ASL and English bilingual users of two different modalities (Emmorey & Wilson, 2004).

Cross-language activation has often been documented for bilingual users, except deaf bilinguals. Deaf bilinguals use their L1, ASL, and an L2, English, languages that have different articulators. ASL accesses the visual modality while most bilinguals depend on the auditory modality. Numerous studies have shown that other bilinguals read successfully in separate languages. Deaf bilinguals lack a written form of ASL as an L1 and, on the surface, may believe ASL has little in common with English phonology, overemphasizing semantics. When both phonological and semantic information were both decoded, ASL-English translations were shown to be effective for cross-language activation in deaf ASL bilinguals (Morford, Wilkinson, Villwock, Pinar, & Kroll, 2011). Goldin-Meadow and Mayberry (2001) stressed that deaf students are capable of using orthographic organization for phonological awareness when they operate their knowledge of literacy, but deaf Chinese readers apparently were more successful reading an orthographic system of the Chinese tapping morphology of the Chinese characters (Shu, Chen, Anderson, Wu, & Xuan, 2003; Tong, McBridge-Chang, Shu, & Wong, 2009).

CONCLUSION

Deaf ASL users are able to comprehend the interwoven fabric of ASL literacy and English literacy after discovering the concept of using ASL rhymes in haikus as a phonological tool. This is an emergent step in literacy, identifying common underlying proficiencies in ASL and English encouraging students to play imaginatively with both ASL and English. Linguistic transfer is maximized and biliteracy is more effectively achieved. Further, this approach can be an effective teaching tool to increase vocabulary, promote language acquisition, and provide motivation to bridge English literature.

REFERENCES

Allen, S. (2008). English and ASL: Classroom activities to shed some light on the use of two languages. In Lindgren, K., DeLuca, D., & Napoli, D. (Eds.), *Signs & voices: Deaf culture, identity, language, and arts* (pp. 139–149). Washington, D.C.: Gallaudet University Press.

Andrews, J., & Rusher, M. (2010). Codeswitching techniques: Evidence-based instructional practices for the ASL and English bilingual classrooms. *American Annals of the Deaf*, 155(4), pp. 407–424.

Bauman, D. (2006). Getting out of line. In D. Bauman, J. Nelson, & H. Rose (Eds.), *Signing the body poetic: Essays on American Sign Language literature.* (pp. 95–117). Berkeley, CA: University of California Press.

Bauman, D., Nelson, J., and Rose, H. (2006). *Signing the body poetic: Essays on American Sign Language literature.* Berkeley, CA: University of California Press.

Blondel, M., & Miller, C. (2001). Movement and rhythm in nursery rhymes in LSF. *Sign Language Studies*, 2(1), 25–61.

Christie, K., & Wilkins, D. (1997). A feast for the eyes: ASL literacy and ASL literature. *Journal of Deaf Studies and Deaf Education*, 2(1), 57–59.

Czubek, T. (2006). Blue Listerine, parochialism, and ASL literacy. *Journal of Deaf Studies and Deaf Education*, 11(3), 373--81.

Emmorey, K. (2002). *Language, cognition and the brain: Insights from sign language research.* Mahwah, New Jersey: Lawrence Erlbaum Associates.

Emmorey, K., & Wilson, M. (2004). The puzzle of working memory for sign language. *Trends in Cognitive Sciences*, 8(12), 521–523.

Emmorey, K. (2007). The psycholinguistics of signed and spoken languages: How biology affects processing. In G. Gaskell (Ed.), *The Oxford Handbook of Psycholinguistics* (pp. 703–721). New York, NY: Oxford University Press.

Emmorey, K., Borinstein, H., Thompson, & Gollan, T. (2008) Bimodal bilingualism. *Bilingualism: Language and Cognition*, 11(1), 43–61.

Emmorey, K., & McCullough, S. (2009). The bimodal bilingual brain: Effects of sign language experience. *Brain and Language*, 109, 124–132.

Fischer, S. (2000). More than just handwaving: The mutual contributions of sign language and linguistics. In K. Emmorey & H. Lane (Eds), T*he signs of language revisited: An anthology to honor Ursula Bellugi and Edward Klima* (pp. 193–213). Mahwah, New Jersey: Lawrence Erlbaum Associates.

Golden-Meadow, S., & Mayberry, R. (2001). How do profoundly deaf children learn to read? *Learning Disabilities Research & Practice*, 16(4), 222–229.

Hall, M., & Bavelier, D. (2010). Working memory, Deafness, and Sign language. In M. M. Marschark & P. Spencer (Eds.), *The Oxford Handbook of Deaf Studies, Language, and Education. Vol. 2*. New York: Oxford University Press.

Hass, R. (1994). *The essential Haiku: Versions of Basho, Buson, and Issa*. New York, NY: Harper Collins Publishers, Inc.

Hauser, P., & Marschark, M. (2008). Language comprehension and learning by deaf students. In M. Marschark & P. Hauser (Eds.), *Deaf Cognition* (pp. 439–457). New York, NY: Oxford University Press.

Hidebrandt, U., & Corina, D. (2002). Phonological similarity in ASL. *Language and Cognitive Processes*, 17(6), 593–612.

Isenhath, J. (1990). *The linguistics of American Sign Language*. Jefferson, NC: McFarland and Company, Inc.

Klima, E., & Bellugi, U. (1979). *The signs of language*. Cambridge, MA: Harvard University Press.

Lederberg, A., & Spencer, P. (2008). Word-learning abilities in deaf and hard-of-hearing preschoolers: Effect of lexicon size and language modality. *Journal of Deaf Studies and Deaf Education*, 14(1), 44–62.

Lindgren, K., Deluca, D., & Napoli, D. (2008). *Signs and voice: Deaf culture, identity, language, and arts*. Washington, D.C.: Gallaudet University Press. DVD

Miyamori, A. (2002). *Classic Haiku: An anthology of poems by Basho and his followers*. Mineola, NY: Dover Publications.

Morford, J., Grieve-Smith, A., MacFarlane, J., Staley, J., & Waters, G. (2008). Effects of language experience on the perception of American Sign Language. *Cognition*, 10(1), 41–53.

Morford, J., Wilkinson, E., Villwock, A., Pinar, P., & Kroll, J. (2011). When deaf signers read English: Do written words activate their sign translations? *Cognition*, 118(2), 286–292.

Paul, P. (2009). *Language and deafness*. Sudbury, MA: Jones and Bartlett Publishers.

Peters, C. (2000). *Deaf American literature: From carnival to the canon*. Washington, DC: Gallaudet Press.

Reichhold, J. (2008). *Basho: The complete haiku—Matsuo Basho*. New York, NY: Kodansha America.

Russo, T., Giuranna, R., & Pizzuto, E. (2001). Italian Sign Language poetry. *Sign Language Studies*, 2(1), 84–112.

Shu, H., Ch–n, X., Anderson, R., Wu, N., & Xuan, Y. (2003). Properties of school Chinese: Implications for learning to read. *Child Development*, 74(1), 27–47.

Simms, L., Andrews, J., & Smith, A. (2005). A balanced approach to literacy instruction for deaf signing students. *Balanced Reading Instruction*, 12, 39–54.

Snodden, A., Cripps, J., & Small, A. (2004). *A parent guidebook: ASL and early literacy*.

Mississauga, ON: Ontario Cultural Society of the Deaf.

Sutton-Spence, R. (2001). Special section on phonology and poetry. *Sign Language Studies*, 2(1), 20–23.

Sutton-Spence, R., & Napoli, D. (2010). Anthropomorphism in sign language: A look at poetry and storytelling with a focus on British Sign Language. *Sign Language Studies*, 10(4), 442–475.

ten Holt, G., van Doorn, A., de Ridder, H., Reinders, M., & Hendriks, E. (2009). Signs in which handshape and hand orientation are either not visible or are only partially visible: What is the consequence for lexical recognition. *Sign Language Studies*, 10(1), 5–35.

Tong, X., McBridge-Chang, C., Shu, H., & Wong, A. (2009). Morphological awareness, orthographic knowledge, and spelling errors: Keys to understanding early Chinese literacy acquisition. *Scientific Studies of Reading*, 12(5), 426–452.

Valli, C., Lucas, C., Mulrooney, K., & Villanueva, M. (2011). *Linguistics of American Sign Language: An introduction*. Washington, D.C.: Gallaudet University Press.

Yasuda, K. (2001). *Japanese Haiku: Its essential natural and history*. Boston, MA: Tuttle Publishing.

Beyond the Sign(s)

What is Lost When Interpreters Miss the Nuances of an African-American Style of Sign

HEATHER CLARK

AFRICAN-AMERICANS HAVE A LONG TRADITION OF USING LANGUAGE as a way to construct identity, from oral stories passed down from generation to generation, to the dozens being played among friends after school to the sidewalk songs young girls create to pass the time. The same holds true for African-Americans who are Deaf and use American Sign Language (ASL) as their primary mode of communication among friends and peers. From signing outside the box, to using exaggerated facial expressions and body movements these nuances and subtleties in the language can alter and change the meaning of what is being conveyed; especially if an interpreter is not aware of the cultural context of what is being said.

Drawing on research conducted with African-American Deaf people in the Seattle area, this paper examines: What does it mean to sign BLACK, what elements mark the language as being 'Black'? Conversely, what does in mean to sign WHITE? How do interpreters stay true to conveying the spirit of what is being said beyond the signs that are being used? How do interpreters voice the nuances of the African-American style of ASL.

LANGUAGE IDEOLOGY

Language ideology can be described as people's beliefs regarding the language people use, emerged as a focal topic of study in the mid-1990s. Kathryn Woodward defines language ideology as "representations, whether explicit or implicit, that construe the intersection of language and human beings in a social world" (1998:3). Part of the ideology about a group's language can include judgments about the people using a particular language (Heath, 1989; Irvine & Gal, 2000; Williams, 1977). For example, during the Ebonics controversy some considered students in the Oakland School District less intelligent because they used an African-American vernacular. Rosina Lippi-Green (1997) writes extensively about the attitudes, beliefs, and discrimination against people who use a non-standard language. She describes the standard language ideology that reinforces the belief in a homogenous spoken language when in reality everyone speaks with an accent. Lippi-Green believes that institutions promoting a standard language ideology are comparable to forcing one to change their gender, race/ethnicity, or religion. While it is legally impossible to ask someone to change their gender, race/ethnicity, or religion, people are nonetheless constantly expected to change their way of speaking.

In Judith Irvine and Susan Gal's (2000) discussion on language ideology and linguistic differentiation, they lay out several processes people use in creating an ideology of language differences. The two that are most relevant in this research are "iconization" and "erasure." Iconization takes a linguistic feature of a person and applies it to an entire group. The feature becomes an icon or representation for every member of the community. For example, I had interviewees describe the African-American variety of ASL as "thuggy" and "wild" because the body language used was different than the mainstream style. These interviewees believed that when the particular linguistic feature was employed everyone who used that style was either "thuggy" or "wild." These participants made sure they did not use any of the distinct features because they did not want to be seen negatively by people outside the African-American Deaf community.

Another process through which linguistic and social categories are linked is erasure, which also supports the belief that there is a homogenous language, by ignoring some variations as if they were non-existent. In the mainstream Deaf community there is a belief, by most, that there is one style of ASL being used by all Deaf people. A unique variety used by many African-Americans is not recognized by the mainstream Deaf community or reflected in its dictionaries or taught in an ASL curriculum. Variations of ASL that could potentially define a separate community are ignored.

LANGUAGE AND IDENTITY

Language and identity go hand in hand, one influences the other. Giles (1973) found that in many instances where people are determining ingroup or outgroup membership, people felt more affinity with people who shared a common language than with those who shared their race/ethnicity. Language choice is considered one of the main ways a person chooses their identity affiliation (Bailey, 2002; Fuller, 2004).

Two key concepts in analyzing language and identity are markedness and essentialism. Markedness emerges when certain categories become the default term for the whole while others are "marked" to signify a difference (Bucholtz & Hall, 2004). For instance "doctor," as the unmarked form, is generally believed to be male whereas "female doctor" must be specified, since a female physician is not the norm, it is a marked category. This same concept occurs with many racial/ethnic communities as well. The unmarked category is typically the dominant culture and marginalized identities often become marked. Simply by placing "African" before "American" marks that group of people as something different than just "American," it is an American that is modified.

Essentialism refers to an ideology that views people who share similar characteristics such as gender, race/ethnicity, or religion as if everyone with those characteristics naturally is the same or behaves the same (Bucholtz & Hall, 2004; Mendoza-Denton, 2002). This concept is challenged in the study of language and identity because linguistic anthropology strives to examine the "complex social and political meanings, with which language becomes endowed in specific contexts" (Bucholtz & Hall, 2004: 370). While essentialist notions can create a sense of sameness among group members, there is also an implicit notion that a group is fundamentally different from another group (Bucholtz & Hall, 2004). Many in society have essentialist views of what it means to be African-American, or what it means to be Deaf. With the globalization of media where such views can be reinforced or challenged, these views do not seem to be on the decline. Knowing this I had to be careful in my own research to avoid falling into essentialism. For instance I could not assume that because someone was African-American and Deaf that they would use an African-American style of ASL, or identify more heavily with one community over another.

There have been a few studies conducted with Deaf individuals who are African-American and one of the primary issues addressed is how they prioritize their multiple identities. Aramburo's (1989) study, which is the most cited in this field, revealed that a majority (87%) of African-American Deaf people prioritized their race/ethnicity over their cultural identity. The remaining 13% identified themselves as Deaf first because they were either raised in a Deaf family, were active in their local Deaf community or were educated in a predominately white environment.

Currently, the majority of the research with African-American Deaf people has been either conducted in the South or on the East Coast, while the Pacific Northwest has been overlooked. Thus, the research I have conducted fills a social and geographical gap in Deaf Studies. Firstly, there has been no research done in the Northwest with individuals who are both African American and Deaf regarding how they identify, or their variation in language use. Secondly, because the sociopolitical landscape of the Northwest is different than in the South and the East Coast, this research can give a better picture of the larger African-American Deaf community. Lastly, my research challenges the notion that ASL is the primary unifying factor for all members of the Deaf community. Individuals I have worked with acknowledge the power in using ASL to connect to a larger community. However, due to their race/ethnicity and variety of ASL, some do not use deafness as their primary identity marker.

AMERICAN SIGN LANGUAGE (ASL)

One of the primary components of defining Deaf culture is the acceptance of ASL as the language of the Deaf community. ASL is used as a way to organize and define the Deaf community and one's membership in the community depends on the language one chooses to use (Kannapell, 1989; Lane et al., 1996; Padden & Humphries, 1988; Wilcox, 1989). ASL is considered a powerful tool to unite the Deaf community because of the cultural beliefs, norms and values expressed through the language. Because of this ASL is considered the "cultural language of the Deaf Community" (Kannapell, 1989:25).

It was not until the 1960s that ASL was recognized as a true language with a rule-governed grammatical structure. William Stokoe (2001), an English professor at Gallaudet University, began noticing his Deaf students making similar mistakes on their English papers. As a result Stokoe decided to research ASL to see if there was a relation, which there was. The students wrote their papers using an ASL grammar structure, not an English one. It was through his seminal research that Stokoe discovered that ASL had a grammatical structure unlike English, which explained the common errors. Stokoe's work provided a basis for the Deaf community to advocate for and take pride in their language. ASL was not merely comprised of hand gestures; it was a bona fide language. Following Stokoe's research, the majority of work done in the Deaf community surrounds language use and the fact that Deaf people consider themselves to be a linguistic minority within the United States (Kannapell, 1989; Lane et al., 1996; Lucas, 1995; Padden & Humphries, 1988; Valli et al., 1989; Wilcox, 1989).

While other aspects of a Deaf person's identity are sometimes recognized, such as race/ethnicity, religion, or sexual orientation, it is the discrimination and lack of access due to the language barriers that galvanize the Deaf community as a whole. This fact explains why most individuals who are Deaf unify around the use, teaching, and promotion of ASL, as it is seen as the barrier that separates them from the mainstream hearing community in the United States. When issues of race/ethnicity arise in the mainstream Deaf community, the perspective taken is usually a colorblind one. This is based on the presumption that race/ethnicity is not the primary defining factor that should be highlighted because it can fragment the community while language access and acceptance are seen as the primary goals.

In many respects Deaf identity and African-American identity share similarities, they are both marked visually. For instance, when a Deaf person chooses to use ASL they are visibly marked as Deaf, similar to African-Americans being marked by their physical traits (i.e. skin color or hair texture). Also in both of these communities there are ways in which an individual can downplay their identity. For a Deaf person they may choose not to use ASL as their primary language, and an African-American may choose not to use African-American English (AAE). However, for all of the similarities between the two identities there is also a difference. Unlike the Deaf person who can choose not to use ASL to perform their identity the African-American individual is born in the body they are and while they can downplay the performance of their identity it is not altogether silenced.

AFRICAN-AMERICAN STYLE OF ASL

Studies conducted with African-American Deaf people highlighting the variety of ASL used among African-Americans in the Southern United States (Lewis, 1998; Valli et al., 1989), which developed as a result of Deaf residential schools being segregated up until the mid-twentieth century (Maxwell & Smith-Todd, 1986; Woodard, 1976). When Woodward (1976) and Maxwell & Smith-Todd (1986) studied African-American Deaf southern signing, their findings were similar in that they both witnessed lexical differences from the language of white Southern signers. The African-American people they interviewed were educated in segregated Deaf residential schools. They both hypothesized that the state of African-American signing is difficult to assess because after the Deaf schools were fully integrated, African-American Deaf people were required to use standard ASL.

One factor that has contributed to the fading out of the unique African-American variety of ASL is that there is no longer a segregated educational setting for African-American Deaf people where they would pass on their variety of ASL. In Aramburo's (1989) study with African-American Deaf people, he noticed some of the participants used what they called 'old signs' when signing amongst themselves, so in this respect some of the southern African-American style may not be completely lost. MacCaskill and Lucas

(2011) conducted a more recent study highlighting the ASL variety currently used among African-Americans in the South.

Other research studies with African-American Deaf people have been conducted on the East Coast, primarily at Gallaudet University in the Washington D.C. area (Aramburo, 1989; Bruce, 1993; Guggenheim, 1993; Hairston & Smith, 1983; Lewis et al., 1995; Valli et al., 1989). These studies focus on the manner in which African-Americans execute the signs they use to distinguish their style of signing from the mainstream white style. Lewis (1995) noticed that when an African-American Deaf participant was asked to describe the differences in American and African clothing, his signing style changed dramatically. When he described the American style of clothing, he had virtually no body movement or facial expressions. He stood straight and in place, faced forward, and did not mouth any signs. In contrast, when describing the African clothing, he employed various African-American signing style elements. He mouthed different signs, his body movements included his torso and shoulders moving forward, he made exaggerated gestures, and bobbed his head back and forth. These are the elements others have mentioned when describing African-American Deaf signing style: not only are facial expressions and body movements more emphatic, but the actual signing space is used to its fullest (Aramburo, 1989; Guggenheim, 1993; Hairston & Smith, 1983).

I asked Marie, an African-American Deaf woman, how she would describe the different signing styles she employed all of the markers that researchers noted. Marie's body language changed, she slouched down in her seat, opened her legs, and used and exaggergated facial expressions. In contrast, when she spoke of the mainstream white style of ASL she straightened up, closed her legs and her facial expressions became less noticeable. How she spoke of the differences was markedly different as well because Marie mentioned that the African-American style was more intense, it was 'thuggy' and used more swear words as opposed to the white style being more superficial and proper.

When I interviewed Phyllis, another participant, about the signing differences she remarked similarly as Marie. She stated that the white style was "proper" and, "normal." She went on further to explain that when she signs using the mainstream style of ASL among other African-American Deaf people some have negatively commented that she signs "white." The notion of "signing white" is similar to how some hearing African-Americans who speak using a mainstream style of English are marked as "talking white."

INTERPRETER'S ROLE

In recognizing that some African-American Deaf peole use a different style of ASL how does the interperter account for the difference while voicing or signing. How does an interpreter change thier voicing to match the physical and visual difference in the signing style? As interpreters, we are charged with conveying the language and spirit of the text so what happens when the interpreter is not familiar with the cultural subtext or signs being used. The Registry of Interpreters for the Deaf (RID) describes an interpreter as someone who has a great knowledge of the English language and the ability to speak clearly, be audibly heard and to portray the feelings and emotion of the speaker, whether voice or sign interpreting.

How can interpreters be culturally relevant but still culturally respectful in situations where terms or slang is being used that may make the interpreter uncomfortable, especially if it is an interpreter from a different race/ethnicity?

In my interpreter training program we did not have many opportunities to practice voicing for a variety of signing styles. The majority of the video clips we used to practice on were middle aged white Deaf people, ocassionaly there may have been a grandparent signing about the Deaf clubs of the past. In all my years of learning ASL and going through my interpreter training program, I can only recal viewing two African-American Deaf people signing, and both of those people did not use an African-American style of signing.

While interviewing Jasmine, Rhonda commented that she watches an interpreter closely to see if their voice matches her signing style, Phyllis commented how disappointed she has been on more than on occasion. She gave an example of making the comment "that boy was trippin' yesterday" while signing this statement she pursed her lips, rolled her eyes and bobbed her head back and forth. While the signing style employed the elments that have been marked as signing African-American, the interpreter voiced in a very monotone voice, "that boy was tripping yesterday." Phylllis felt the hearing person was not able to get the true meaning of the statement.

VOICING AFRICAN-AMERICAN STYLE OF ASL

I was asked to interpret a traditional 'homegoing' service for an African-American Deaf woman who was very beloved in the community. The service took place at a large church and because of the mixed audience (hearing/Deaf) the interpreter coordinator made sure there were five interpreters, three were assigned to provide voice-to-sign interpretation and two were assigned to provide sign-to-voice interpretation. The two voice inter-preters were white women and the three voice-to-sign interpreters were African-American women; I was one of the voice-to-sign interpreters. Dur-ing the service, there was time allotted for people who knew the deceased to offer reflections, Derick, a young African-American Deaf man who grew up with her came up to share his reflections. When he got to the pulpit all he could do was look down at the casket. He was visibly emotional and the only two signs he could muster were MY and GIRL. Several times, one could see him begin to sign some something but the only thing Derick could do was cry, shake his head and pat his chest, signing MY, MY, MY after which he signed GIRL, once Derick stopped and started this same sentence a few times he simply spread his arms wide and looked down at the casket.

The voice interpreter eventually said, in an extremely monotone voice "she was a good friend of mine, a very good friend of mine." Technically that is not what Derick said, he technically said, "my girl." This seemingly sim-ple phrase in the African-American community expresses much more than simply 'my girl' or 'she is a very good friend of mine.'

As interpreters how much poetic license do we have? How do we convey not only the signs being used but also the spirit and meaning of what is being signed? I have discussed this experience with others who were in attendance and shared with them what the voice interpreter said. In no way do I con-demn the interpreter; she did the best she could given the circumstances. I have not discussed this incident with her, so I am not sure why she or her interpreter teammate felt the sentence she voiced was the most adequate interpretation. I am left wondering why she did not voice what he signed, or said I am at a loss for words as opposed to putting words into his mouth. Was she uncomfortable with how he was signing or the emotion of his signs?

CONCLUSION

The goal of this paper is to explore how some African-American Deaf peo-ple use language to integrate both their cultural and racial/ethnic identities. Using an African-American style of ASL not only differentiates them from the mainstream Deaf community; it also connects them to the larger hearing African-American community.

This paper explores African-American Deaf people in the Pacific North-west who play with ASL as a way to differentiate themselves from the main-stream Deaf community and unite them to the larger African-American community.

What happens if an African-American Deaf person chooses to use the word NIGGAH in the context of a conversation, does the hearing white interpreter voice "niggah" or do they do what many hearing people do and say the 'n' word in its place?

(All names used in this article are pseudonymns and have been chosen by the participant.)

REFERENCES

Aramburo, A.J. (1989). Sociolinguistic Aspects of the Black Deaf Community. In C. Lucas (ed.) *The Sociolinguistics of the Deaf Community*, New York, NY: Academic Press, 103–122.

Bailey, B. H. (2002). *Language, Race and Negotiation of Identity: A Study of Dominican Americans.* New York: LFB Scholarly Publishing LLC.

Bartha, C. (2005). Language Ideologies, Discriminatory Practices and the Deaf Community I Hungary. In J. Cohen, K. Y. McAlister, K. Rolstad, and J. MacSwan (eds.), ISB4: *Proceedings of the 4th International Symposium on Bilingualism.* Somerville, MA: Cascadilla Press, 210–222.

Bruce, J. (1993). A Comparative Study of Backchanneling Signals Between an African American Deaf Speaker and African American and White Deaf Speakers. In E. Winston (ed). *Communication Forum (vol 2).* Washington, D.C.: Gallaudet University, 1–10.

Bucholtz, M. & Hall, K. (2004). Language and Identity. In A. Duranti (ed.) *A Companion to Linguistic Anthropology.* Malden, MA: Blackwell Publishing, 369–394.

Fuller, J. M. (2007). Language Choice as a Means of Shaping Identity. *Journal of Linguistic Anthropology*, 17(1): 105–129.

Guggenheim, Laurie. "Ethnic Variation in ASL: The Signing of the African American and How it is Influenced by Conversation Topic," In E. Winston (ed.) *Communication Forum (vol 2).* Washington, D.C.: Gallaudet University. 1993. 51-76.

Hairston, E. & Smith, L. (1983). *Black and Deaf in American: Are We that Different.* Silver Springs: T.J. Publishers, Inc.

Irvine, J. T. & Gal, S. (2000). Language Ideology and Linguistic Differentiation. In P. V. Kroskrity (ed.) *Regimes of Language Ideologies, Polities, and Identities.* Santa Fe, NM: School of American Research Press, 35–83.

Kannapell, B. (1989). Inside the Deaf Community. In S. Wilcox (ed.) *American Deaf culture.* Burtonsville: Linstok Press, 21–28.

Labov, W. (1972). *Language in the Inner City; Studies in the Black English Vernacular.* Philadelphia: University of Pennsylvania Press.

Lewis, J., Palmer, C. & Williams, L. (1995). Existence of and Attitudes Toward Black Variations of Sign Language. In L. Byers, J. Chaiken, & M. Mueller (eds.) *Communication Forum (vol 4).* Washington, D.C.: Gallaudet University, 17–48.

Lewis, J. G. (1998). Ebonics in American Sign Language Stylistic Variation in African American Signers. *Deaf Studies V: Toward 2000 Unity and Diversity. Conference Proceedings April 17-20, 1997*, Washington, D.C., 229–239.

McCaskill, C., Lucas, C., Bayley, R., & Hill, J. (2011). *Hidden Treasures: The History and Structure of Black ASL.* Gallaudet University Press.

Maxwell, M. & Smith-Todd, S. (1986). Black Sign Language and School Integration in Texas. *Language in Society* 15, 81–94.

Padden, C. & Humphries, T. (1988). *Deaf America: Voices from a Culture.* Cambridge, MA: Harvard University Press.

Padden, C. & Humphries, T. (2005). *Inside Deaf Culture.* Cambridge, MA: Harvard University Press.

Parasnis, I. (1996). *Cultural and Language Diversity and the Deaf Experience.* Cambridge; New York: Cambridge University Press.

Stokoe, Jr., W. C. (2001). *Language in Hand: Why Sign Came Before Speech.* Washington, DC: Gallaudet University Press.

Valli, C., Reed, R., Ingram, Jr., N., & Lucas, C. (1989). Sociolinguistic Issues in the Black Deaf Community. In C. Lucas (ed.) *The Sociolinguistics of the Deaf Community.* New York, NY: Academic Press. 42-66.

Wilcox, S. (1989). *American Deaf culture.* Burtonsville: Linstok Press.

Woodward, K. A. (1998) Introduction: Language Ideology as a Field of Inquiry. In Bambi B. Schieffelin, Kathryn Ann Woolard, and Paul V. Kroskrity (eds.) *Language Ideologies: Practice and Theory.* Oxford studies in anthropological linguistics, 16. New York: Oxford University Press. 3-47.

Language Transfer Among Deaf L2 Writers

KIMBERLY A. WOLBERS, PH.D; SHANNON C. GRAHAM;
HANNAH M. DOSTAL, PH.D.; AND LISA M. BOWERS

DEVELOPING SECOND LANGUAGE (L2) WRITERS USE MULTIPLE STRAT-
egies to make sense of morphological and syntactical structure variations, and
will frequently embed L1 (primary language) features in L2 writing (Bhela,
1999; Valdes, 2006). This language transfer phenomenon occurs among deaf/
Deaf and hard of hearing (d/Dhh) writers, whereby American Sign Language
(ASL) structures are utilized in English writing (Wolbers, 2008, 2010).
Unlike languages that have a written form, ASL is manual and visual in
nature, thus providing a unique area for research and discussion on writing trends of d/Dhh L2 writers. The purpose of this paper is two-fold: (1) to
describe language transfer occurrences in the writing of d/Dhh adolescents
who have had varying exposure to ASL and (2) to present the impact of Strategic and Interactive Writing Instruction (SIWI) on various language transfer tendencies over one year of academic instruction.

ASL IN ENGLISH TEXT

American Sign Language constitutes a grammatically complex system and
includes all elements of language as similar to spoken languages (Stoke
1960). The visual nature of ASL also allows for the incorporation of other
features such as non-manual markers and space. As such, ASL and English are entirely different languages and "…it would be highly unusual for an
ASL sentence ever to have exactly the same grammatical structure as an English sentence" (Liddell, 2003, 2). This makes it possible to identify some ASL
features in English writing.

An example of ASL features existing in English text comes from the *Deaf Way II Anthology (Vol II)* (Stremlau, 2002), which is a literary collection of d/Dhh writers' works. This collection includes a poem, entitled "Salt in the Basement: An American Sign Language Reverie in English," written by Willy Conley. The author of this poem purposefully transliterated American Sign Language features into text:

> me little, almost high wash-wash machine
> down basement, me have blue car
> drive drive round round
>
> happen summer
> me inside blue car
> drive round round
> basement
>
> me drive every corner
> drive drive drive
> then BOOM! Me crash (Conley 2002, 184)

In this brief excerpt, the author includes several ASL phrases. "Wash-wash machine" is an example of substitution for "washing machine," to which the sign for "wash" is repeated two, maybe three times, depending on the context. "Drive drive round round" would likely be signed using classifiers to describe the movement of the car. Based on one perspective, this statement could be translated to English as, "Driving in a circular motion." "Happen summer" in the second section is an example of how "happen" can function as a conjunction in ASL (Fischer & Lillo-Martin, 1990). The poem nicely illustrates the occurrence of ASL grammatical features incorporated into written English.

More of what we know about the use of ASL features in English writing comes from studies of children of Deaf adults (CODAs). Bishop and Hicks (2005) examined the written email conversations between CODAs who tended to use a purposeful mixture of both ASL and English. The analysis identified ASL characteristics in their writing and visual descriptions of ASL signs. They found, for example, that 146 of the 275 lines used unique ASL glossing, a notation method to translate individual signs into text (Valli, Lucas, Mulrooney, & Villanueva, 2011). One example of ASL gloss in Bishop and Hicks (2005) is NOT MY TASTE. The English translation could be "not my preference." There were also English features that were commonly dropped. Of the 275 lines analyzed, the most common features were dropped subjects (69) (e.g., "Hope lots of room on plane"), dropped copulas (62) (e.g., "That nice"), and dropped determiners (59) (e.g., "That point"). Dropped subjects in English could be explained because the "subject is understood through context" (Bishop & Hicks, 2005, 205). While not as frequent, objects were also dropped and could reflect the use of prior placement of objects in space or eye gaze when using ASL. Visual representations in ASL such as space, facial expression, and body language may not be literally translated into English and result in these drops.

TRENDS AMONG DEVELOPING D/DHH WRITERS

Research on d/Dhh writers reveals common writing trends. For instance, text is typically shorter, and sentences comprise repetitions of basic grammatical structure (Marschark, Lang, & Albertini, 2002; Marschark, Mouradian, & Halas, 1994). New topics are introduced without producing fully developed ideas, and content-oriented vocabulary is targeted over functional words (Wilbur, 2000). Additionally, d/Dhh writers struggle with verb inflections, verb tenses, and passive voice (Bishop & Hicks, 2005). Additional words are added out of context, necessary words are not considered, and there are substitutions of text or phrases (Bishop & Hicks, 2005; Paul 1998).

It is believed that developing d/Dhh writers face challenges when producing text in English, and draw on ASL (L1) linguistic knowledge to do so. Language transfer is common among developing L2 writers (Baker & Jones, 1998). The basis of this phenomenon suggests that L2 writers use L1 to generate or communicate ideas prior to or during production of text. Developing a sophisticated understanding of a L2 generally diminishes the language transfer occurrences, suggesting that as writers improve knowledge of L2 and metalinguistic awareness, there are fewer features of L1 in their writing (Baker & Jones, 1998).

Researchers and practitioners have identified language transfer trends in d/Dhh students' writing, whereby individuals with varying fluency levels of ASL as L1 embed American Sign Language patterns in English text. Nover and Andrew's (1999) Star Schools Project Report includes teachers' reflections on implementing ASL/English bilingual methodology for d/Dhh students and examples of ASL features in d/Dhh writing.

> I not know much about Earth. I have no feel about Earth, but I finish learn about Earth. People need care for home. People need respect. People nice to Earth. Animals can live long if animals eat healthy food, drink clean water and breathe clean air. Animals live Free. Each help people and animal live. Each is very pretty because blue water, colors many different. Earth need nicely. Earth not need mess. (99).

In this excerpt, sentences are simpler, ideas are not fully developed, and some content across the sentences is repetitious (e.g., Earth). The content words are strong, much more so than functional words. For example, in this statement, "People need respect. People nice to Earth," the meaning of these two sentences is comprehensible, yet functional words (e.g., infinitives, determiner) are missing. There is also inclusion of ASL gloss or patterns such as the statement FINISH LEARN. In ASL, FINISH is a way to show past tense and is provided before the verb LEARN. Once established, tense is not repeated throughout a narrative. In English, we may write, "I learned," and the writer must use past tense consistently throughout that writing. Another example of ASL structure is COLORS MANY DIFFERENT. This is a linguistic element of ASL to which the topic or noun is conveyed before the details. In this example, the details are MANY DIFFERENT. In English, a possible translation would be "There were many different colors," whereby "many different" precedes the noun.

Singleton, Morgan, DiGello, Wiles, & Rivers (2004) conducted a study on quality of L2 text based on ASL proficiency. ASL structure was identified in writing samples. For example, WHO WIN TURTLE could be an example of an ASL rhetorical question and RABBIT SLEEP could be described as topicalization, where the topic precedes the details. Bailes (2001) also included some writing samples from deaf L2 writers that illustrate ASL features in English text. One student wrote, "If dog no food what do?" This could be another example of a rhetorical question. This same student also wrote "invented sled dog." In this phrase, the determiner is omitted and the subject is dropped. Additionally, the adjective-noun is flipped and should be written as "dog sled."

In prior literature, there are intentional uses of ASL in English writing such as those in ASL literary collections and in CODA email conversations, and there are unintentional uses of language transfer among d/Dhh developing writers. For this paper, we will examine the various kinds of ASL features found in d/Dhh adolescent writing existing as natural language transfer occurrences. Then we will investigate the impact of heightening metalinguistic awareness and promoting L2 implicit competence through the use of SIWI to reduce the unintentional occurrences of ASL features in writing.

STRATEGIC AND INTERACTIVE WRITING INSTRUCTION

Strategic and Interactive Writing Instruction (SIWI) is a classroom approach to teaching d/Dhh students to write for a variety of purposes and audiences. There are three main driving principles of SIWI. First, SIWI draws on twenty years of evidence-based research with strategy instruction in writing (Englert, Raphael, Anderson, Anthony & Stevens, 1991; Graham, 2006), whereby the strategies or processes of expert writers are explicitly taught to novice writers who do not yet evidence usage of the strategies independently. It may be that students, for example, benefit from explicit instruction on ways to plan for writing. While students engage in practice, they may rely on procedural facilitators that prompt them to engage in planning behaviors until the actions become routine.

Secondly, SIWI builds on a substantial foundation of research in interactive writing (Englert & Dunsmore, 2002; Englert, Mariage, and Dunsmore, 2006; Mariage, 2001; Wolbers, 2007). During collaborative writing, teachers, and sometimes students, model, think-aloud and scaffold students with the writing process and with the use of more advanced writing skills. Over time, the teacher steps back and transfers more responsibility to students when engaged in shared or independent writing activity.

Lastly, SIWI has instructional components that respond to the unique language needs of d/Dhh individuals. Informed by Krashen's (1994) language input hypothesis, SIWI incorporates explicit language teachings that build students' metalinguistic knowledge, and also provides opportunities for implicit acquisition of L2. When there are students who use ASL to communicate and do not yet effectively code-switch to English when engaged in writing, teachers use a two-surface approach to handle language expressions during SIWI. That is, one surface is where the group co-constructs the English text and another surface is where ASL ideas are held. Expressions that are close approximations of English and only require minor revisions to be grammatically accurate may be added to the English board. Expressions that are more like ASL in form are "parked" on the ASL board in either ASL gloss, picture, drawing, or video. The teacher will then guide the class in a translation activity, moving the idea from ASL to English, and subsequently adding to the English text. During this process, participants build their understandings of the grammars of ASL and English through explicit teachings of the languages and language equivalence.

Teachers also implement *print-based sign* rereadings of the text to allow for L2 implicit competence. It is important that students have an opportunity to acquire English implicitly, for there are many aspects of English that cannot be explicitly taught. Often these are the intangibles that hearing individuals claim "just sound right or wrong." While rereading the text is important to the revision process, it is also a way d/Dhh students come to know how English looks, feels and sounds, similar to a hearing writer. Print-based sign is not a way of naturally communicating but a nuanced and complex method of signing with text support. It calls for students to pay attention to the exact written English (in all its complexity) and express the corresponding meaning through a manual mode. While reading, the teacher uses one hand to point to the printed text and one hand to sign. Students may prefer to also voice or move their mouths to replicate the words they are reading. Since the text during collaborative writing is generated by the students based on their own ideas, the English is comprehensible and provides meaningful input.

SIWI has been implemented with students who have mild to severe hearing losses and who use various communication methodologies such as ASL, speech, English-based sign, or a mixture of these. Prior SIWI research has led to improved expressive ASL and written English outcomes at the word, sentence, and discourse levels (Dostal, 2011; Wolbers, 2007, 2008, 2010; Wolbers, Dostal & Bowers, 2011). Although SIWI has led to a number of language and writing gains, it is unclear the impact SIWI has on language transfer, or the use of various ASL features in written English.

METHOD

Two research questions guided the current study: (A) What ASL features are prevalent in L2 writing among d/Dhh adolescents? (B) How do these features change during one year of SIWI? A language arts instructor provided SIWI for one academic year. Four genres of writing were introduced (personal narrative, narrative, expository, and persuasive). A total of 360 writing samples were collected at pre, mid, and post intervention. For this study, researchers used personal narrative samples only (n = 90), as no new ASL features were identified in the other genre samples.

STUDENT PARTICIPANTS

There were a total of twenty-nine d/Dhh students in grades six through eight at a southeastern residential school for the deaf. Students had a mean age of 13.2 years, a mean SAT-HI reading comprehension score of 2.7, and a mean hearing loss of 88dB (33dB aided). The communication policy at the school was total communication, which was primarily enacted by teachers as simultaneous communication (Sim-Com). However, the majority of students were exposed to ASL throughout the day from deaf adults, during student conversations, and during residential hours. During SIWI lessons, the teacher frequently integrated ASL into lessons by using the participants' expressions of ASL to explicitly draw comparisons and distinctions between ASL and English.

PROCEDURES AND ANALYSIS

Three researchers blind reviewed the pre-, mid- and post-writing samples (n=90) to identify specific ASL features at the phrase level. Two researchers were hearing and fluent L2 users of ASL, and one researcher was a deaf, native user of ASL. The researchers first reviewed each of the writing samples by T-unit and marked phrases that were of ASL nature. A t-unit is an independent clause and any subordinate clauses that cannot stand on its own (Hunt, 1965). The team then came to a consensus on all occurrences of ASL features identified in the writing. Because many d/Dhh adolescents exhibit L1 expressive language delays which have an impact on writing, we coded only those instances of clearly identifiable ASL features of expression, rather than simply any non-English expressions or dropped English.

The identified ASL phrases were then compared with pre-defined codes from the literature (Bishop & Hicks, 2005; Valli, Lucas, Mulrooney, & Villaneuva, 2011). As can be seen in Table 1, six linguistic features of ASL were drawn from the literature to support the current research. Codes for the current study included: unique glossing and substitution, plurality and adverbs, adjectives, topicalization, conjunctions and rhetorical questions. We provide a description and an example to illustrate each of these in Table 2. Besides unique glossing and substitution, the categories are all representative of ASL syntactical features. Each of the ASL occurrences identified was coded as one of the six categories. If, however, an identified ASL feature did not fit the description of any of the six categories and did not occur more than once to substantiate its own category, it was labeled as "other."

Valli, Lucas, Mulrooney, & Villaneuva (2011)	Bishop & Hicks (2005)
Topic/comment**	Irregular inflections (S-V agreement)
Tenses	Dropped subjects
Adjectives/Adverbs**	Dropped copula
Pronouns	Dropped determiners
Conjunctions**	Dropped auxiliaries and modals
Interjections	Dropped prepositions
Pluralization	Dropped infinitives
Rhetorical questions**	Dropped objects
WH questions	Unique glossing and novel lexicon**
Negation	Visual description of ASL sign**
Substitution	

Table 1: ASL Features Identified in the Literature (** denotes influenced codes in current research)

Code	Definition	Example
Unique Glossing and Substitution (UG/S)	Translation of signed utterance into text (typically one gloss) that is based on common cultural trends lacking clear ASL syntactical "rules" or uncertainty of English equivalence.	• TOUCH FLORIDA FINISH (TOUCH is commonly used in place of "visited") • GREW UP TOGETHER SINCE 11 YEARS (SINCE is used in place of "for")
Plurality and Adverbs (IV)	Reduplication or emphasis to represent pluralization of nouns or temporal frequency of verbs. This code is similar to unique glossing but has a clear linguistic explanation.	• HOUSE HOUSE ALL OVER • plurality (many houses) and use of space • SIT SIT LONG TIME • verb inflected through temporal frequency (recurring/continuous)
Adjectives (ADJ)	Noun precedes descriptor. This is similar to topical-ization but on word level (i.e., typically adjacent words).	• She lives in a HOUSE BLUE • MOVIE FUNNY • COLORS MANY DIFFERENT (Nover and Andrews, 1999) • AGE 1 • MORNING 1:00
Topicalization (TC)	Broad ideas precede details on sentence level. This code is similar to adjectives (noun-descriptor). The difference is the overall idea in the sentence precedes details.	• IF DOG NO FOOD WHAT DO? (Bailes, 2001) • HOMEWORK I DETEST
Conjunctions (CONJ)	ASL gloss that joins or "glues" together two ideas. Non manual markers accompanying the conjunction are characterized as raised eyebrows, head tilt, with a pause before starting the second idea.	• ALL CAN GO UNDERSTAND ONLY CHILDREN (translated as "but" in English; common conjunctions are BUT, UNDERSTAND, HAPPEN, WRONG; Fischer and Lillo-Martin, 1990)
Rhetorical Questions (RH)	Not a true question. Statement includes a response.	• I BOUGHT SHOES WHY OLD SHOES DON'T FIT ANYMORE

Table 2: ASL Code Descriptions and Examples

Twenty-five percent of the ASL occurrences were triple-coded by the researchers, and inter-rater reliability was calculated at 94.7%. Discrepancies were resolved among research members, and the agreed upon codes were used in the analysis. Once the various types of ASL expressions occurring in d/Dhh student writing were identified and categorized, we tallied total frequency counts by category and by category for pre-, mid-, and post-academic year.

RESULTS

Research Question 1: What ASL features are prevalent in L2 writing among d/Dhh adolescents?

There were thirty-nine ASL occurrences in the writing samples at pre-intervention. As illustrated in Figure 1 by percentage of codes, unique glossing and substitution accounted for nearly half of the codes in pre-intervention writing samples at 41.0%. All other categories related to syntactical aspects of ASL, and represented 59.0% of the ASL occurrences at pre-intervention. Of the syntax-related categories at pre-intervention, adjectives occurred most frequently (65.2%), and then plurality and adverbs (8.7%), topicalization (4.3%), and conjunctions (4.3%) (Figure 2). Additional syntactical structures included in "Other" accounted for 17.4% of the ASL features. Some examples of ASL expressions labeled "Other" included AND MY FATHER DEYWARE BUSTER, NEXT DAY WE GO TO ISLAND CAMP, and CAN'T MOVE THAT WHY. Rhetorical questions, while absent in pre-intervention samples, were identified at post-intervention (four instances in two samples).

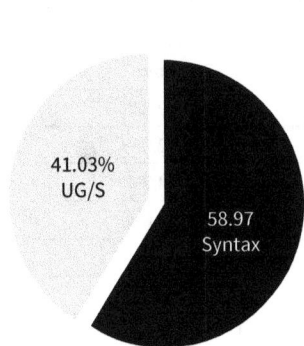

Figure 1. Percentages of ASL syntax and unique glossing/substitution (UG/S) at pre-intervention.

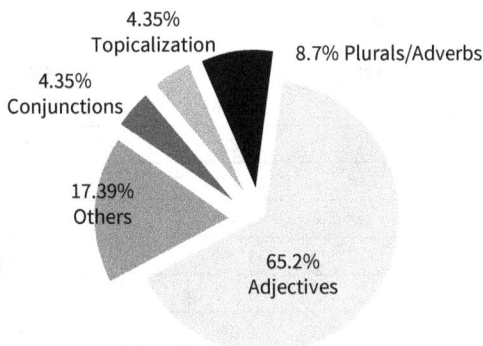

Figure 2. Percentages of ASL syntactical structures identified in pre-intervention writing samples at pre-intervention

Research Question 2: How do these (ASL) features change over one year of SIWI?

A negative linear trend (Figure 3) could be identified for both ASL syntax categories (total pre: 26.7%, mid: 16.3%, and post: 12.8%) and unique glossing and substitution (pre: 18.6%, mid: 16.3%, and post: 9.3%). Percentages were calculated based on the total number of ASL occurrences in student writing during the year (n = 86). Four of the six categories decreased by more than 50%, including unique glossing and substitution, adjectives, conjunctions, and plurality and adverbs. Table 3 lists percentages for each of the syntactical structures at pre-, mid-, and post-intervention. The two remaining categories did not decrease over time. Topicalization slightly increased from pre (1.2%) to mid (7.0%) and then decreased at post (3.5%). As mentioned earlier, rhetorical questions were not indicated at pre or mid, but slightly increased to 4.6% at post (Figure 4).

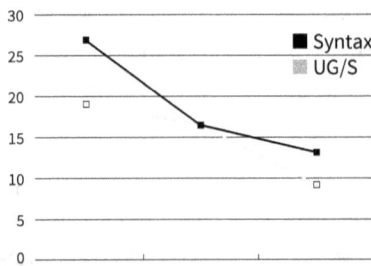

Figure 3. Percentages of ASL syntax and unique glossing and substitution (UG/S) at pre-, mid-, post-intervention.

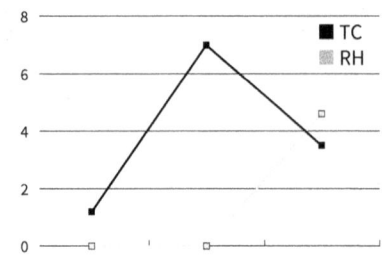

Figure 4. Patterns of topicaliation (TC) and rhetorical questions (RH) at pre-, mid-, and post-intervention.

ASL features	Pre	Mid	Post
UG/S	18.6%	16.3%	9.3%
Syntax	26.8%	16.3%	12.9%
ADJ	17.4%	8.1%	4.7%
IV	2.3%	0.0%	0.0%
TC	1.2%	7.0%	3.5%
CONJ	1.2%	0.0%	0.0%
RH	0.0%	0.0%	4.6%
Other	4.7%	1.2%	0.0%

Table 3: Percentages of unique glossing/substitution and syntax at pre, mid, and post-intervention

DISCUSSION

For students in the current study, ASL surfaced in their writing most frequently as unique glossing and substitution, more than any of the ASL syntactical categories (i.e., plurality and adverbs, adjectives, topicalization, conjunctions and rhetorical questions). Unique glossing and substitution was often the result of including ASL specific lexicon in English.

The expressions are appropriate and acceptable in ASL but sound awkward and are sometimes grammatically incorrect when utilized in the same way in English expressions. A few examples (with the unique word/s italicized) include "I was born *full* deaf," "Justin say that *invent*," "Later she got pregnant again and *borned* Hunter," "She fell *herself*." Because these occurrences happened at the word level, they were perhaps the least intrusive examples of language transfer in the students' writing, and the reader may not necessarily need to be a user of ASL to understand the expression. Other ASL features included in writing samples that were more syntactical in nature such as, "college I all day sit," may be considered more intrusive and difficult to understand without knowledge of the ASL grammar element, topicalization. With this element, the topic of an idea is conveyed prior to providing details. In this example, "college" is the topic whereas "I all day sit" is the description about this topic. ASL syntactical structures such as topicalization found in writing samples could be misperceived as "bad grammar." Yet, these occurrences were less prevalent in student writing.

There did exist an overall decline in both unique glossing and substitution and ASL syntax in d/Dhh adolescent writing after one year of SIWI. This may suggest that d/Dhh students improve their metalinguistic awareness of both languages and increase their implicit English competence as a result of SIWI. Subsequently, they have greater ability to distinguish ASL ways of expression from English.

Teachers can promote metalinguistic awareness among their students by "switching back and forth between the two languages, making explicit comparisons between their rules and structure" (Bailes, 2001, 159). During SIWI, teachers utilize a two-surface approach, which provides additional visual and spatial distinctions for students. Students are not excluded from participating in the co-construction of text if they cannot phrase their ideas in English. Rather, the environment is accepting of ASL expressions, and students' contributions are the focus of explicit metalinguistic instruction. After engaging students several times in guided translation, the teacher begins to step back so students can take up more control over identifying ASL expressions and finding their English equivalents, which then transfers to independent writing.

It may also be that students become more implicitly competent in English as a result of using SIWI's print-based sign to reread the English text several times a lesson. Ideas for the text are generated, translated and constructed by the students primarily but also guided to some extent by the teacher. Therefore, the English text often serves as meaningful and comprehensive language input just beyond the students' level, otherwise known as input + 1 which promotes second language acquisition (Krashen, 1994). As students grow in their ability to use English to express complex thoughts and ideas, they need to rely less on their ASL.

There were two ASL features that did rise slightly in students' writing over time — topicalization (i.e., pre 1.2%, mid 7%, and post 3.5%) and rhetorical questions (i.e., pre 0%, mid 0%, and post 4.6%). The percentages were small compared to the other ASL categories, but did show a different pattern over time. This may have happened as a result of students writing more complex sentences (Wolbers, Dostal, & Bowers, 2012) at the end of the year compared to the beginning. Rhetorical questions, in particular, are a way of adding more adverbial or adjectival phrases (e.g., *when* I have flu last Thursday) or a way of conjoining clauses (I bought shoes *why* old shoes don't fit anymore).

Another explanation for the unexpected but small rise in these ASL features is that some of the d/Dhh students at the beginning of the year were severely language delayed in ability to express their ideas using either ASL or English. Research shows that SIWI leads to gains in student's expressive ASL abilities among students who are language delayed (Dostal, 2011; Dostal & Graham, 2012), and this likely has an impact on how much students expressed in their writing and in what way. Total word count more than doubled from pre- to post-writing samples for typically low-achieving students (Wolbers, Dostal & Bowers, 2012), and thus we were likely to see a greater occurrence of ASL features in the pieces of text written by these students.

EDUCATIONAL IMPLICATIONS

Through this study, we were able to identify and describe the various ways that students use ASL in their English writing. This may be helpful to educators of the d/Dhh who also witness instances of language transfer in their students' writing. Once identified, we can begin to understand the nature of ASL glossing or syntactical influence on writing, and respond with explicit instruction on ASL and English. SIWI is one approach to teaching students to write that embeds techniques for developing metalinguistic knowledge of ASL and English, promoting implicit competence of English and guiding students with translation between languages.

The teacher may additionally create visual scaffolds that help students distinguish between ways of expression in ASL and English. For example, in the current study, students used an ASL way of expressing adjectives approximately 30% of the time. Examples include SHOES NIKE, I WAS AGE 5 OR 4, BREAK SCHOOL and SCHOOL MIDDLE. A visual scaffold might include a description and a demonstration of acceptable ways of signing on one side, and then have a description and a demonstration of acceptable ways of writing adjectives in English on the other side. The teacher can then prompt students to use the visual scaffold during guided writing until they become more independent in their understanding of how to express the concepts in each language.

LIMITATIONS AND FUTURE DIRECTIONS

In the current research, we reviewed the writings of 29 d/Dhh adolescents to determine the types of ASL features that exist in their writing. We were able to identify six different ways that students use ASL in their writing of English. While we did provide an initial description and discussion of this L2 phenomenon that occurs among d/Dhh students, we do not claim the findings to be fully comprehensive of all possible ASL features in writing. Subsequent studies might draw from a larger group of d/Dhh students. Future studies might also compare the prevalence of language transfer in the writings of students who are enrolled in Total Communication versus Bilingual programs. We anticipate that language transfer is more prevalent in Total Communication programs, since Sim-Com is often used with students, and that language input, in essence, is a blending of ASL and English features. Additionally meta-linguistic teachings are less commonly a trait of Total Communication programs.

REFERENCES

Bailes, C. N. (2001). Integrating ASL-English Language Arts: Bridging Paths to Literacy. *Sign Language Studies* 1:147–174.

Baker, C., & Jones, S. (1998). *Encyclopedia of Bilingualism and Bilingual Education.* Clevedon, UK: Multilingual Matters.

Bhela, B. (1999). Native Language Interference in Learning a Second Language: Exploratory Case Studies of Native Language Interference with Target Language Usage. *International Education Journal* 1:22–31.

Bishop, M. & Hicks, S.. (2005). Orange Eyes: Bimodal Bilingualism in Hearing Adults from Deaf Families. *Sign Language Studies* 5:188–230.

Conley, W. (2002). Salt in the Basement: An American Sign Language Reverie in English. In T. Stremlau (ed.) *The Deaf Way II Anthology: A Literary Collection by Deaf and Hard of Hearing Writers (Vol 2),* 171–188. Washington, D.C.: Gallaudet University Press.

Dostal, H. (2011). *Developing Students' First Language through a Second Language Writing Intervention: A Simultaneous Approach.* Unpublished dissertation, University of Tennessee.

Dostal, H. & Graham, S. C. (2012, February). *Communicating Like a Scientist: Discursive Practices of Middle School Deaf Students in the Context of Strategic and Interactive Writing Instruction.* Paper presented at the Association of College Educators of the Deaf and Hard of Hearing, Jacksonville, FL.

Englert, C. S. & Dunsmore, K. (2002). A Diversity of Teaching and Learning Paths: Teaching Writing in Situated Activity. In J. Brophy (ed.) *Social Constructivist Teaching: Affordances and Constraints*. Boston: Elsevier.

Englert, C. S., Mariage, T. V. & Dunsmore, K. (2006). Tenets of Sociocultural Theory in Writing Instruction Research. In C. A. MacArthur, S. Graham and J. Fitzgerald (eds.) *Handbook of Writing Research*, 208–221. New York: Guilford Press.

Fischer, S. & Lillo-Martin, D. (1990). Understanding Conjunctions. *International Journal of Sign Linguistics* 1:71–80.

Graham, S. (2006). Strategy Instruction and the Teaching of Writing: A Meta-analysis. In C. A. MacArthur, S. Graham and J. Fitzgerald (eds.), *Handbook of Writing Research*, New York: The Guilford Press.

Hunt, K, W. (1965). *Grammatical Structures Written at Three Grade Levels*. NCTE Research Report 3, Champaign, IL: National Council of Teachers of English.

Krashen, S. D. (1994). The Input Hypothesis and its Rivals. In N. C. Ellis (ed.) *Implicit and Explicit Learning of Language*, 45–77. London: Academic Press Limited.

Liddell, S. K. (2003). *Grammar, Gesture, and Meaning in American Sign Language*. Cambridge: Cambridge University Press.

Marschark, M., Lang, H. G., & Albertini, J. A. (2002). *Educating Deaf Students: From Research to Practice*. New York: Oxford University Press.

Marschark, M., Mouradian, V., & Halas, M. (1994). Discourse Rules in the Language Productions of Deaf and Hearing Children. *Journal of Experimental Child Psychology* 57:89–107.

Mariage, T. V. (2001). Features of an Interactive Writing Discourse: Conversational Involvement, Conventional Knowledge, and Internalization in "Morning Message." *Journal of Learning Disabilities* 34:172–196.

Nover, S., & Andrews, J. (1999). *Critical Pedagogy in Deaf Education: Bilingual Methodology and Staff Development: Year 2 (1998–99)*. Santa Fe: New Mexico School for the Deaf.

Paul, P. (1998). *Literacy and Deafness: The Development of Reading, Writing, and Literate Thought*. Boston: Allyn and Bacon.

Singleton, J. L., Morgan, D., DiGello, E., Wiles, J., & Rivers, R. (2004). Vocabulary Use by Low, Moderate, and High ASL-proficient Writers Compared to Hearing ESL and Monolingual Speakers. *Journal of Deaf Studies and Deaf Education* 9:86–103.

Stokoe, W. C. (1960). Sign Language Structure: An Outline of the Visual Communication Systems of the American Deaf. *Studies in Linguistics: Occasional Papers 8*. Buffalo: University at Buffalo.

Stremlau, T. M. (2002). *The Deaf Way II Anthology: A Literary Collection by Deaf and Hard of Hearing Writers (Vol 2)*. Washington, D.C.: Gallaudet University Press.

Wilbur, R. B. (2000). The Use of ASL to Support the Development of English and Literacy. *Journal of Deaf Studies and Deaf Education* 5:81–104.

Wolbers, K. (2007). Using Balanced and Interactive Writing Instruction to Improve the Higher Order and Lower Order Writing Skills of Deaf Students. *Journal of Deaf Studies and Deaf Education* 13:255–277.

Wolbers, K. (2008). Strategic and Interactive Writing Instruction (SIWI): Apprenticing Deaf Students in the Construction of English Text. *ITL International Journal of Applied Linguistics* 156:299–326.

Wolbers, K. (2010). Using ASL and Print-based Sign to Build Fluency and Greater Independence with Written English among Deaf Students. *L1-Educational Studies in Language and Literature* 10:99–125.

Wolbers, K., Dostal, H., & Bowers, L. (2012). "I was Born Full Deaf." Written Language Outcomes after One Year of Strategic and Interactive Writing Instruction (SIWI). *Journal of Deaf Studies and Deaf Education* 17:19–38.

Valdes, G. 2006. Bilingual Minorities and Language Issues in Writing: Toward Profession Wide Responses to a New Challenge. In P. K. Matsuda, M. Cox, J. Jordan, and C. Ortmeier-Hooper (eds.) *Second-language Writing in the Composition*, New York: Bedford/St. Martins.

Valli, L., Lucas, C., Mulrooney, K. J., & Villanueva, M. (2011). *Linguistics of American Sign Language: An Introduction (5th ed.)*. Washington, DC: Gallaudet University Press.

What Was
Dr. Klopping's Secret?

BRIAN MALZKUHN

AS LANGUAGE AND CULTURE ARE SO INTERWOVEN AND INSEPARABLE, it can be argued that ASL is the language of Deaf people who depend on the visual aspects of ASL. ASL is communicated through eyes and hands along with facial expressions in a given signing space. Although Deaf Culture is ASL-based and not English-based, many Deaf people are bilingual. It is virtually impossible to expect literacy and fluency in ASL without Deaf people as well as to remove ASL from Deaf people. Hiring Deaf people to work at a deaf school cannot help but produce a rich ASL environment, that promotes higher learning and bilingualism. Having a language is everything!

PAST TO PRESENT

What was Dr. Klopping's secret? I moved to California from Michigan when I was seven, to attend the *alma mater* of my deaf father, the California School for the Deaf, Berkeley. In 1957, CSD Berkeley was like any deaf school in America, employing a strictly oral method in primary and elementary schools for all deaf children and a separate program for children who were unable to learn speech and lip-reading skills (then considered 'non-college material,' or put on the 'vocational track.') Moving into the junior high school, deaf children were permitted to sign and speak at the same time in English order — the simultaneous method — and finally enjoyed signing in the classroom. In the eighth grade, I had my very first Deaf teachers in science and mathematics classes. In high school, we had Deaf teachers in science, social science, mathematics, and vocational classes. They used ASL vocabulary in English grammatical order. Unlike hearing teachers, deaf teachers did not voice while signing. (We never had Deaf teachers in English classes because at that time, the philosophy of deaf education was that hearing teachers must teach English to deaf children as a role model of language. Always English.) In the dormitories, we had many Deaf counselors who were fluent in ASL; in athletics, we had deaf coaches coaching who used fluent ASL. I graduated in 1968, and headed towards Gallaudet University.

After teaching at both CSD Riverside and CSD Berkeley (later Fremont) for twelve years, I entered the private sector for a few years. Eventually, I returned to teaching ASL full time at Ohlone College where there was a strong working relationship between the Ohlone College Deaf Center and CSD Fremont. I taught ASL to many students at Ohlone who later became interpreters and teachers and counselors at Fremont. I also taught ASL to CSD staff (from kitchen to groundskeepers to janitors to secretaries) while at Ohlone. Students from my ASL storytelling classes told ASL stories to elementary children at Fremont. Many students volunteered at Fremont, a wonderful way to enhance their ASL level all the way to proficiency.

Now, though I am "retired" after a three-year stint of teaching ASL at Gallaudet University, this is my fortieth year of teaching experience and I am still a substitute teacher at CSD!

DR. KLOPPING'S ORIGINS

Dr. Henry Klopping was the director of the Teacher Preparation Program at the San Fernando Valley State College in Northridge, California in 1972. Upon graduating from Gallaudet College in May 1972, I enrolled in the TPP and had Dr. Klopping in my first class, "Psychology of Education of Exceptional Children." I was impressed to see him signing and speaking at the same time in class although there were interpreters available. Having interpreters in classes was a new experience for me. Two things happened during that summer: the college changed its name to California State University, Northridge (CSUN), and Dr. Klopping moved to Washington, D. C. to work as Dean of Men at Gallaudet College! I believe that the three-year stint of Dr. Klopping at Gallaudet College was instrumental in his professional life.

In 1975, Dr. Klopping was hired as the Superintendent at CSD Berkeley. His first task was hiring Kenneth Norton, an adjustment teacher, to Dean of Students, the very first deaf person to hold a top-level administrative position at CSD. Thanks to Dr. Klopping's previous positions at CSUN and Gallaudet College, he knew many deaf people and there was a mass gathering of deaf teachers from all over the country to accept teaching positions at Berkeley in his first five years before moving to Fremont.

Dr. Klopping developed his Deaf Education philosophy (Total Education, an upgrade of Total Communication and a forerunner of bilingualism). It was published in *The California News* and he gave presentations in various places, especially at CSD Riverside where I was a high school mathematics teacher in my third year. When I moved north to Berkeley in 1976, I was among twenty-five deaf new employees at the school, many of them fellow college friends and alumni! Fremont was becoming "Gallaudet West"!

Total Communication focuses on holistic language exposure, from signing to speaking to gesticulating to acting out to drawing, Total Education encompasses every place of students during the day: the classroom, the dining room, vocational classes, physical education classes, athletic practice, dormitory life, clubs, organizations, and speech training. Dr. Klopping believed that students needed exposure to signed language, 24/7 from all staff and faculty. Education did not stop in the classroom, Dr. Klopping believed, but continued outside of the classroom into sports and clubs and organizational activities. In other words, 90% of a student's education occurs *outside* of the academic classroom.

To me, this philosophy is truly a forerunner of bilingual-bicultural education, the educational buzzword of the late 1980s, that Fremont adopted across campus, elevating ASL to equal status with English. In order to get everyone involved in a bilingual program, CSD trained all its faculty, staff, and administrators in service training and absorbed the philosophy best to meet deaf students' needs by learning in a visual mode. Parents and alumni were also a part of the growth; through the next ten to fifteen years, Fremont was a paradigm of Deaf education and a national and internatoinal model for all Deaf schools. Before long, everyone on campus used ASL and adopted the cultural appropriateness of signing in front of deaf children at all times. ASL classes are offered on campus weekly to anyone who wants to improve signing skills. Thanks to the affiliation with Ohlone College, members of the community and parents or siblings of Deaf children can become staff or faculty members at CSD Fremont.

DR. KLOPPING'S PHILOSOPHY IN DEAF EDUCATION

Dr. Klopping realized there was a correlation between ASL and deaf employees who could serve as visual language role models for deaf children. Bilingual/bicultural specialists Marlon Kuntze and Ed Bosso helped Dr. Klopping initiate a new campus philosophy in 1990. Dr. Klopping saw the potential of the highest quality education made available to deaf children and CSD Fremont has since been stellar in its accreditation efforts, with continual renewal, showing excellence in all areas.

Prior to Dr. Klopping's arrival at Fremont, 16% of workers (forty-two out of two hundred and sixty four employees) on CSD campus were deaf. There were no deaf secretaries or facility staff (groundskeepers, kitchen staff, janitors), only one deaf administrator (Ken Norton as Dean of Students), one deaf principal (Dean Swaim in high school department), and one deaf teacher in the elementary department.

POSITION	NO. OF DEAF/HEARING EMPLOYEES	PERCENTAGE OF DEAF EMPLOYEES
Administrators	1 deaf, 3 hearing	25%
Secretaries	0 deaf, 17 hearing	0%
Principals	1 deaf, 4 hearing	20%
High School Teachers	11 deaf, 14 hearing	44%
Jr. High School Teachers	2 deaf, 6 hearing	25%
Elementary Teachers	1 deaf, 11 hearing	8%
Special Unit Teachers	2 deaf, 6 hearing	25%
Vocational Teachers	7 deaf, 8 hearing	47%
Total Teachers	**23 deaf, 45 hearing**	**34%**
Academic Supporting Services	3 deaf, 15 hearing	17%
Supervising Instructional Counselors	1 deaf, 4 hearing	20%
Dorm Counselors	13 deaf, 38 hearing	26%
Staff	0 deaf, 96 hearing	0%
Overall Totals	**42 deaf, 222 hearing**	**16% deaf**

Table 1: Deaf vs hearing employee totals prior to Dr. Klopping's arrival on campus

In terms of true contact with deaf children, there were forty-two deaf and one hundred and twenty six hearing employees, or 25% deaf in contact with deaf children on campus. By the end of Dr. Klopping's tenure in 2011, the percentage of Deaf language role models on campus grew dramatically; Table 2 displays position names, deaf or hearing employees in specific positions, and percentage of deaf employees by specialty.

POSITION	NO. OF DEAF/HEARING EMPLOYEES	PERCENTAGE OF DEAF EMPLOYEES
Administrators	2 deaf, 5 hearing	29%
Principals	9 deaf, 1 hearing	90%
Office Technicians on campus	9 deaf, 13 hearing	41%
Teacher Specialists on campus	11 deaf, 19 hearing	37%
Student Assistants on campus	15 deaf, 7 hearing	68%
High School Teachers	13 deaf, 5 hearing	72%
Teaching Assistants	3 deaf	100%
Adjustment Teacher	1 deaf	100%
Office Technicians	1 deaf, 1 hearing	50%
Middle School Teachers	12 deaf, 2 hearing	86%
Teaching Assistants	2 deaf	100%
Adjustment Teacher	1 deaf	100%
Office Technicians	1 deaf	100%
Career Technical Education Teachers	9 deaf	100%
Teaching Assistants	2 deaf, 1 hearing	67%
Office Technician	1 deaf	100%
Physical Education Teachers	9 deaf, 1 hearing	90%
Office Technician	1 hearing	0%
Elementary School Teachers	7 deaf, 7 hearing	50%
Teaching Assistants	3 deaf	100%
Adjustment Teacher	1 deaf	100%
Office Technician	1 deaf	100%
Early Childhood Education Teachers	7 deaf, 1 hearing	88%
Teaching Assistants	3 deaf, 2 hearing	60%
Office Technician	1 deaf	100%
ECE Curriculum Specialist	1 hearing	0%
Speech Teacher	1 hearing	0%
Special Needs Teachers	11 deaf, 3 hearing	86%
Teaching Assistants	3 deaf	100%
Office Technician	1 hearing	0%
Career Center Teachers	3 deaf, 2 hearing	60%
Counselors	3 deaf	100%
Job Placement	1 deaf	100%
Teaching Assistants	1 deaf, 1 hearing	50%
Interpreter	1 hearing	0%
Office Technician	1 hearing	0%

Curriculum and Media Services		
Teacher Specialists	7 deaf, 4 hearing	64%
Library Assistant	1 deaf	100%
Communication		
Teachers:	2 hearing	0%
Teacher Specialist	1 hearing	0%
Total Teachers	**87 deaf, 32 hearing**	**73% deaf**

POSITION	NO. OF DEAF/HEARING EMPLOYEES	PERCENTAGE OF DEAF EMPLOYEES
Department of Pupil Personnel Svc	2 deaf, 5 hearing	29%
Guidance Counselors	4 deaf, 4 hearing	50%
Clerical Staff	1 deaf, 5 hearing	16%
Professional Staff (psychologists, behavioral specialist, diagnostic teachers, audiologist, social worker, IEP coordinator))	4 deaf, 3 hearing	57%
Supervisors of Residence Programs:	11 deaf, 2 hearing	85%
Cottage counselors:	57 deaf, 14 hearing	80%
Facility Staff (maintenance, janitorial, kitchen, groundskeeper, electrical)	20 deaf, 98 hearing	17%
Nurses	0 deaf, 6 hearing	0%
[note: Rev. Thomas Coughlin & Jody Hamilton, nurses and Dr. Frank Hochman, a doctor were deaf working at the school infirmary.]		
Overall Totals:	**240 deaf, 195 hearing**	**55% deaf**
Overall Totals in Contact with Deaf Children:	**19 deaf, 86 hearing**	**72% deaf**

Tables 2a/b: Deaf vs hearing employee totals after Dr. Klopping's tenure (Jun/Sep 2011)

DR. KLOPPING'S VISION FOR EMPLOYEES

In 1976, Dr. Klopping told me that I had not been allowed to attend the national Jr. NAD Convention in Virginia because CSD Riverside was aware I would be moving to Berkeley in the fall. However, he asked me if I would be interested in accompanying students to the Close Up program in Washington, D.C. I was thrilled at the prospect seeing some family members again but more importantly, showing students around the campus of Gallaudet University. The trip was unforgettable! In 1978 when my wife was accepted into Gallaudet University's school counseling masters program, and knowing that she would be away for as much as up to two years, I decided to apply for the Alumni Relations Coordinator position in the Gallaudet University Alumni Association.

Dr. Klopping came to me, wishing me the best of luck for the job interview. He said that although he wanted for me to stay at Fremont teaching mathematics in the high school department, he understood the golden opportunity to experience the unique job at a national level and supported me. I was truly inspired by this. I never got the job so I remained at CSD, much to Dr. Klopping's delight!

Dr. Klopping had a vision of promoting Deaf and hearing candidates in deaf schools or programs; it reminded me of the very concept I embraced during my two-year hiatus in a networking business where we all pushed our downlines up to build our business. Dr. Klopping passionately hired good people and trained them to move to higher positions at other schools; former employees or students who became superintendents include

- James Tucker; Maryland School for the Deaf
- Michael Finneran; Mississippi School for the Deaf and Austine (Vermont) School for the Deaf
- Ed Bosso; Delaware School for the Deaf; Vice President of Laurent Clerc National Deaf Education Center at Gallaudet University
- Ronald Stern; New Mexico School for the Deaf
- Malcolm Grossinger; California School for the Deaf, Riverside
- Sean Virnig; California School for the Deaf, Fremont

Dr. Klopping also believed that higher education was the path to further employment placement. Several others obtained or (at this writing) are in the process of receiving doctoral degrees (* indicates CSDF student):

- Dr. Benjamin Bahan
- Dr. Marlon Kuntze*
- Dr. Nathie Marbury
- Dr. Florence Burke
- Dr. Dawn Riley
- Dr. Diane Morton
- Dr. Debbie Golos
- Dr. Ronald Stern
- Andrew Phillips*, JD (also passed bar exam)

Former CSDF students in Ph.D. programs include Sean Virnig (University of Minnesota), Brendan Stern (Catholic University of America), Matthew Malzkuh, and Julie Cantrell Mitchiner (both at George Mason University).

Several former Fremont employees and students (*) have moved on to teach and work at universities:

- Dr. Benjamin Bahan (Gallaudet University)
- Dr. Marlon Kuntze* (Boston University; Gallaudet University)
- Matthew Malzkuhn* (Gallaudet University)
- Brian Malzkuhn* (Gallaudet University)
- Benjamin Jarashow* (Gallaudet University; Utah Valley University)
- Brian Morrison* (Utah Valley University)
- Melissa Malzkuhn* (Gallaudet University)
- Brendan Stern* (Gallaudet University)
- Vaughn Hallada (University of Wisconsin, Milwaukee)
- Dr. Diane Morton (Gallaudet University)
- Dr. Lori Rush (Gallaudet University)
- Anne Marie Baer* (Gallaudet University)
- Dr. Barbara White (Gallaudet University)
- Angela Vogler* (Gallaudet University)
- James Tucker (Gallaudet University)
- Kristen Cantrell Mitchiner* (Gallaudet University)

IN CONCLUSION OF HIS ERA

Dr. Klopping's ideals and work have reverberated throughout the CSD Berkeley/Fremont community. He passed the torch on to his former student, Sean Virnig, who came to CSD from Texas and Minnesota as CSD's tenth Superintendent in July 2011.

Dr. Klopping is an avid Deaf rights supporter and was visible in the Deaf President Now (1988) and Unity for Gallaudet (2006) movements by allowing many faculty and staff members (whose children were students at Gallaudet University) to fly out to Washington, D.C. to join in the campus movements. He and his wife Bunny have been frequent attendants at NAD conferences, California Association of the Deaf conferences, World Federation of the Deaf conferences, and even here at Deaf Studies *Today!*

THE SECRET IS REVEALED!

By now, you must have figured out the secret, which is, for the sake of survival of a Deaf school, it must have Deaf employees — at least a fifty/fifty breakdown of teachers and counselors — on campus, both in classrooms and in dormitories, as sign language models for deaf children. Language and mathematics are the heart of education. What is the language that deaf children use? It is obvious that it is American Sign Language, a natural and visual language. Deaf teachers and counselors are proficient in ASL and hearing colleagues must be able to sign as well.

DISCUSSIONS AND THOUGHTS

To analyze the success or validity of a program, we need to see a transformation over time. Five years is too short. Since Dr. Klopping held his superintendency position for thirty-six years, we get a chance to verify his insight of hiring deaf workers (and hearing workers who are ASL signers) to be in touch with deaf children, pre-K through 12. Deaf students have constant exposure to visual language from day one to graduation. During Dr. Klopping's tenure, CSD saw a language transformation from an oral method (elementary school), through Simultaneous Communication, Total Communication to SEE to an ASL/bilingual approach. At long last, pre-K and elementary children enjoy full language exposure with teachers and counselors day in and day out.

I cannot help but think that there is a direct correlation between the number of Deaf employees and the number of Deaf students at a school. The more Deaf faculty, administrators, counselors and staff, the more students tend to respond in this relationship. As parents came to visit the CSD Fremont campus with their children for the first time. nearly all of them were blown away by the quality of education, bilingualism, and quantity of qualified Deaf faculty, administrators, and counselors on campus; their children virtually implored their parents to let them enroll at CSD. I do not wish to criticize our hearing counterparts working at CSD as they are as vital in leading quality education to deaf children, however, a healthy number of Deaf people visibly available to deaf children as role models of language and leadership is critical to health of a deaf school/program.

I have seen a deaf school with one deaf superintendent, one deaf teacher, and one deaf counselor on a campus of ninety deaf children. It has since closed down. Is it possible to assume that parents of deaf children, seeing a very small number of deaf employees at a school, prefer to send them to a mainstreamed (public) school? A small sample of deaf employees turns away potential deaf children to public schools where ASL models (deaf or hearing) are not prevalent. CSD is living proof of that a Deaf school model is here to stay in Fremont and is attractive to both deaf and hearing parents of prospective deaf students, near and far (as far as Maryland)! New parents see CSD deaf principals, deaf academic administrators, deaf counselors (cottage and school), and deaf coaches as the role models for their deaf children: "You see us as your child grows."

REFERENCES

Norton, K. W. (2000). *The Eagles Soar to Enlightenment—2000, History of CSD-San Francisco, Berkeley, Fremont from 1860 to 2000*. Fremont, CA: California School for the Deaf.

Various documents from the Museum at the California School for the Deaf, Fremont; *The California News* and CSD Yearbooks (1975–2011).

APPENDIX A

Listed here are several of CSD Fremont's accomplishments in local, state, national, and international sports, academics, commercial, and professional arenas during the Klopping era. Brackets [ ] indicate overall or total championships from league to tournaments whereas parentheses ( ) indicate specific categories like the Western States Basketball Classic and Hoy, etc. Deaf national champions are named more subjectively than objectively by Barry Strassler, an editor of DeafDigest, Inc. and in recent years, the National Deaf Interscholastic Athletic Association started announcing National Champion winners.

STATE AND LOCAL ATHLETIC LEAGUE CHAMPIONSHIPS AND PLACEMENTS
Football [4]
- 1978, 1991, 2002 League Champions (also Bay Football League Champions)
- 1991 NCS Class B Champions; 2002 NCS Class B 2nd Place
- 1982 Bay 6 JV Football Co-Champions

Girls' Volleyball [3]
- 1979, 1994 League Champions (JV); 2008 Co-Champs

Cross Country state qualifiers
- 1989 Merrill Samuels
- 1994 Jason Hardy
- 1996 Jose Gutierrez
- 1998 Brice Pruyn (state medaled) 7th place

Boys' Basketball [22]
- 1986 League Champion
- 1981, 1983, 1984, 1985, 1986, 1987, 1988, 1989, 1993, 1994, 1995, 2000, 2004, 2005, 2006, 2007, 2008, 2009, 2010, 2011 Western States Basketball Classic Champions (20; originated by Dr. Klopping in 1977)
- 2006 Clerc Classic Champion

Girls' Basketball [14]
- 1995 League Co-Champion
- 2008–2009 NCS Division VI 2nd Place
- 1983, 1986, 1990, 1991, 1998, 2001, 2003, 2004, 2005, 2006, 2010, 2011 Western States Basketball Classic Champions (12)

- 1995 King's Academy Christmas Tournament Champion

Cheerleading [8]
- 1986, 1994, 1995, 2001, 2008, 2010, 2011 Western States Basketball Classic Champions (7)
- 2000 Clerc Classic Champion
- Mona Mayes Viera, cheerleader with Oakland Raiders!!

Boys' Track [19]
- 1976, 1977, 1978, 1981, 1983, 1984, 1986, 1987, 1988, 1989, 1990, 1991, 1992, 1993, 1994, 1995 League Champions
- 1984, 1986 NCS Class A Championship; 1995 NCS Class A 2nd Place
- State Qualifiers: Norman Edwards (Triple Jump, 1986); Merrill Samuels (400m and 200m, 1990)
- 2009 Berg Seeger Champs

Girls' Track [11]
- 1980, 1981, 1983, 1984, 1986, 1987, 1988, 1990, 1991, 1992, 1993 League Champions
- 1987 NCS Class A 2nd Place
- State Qualifier: Ashley Griffith (High Jump, 2005, 2006)

Baseball [8]
- 2007 League Champion
- 2007 BCL East Division II Champion
- 2001, 2002, 2003, 2004, 2007, 2008, 2010 Hoy Classic Champions (7)

Girls' Softball [5]
- 1998 BCL East Champion; 2007 BCL East Division II Champion
- 2001, 2003, 2009 Hoy Classic Champions (3)

Special Awards [2]
- 2010–2011 BCL CIF Sportsmanship Champion
- 2010 Scholastic Football Division V in Highest GPA

DEAF ATHLETIC NATIONAL CHAMPIONS [30]
- 1986, 1987 Girls' Track (2)
- 1987, 1988, 1989, 1990, 1991, 1992, 1994, 1995, 1996 Cross Country (9)
- 1985, 2002 Football (2)
- 1993, 2001, 2002, 2007, 2008, 2010 Baseball (6)
- 1990, 1995, 1998, 2001, 2003, 2009 Softball (6)
- 1990 Girls' Volleyball (1)
- 1985, 2006 Boys' Basketball (2)
- 2001 Girls' Basketball (1)
- 2005 Wrestling (1)

DEAF ATHLETIC NATIONAL PLAYER OF THE YEAR AWARDS
- 1993 Mark King, Boys' Basketball
- 1986 Lynn Barlow, Girls' Track, Girls' Cross Country
- 1988 Quilla Mosley, Girls' Volleyball
- 1989 Karen Gilbert, Girls' Volleyball

- 1989 Merrill Samuels, Boys' Cross Country
- 1994 Nora Yates, Girls' Volleyball
- 1995 Jason Hardy, Boys' Cross Country
- 1996 Jose Gutierrez, Boys' Cross Country
- 2005 Michael Lizarraga, Boys' Basketball
- 2008 Shane Nevins, Baseball
- 2009 Alicia Johnson, Softball

DEAF ATHLETIC NATIONAL COACH OF THE YEAR AWARDS
- 1986 Ken Pedersen, Track
- 1987 James Koetz, Cross Country
- 1988 Robert Ellis, Girls' Volleyball
- 1989 Pat Bernstein, Softball
- 1989 Ron Obray, Baseball
- 1993 Ken Pedersen, Boys' Basketball
- 1993 Mike Pereira, Baseball
- 1994 Kevin Bella, Softball
- 2001, 2009, 2010 Deb Ayers, Girls' Basketball
- 2006 Oskar Schugg, Boys' Basketball
- 2008 Saul Gevarter, Baseball
- 2009 Michelle Malcolm, Softball

DEAF YOUTH ATHLETIC CHAMPIONSHIPS AND PLACEMENTS
With Dr. Klopping's blessing, the elementary and middle school athletic programs started in early 2000s [7]:
- 2006 Girls' and Boys' Basketball 5/6th Grade Fremont District Tourney Championships
- 2009, 2010, 2011 Boys' Basketball, 2010, 2011 Girls' Basketball The Iron Five Tournament for middle school athletes
- 2006–2009 Fremont Middle School Football League (Fremont, Union City and Newark) Bengals
- 2006–2009 Middle School Cheerleading, Fremont Football League
- 2010 Golden State Conference Youth Football League, 2nd place

INTERNATIONAL DEAFLYMPICS PARTICIPATION
Former CSD students, faculty, staff Deaflympians, coaches, or directors
- 1977 Bucharest: Craig Healy (Javelin), Ronald Stern (Men's basketball), Bob Skedsmo (Cycling)
- 1979 Meribel: Leslie Romak (Giant slalom, Slalom downhill), Doug Dickinson (Giant slalom, Slalom downhill)
- 1981 Koln: Mike Peterson (400m hurdles)
- 1983 Madonna di Campiglio: Doug Dickinson (Giant slalom, Super giant slalom)
- 1985 Los Angeles: Ron Bye (water polo), Charles Holmes (Men's volleyball); Graham Koetz (Cycling), Richard Machado (Cycling), Alvin Spain, Thomas Withrow (Hammer), Daryl Wetzel (Men's basketball); James Koetz (Track coach), Bob Skedsmo (Cycling coach)
- 1989 Christchurch: Jon Schmitz (Cycling), Paul Wood (Cycling), Rodney Pedersen (Men's basketball), Mike Bauer (wrestling), Norman Edwards (Team handball), Jason Ingraham (Team handball), Scott O'Donnell (Team handball), Jude

Castaneda (Wrestling), Justin Coleman (Pole vault), Richard Machado (Cycling), Daniel Rosenthal (Marathon), Merrill Samuels (Track), Charles Holmes (Men's Volleyball), Daryl Wetzel (Team Handball), Thomas Withrow (Shot), Ralph Fernandez (Cycling), Craig Salenon (Water Polo); Ron Stern, Director of Team Development for Team USA, Bob Skedsmo (Cycling coach)

- 1991 Banff: Doug Dickinson (assistant coach and technician)
- 1993 Sofia: Paul Wood (Cycling), Jon Schmitz (Cycling), Norman Edwards (Team handball), Scott O'Donnell (Team handball), Jodee Dike (Women's basketball), Charles Holmes (Men's volleyball & flag bearer), Alexander Ash (Cycling), Ron Bye (Water polo), Thomas Withrow (Hammer), Daryl Wetzel (Men's basketball); Ron Stern, Director of Team Development for Team USA; Jack Lamberton, Logistics Officer, Bob Skedsmo, CISS Technical Director
- 1995 Yllas: Doug Dickinson (assistant coach and technician), Ron Stern, Director of Team Development for Team USA, Jack Lamberton, Team Director
- 1997 Copenhagen: Jodee Dike (Team bowling), Charles Holmes (Men's volleyball), Paul Wood (Cycling), Karen Gilbert (Women's volleyball), Dyan Kovacs (Women's volleyball), Scott O'Donnell (Team handball), Tyrone Kovacs (Team handball), Cy Saunders (Team handball), Ron Bye (Water polo), Thomas Withrow (Hammer); Ron Stern, Director of Team Development for USA teams, Jack Lamberton, Team Director, Bob Skedsmo, CISS Technical Director
- 1999 Davos: Doug Dickinson (assistant coach and technician)
- 2001 Rome: Scott O'Donnell (Team handball), Tyrone Kovacs (Team handball), Norman Chan (Team handball), Kevin Kovacs (Team handball), Dyan Kovacs (Women's volleyball), Paul Wood (Cycling), Nixo Lanning (Team handball), Sarah Parker (Team handball), Jeanne Dike (Team handball), Jodee Dike (Team handball), Thomas Withrow (Hammer); Bob Skedsmo, CISS Technical Director
- 2003 Sundsvall: Sheila De La O (Snowboarding), Clint Dickinson (Skiing), Nixo Lanning (Snowboarding), Keith Doane (Skiing); Jack Lamberton, Vice President of International Affairs Chef de Mission for Team USA
- 2005 Melbourne: Paul Wood (Cycling), Ashley Griffith (Track), Barbara Hyde (Women's Basketball), Jeff Bibb (Team handball), Ty Kovacs (Team handball), Rory Osbrink (Cycling), Norman Chan (Team handball), Adam Jarashow (Team handball), Dyan Kovacs (Women's volleyball), Sarah Parker (Women's beach volleyball), Brendan Stern (Men's basketball); Jack Lamberton, Vice President of International Affairs Chef de Mission for Team USA; Bob Ellis, Team Director; Bob Skedsmo, CISS Technical Director; Stuart Ikeda, Information Technology Specialist
- 2007 Salt Lake City: Jodee Dike (Curling), Karen Officer (Curling), Nixo Lanning (Snowboarding); Doug Dickinson, Head Coach; Jack Lamberton, Vice President of International Affairs Chef de Mission for Team USA
- 2009 Taipei: Paul Wood (Cycling), Nixo Lanning (Women's Basketball), Barbara Hyde (Women's Basketball); Jack Lamberton, Vice President of International Affairs Chef de Mission for Team USA, Bob Skedsmo, CISS Technical Director

ACADEMIC BOWL NATIONAL CHAMPIONS [2]
- 1998 Melissa Malzkuhn, Shoshanna Stern, Jesse Saunders, Jerry Pua, coach Gary Olsen
- 1999 Adam Jarashow, Melissa Malzkuhn, Brendan Stern, Megan Malzkuhn, Jane Jonas, Adam Jarashow, coach Jack Lamberton

AUTHORS, PUBLISHERS, PRODUCERS

Former employees or students publishing commercial artwork, books, and/or DVDs:

- Don Baer, sculptor, created life-size wax figures of historical Deaf people (Thomas H. Gallaudet, Laurent Clerc, Alice Cogswell, Willam E. "Dummy" Hoy, Laura Redden Searing, Juliette Gordon Low, Andrew Foster, Laura Dewey Bridgman, Fredrick C. Schreiber, Bernard Bragg, Erastus "Deaf" Smith)
- Dr. Ben Bahan, co-author with Harlan Lane and Robert Hoffmeister, *A Journey into the Deaf-World* (2000); co-author with Carol Neidle, Judy Kegl, Dawn MacLaughlin and Robert Lee, *The Syntax of American Sign Language: Functional Categories and Hierarchical Structure* (1999); co-author/director with Dirksen Bauman, *Audism Unveiled* (2008); co-author/producer with Dr. Sam Supalla, *Bird of a Different Feather* and *For a Decent Living* (1994)
- Dr. Roy K. Holcomb, co-author with Dr. Thomas K. Holcomb and Samuel K. Holcomb, *Deaf Culture Our Way* (1995)
- Melissa Malzkuhn, producer, *Tara's Story* (2007), international and national award-winning documentary film on Tara Holcomb at the 2006 Gallaudet University Protest
- Megan Matovich, developer, www.whysign.com
- Mark Nelson, developer, www.csdalumni.org
- Kenneth Norton, author, *The Eagles Soar to Enlightenment* (2000), *History of CSD-San Francisco, Berkeley, Fremont from 1860 to 2000*
- Theron Parker, co-producer with Mindy Parker *Have ASL, Will Travel, Folklore from around the World*; *Little Deaf Spies*; *In the Minds of Ed and Theron*
- Bernice Singleton, authored a book *Signs of Courage: Deaf Survivors of Breast Cancer* (2001)
- Ralph Singleton, co-author with Judy Singleton, *Underwater Sign Communication* (2002)
- Louise Stern, author, *Chattering: Stories* (2010)
- Mark Wood, produced *Forget Me Not, Wrong Game, Legend of The Mountain Man, Gerald, Black Sand, Versa Effect* [all DVDs, at least 90% deaf cast and behind scenes; films shown in many places in America]

PRESIDENTS, DIRECTORS, CHAIRS, AND ORGANIZATION FOUNDERS

Former employees or students who have served as presidents, directors, or founders of state, national or international organizations:

- Celia May Baldwin, Gallaudet University Board of Trustees; vice-president of National GUAA, president of CAL-ED
- Celia May Baldwin, Lon Kuntze & Deirdre Kennedy, directors of 1988 national Jr. NAD ConventioN
- Celia May Baldwin & Michele Berke Holcomb, co-chairs of 1996 CAL-ED/IMPACT Conference
- Richard Bonheyo, secretary of national Deaf Senior Association
- Mike Finneran, president & board member of Convention of American Instructors of the Deaf
- Leo Jacobs, pioneer of California's Deaf Awareness Month; director of Outreach
- Michelle Boren Hughes, chair of the 2011 50th Biennial CAD Convention
- Dr. Henry Klopping, President of CEASD (Conference of Educational Administrators Serving the Deaf)
- Jack Lamberton, Chef de Mission for Team USA; International Commission for

Sports of the Deaf (ICSD); president of USA Deaf Sports Federation
- Gil Lentz, founder and president in American Deaf Golf Education Foundation and instructor of over two hundred international deaf/hard of hearing golfers
- Melissa Malzkuhn, founder of DYUSA (Deaf Youth USA); executive secretary of World Federation of the Deaf Youth Section
- Megan Malzkuhn, president of DYUSA
- Ginny Malzkuhn and Brenda Call, co-chairs of 2007 CAL-ED Conference
- Megan Matovich, president of Norway Association of the Deaf
- Barbara Morrison, Chair of CSD's 150 Year Celebration
- Ralph Neesam, Project Coordinator for Kellogg/Gallaudet Project at CSD
- Donald Parodi, founder of The Donald N. Parodi Memorial Charitable Trust; benefits the CSD Fremont community in charitable, scientific, literary and/or educational projects
- Andrew Phillips, lawyer, The National Association of the Deaf
- Alyce Slater Reynolds, president of National GUAA
- Buddy Singleton, president of CAD
- Ralph Singleton, president of CAD

FORMER EMPLOYEES OR STUDENTS RECEIVING SPECIAL AWARDS
- Ralph Jordan, 1978 Laurent Clerc California Deaf Teacher of the Year by National Center on Deafness, CSUN
- Mark Nelson, 1980 Mervin Garretson Publications Award by Jr. NAD for CSD School Newsletter, "The Bear Hunt"
- Mark Nelson, 1981 Jr. NAD Byron B. Burnes Leadership Award by Gallaudet University Kappa Gamma Fraternity
- Bernadette Attletweed, 1983 Laurent Clerc California Deaf Teacher of the Year by National Center on Deafness, CSUN
- Deirdre Kennedy, 1986 Laurent Clerc California Deaf Teacher of the Year by National Center on Deafness, CSUN
- Kenneth Norton, Supervisor Performance Award by California State Department of Education in recognition of an exceptional contribution to state government as an exemplary during the 1988-89 Fiscal Year
- Julian "Buddy" Singleton, winner of CDE Superior Achievement Award
- Julian "Buddy" Singleton, 1985 California Deaf Teacher of the Year
- Celia May Baldwin, 1994 State Schools Administrator of the Year by IMPACT
- Deirdre Kennedy, 2004 Administrator of the Year from California Educators of the Deaf and Hard of Hearin
- Jane Newkirk, 2004 Professional of the Year by IMPACT
- Kenneth Norton (with Audree Norton), 2006 Pauline 'Polly' Peikoff Service to Others Award by GUAA
- Celia May Baldwin, 2008 CAL-ED Administrator of the Year by CAL-ED (California Educators of the Deaf)

FORMER EMPLOYEES OR STUDENTS IN THE ADVOCACY, DRAMATIC ARTS, AND ENTERTAINMENT INDUSTRIES
- Joey Baer, community leader
- Joel and Jed Barish, founders of DeafNation, featuring booths of all sorts related to Deaf-World and ASL entertainments for everyone
- Mark Bella, vice president of Sales, Purple Communications

- Michael Davis, performer/dancer, national one man show "Janitor," performer, The Wild Zappers, all-male dance troupe; a guest appearance on television drama series "Cold Case"
- Jon Kovacs, founder/actor, Rathskellar
- Melissa Malzkuhn, managing editor, Deaf Studies Digital Journal, www.dsdj.gallaudet.edu
- Priscilla Poynor Moyers, owner, Allies for Communication Equality, LLC, interpreting agency
- Ron Obray, founder, Hands On Interpreting
- Michael Pementel, official sports photographer, University of California at Berkeley, featured in Sports Illustrated
- Judy Pratt, actress, PBS series "The Voyage of the Mimi"
- Shoshanna Stern, television and film actress, "Jericho," "Lie to Me," "Hamill"

Language Attitudes in the American Deaf Community: An Overview

JOSEPH C. HILL

WITHIN A POPULATION OF DEAF AND HARD-OF-HEARING INDIVIDUALS in the United States, there is a community in which members consider themselves a cultural and linguistic minority with ASL as a language. The members naturally gravitate toward each other because of their shared experience of deafness and of the bond they share through communicating in ASL. Nevertheless, the Deaf community is not entirely composed of deaf ASL signers who were born to deaf parents, exposed to ASL during the critical age of language acquisition, and attended deaf school. Many members of the community have hearing parents and have attended mainstream education programs that might use English-based signing systems or contact signing instead of ASL. Some members are late deafened, meaning that they were exposed to spoken English in the earlier years of their lives before they lost their hearing. Some members were raised to communicate orally before they decided to learn ASL. With the diversity in the Deaf community in terms of education, family, and social backgrounds, it is likely that they have different ideas of what ASL is and who uses ASL and the differences may explain the attitudes they possess about ASL. This raises the research question in the study: *What are the linguistic and social factors that govern attitudes toward signing in the American Deaf community?*

This question is important to consider because there are different viewpoints in the American Deaf community regarding the acceptance of the signing forms and features that are deemed standard or vernacular as ASL and the rejection of the forms and features as not ASL (typically English-based). The social factors are also important to consider because identities are stereotypically associated with the types of signing possessing particular forms and features. Attitudes toward language varieties are generally influenced by the process of language standardization (Garrett, 2010:7). When one language variety is deemed "standard," that impacts (usually devalues) the status of other language varieties and of social groups using those language varieties in a particular context (ibid.) and members of society, regardless of their social status, consciously or unconsciously "subscribe to the ideology of the standard language" (Milroy, 2001:535) because of their belief in correctness. In addition, prestige is acquired through the process of standardization in a given society in a given time and it is most often associated with a social group with weighty influence in the society. With English being viewed as a standard language with an overt prestige, it has a tremendous effect on perceptions of the status and linguistic structure of ASL in the American Deaf community as well as the mainstream American society.

SOCIAL AND HISTORICAL CONTEXTS OF ASL

In the history of deaf education in America, there was great pressure to remove ASL as a medium of instruction and replace it with an oral form of English language. Years later when that failed in some places, there has been "agreement" to use signed communication in classrooms with deaf and hard of hearing students but only a visual method based on English. Even though ASL was still used, however surreptitiously for the reason of covert prestige (which is the advantage of using a stigmatized language variant favored by a particular community in terms of cultural solidarity), the general avoidance or suppression of ASL by educators and administrators sent a message to deaf and hard-of-hearing students that English was better than ASL and English in the written and oral forms was how they could succeed in American society. For a long time, deaf and hard-of-hearing children and adults internalized this negative thinking about ASL until research by William Stokoe showed that ASL is a valid linguistic system.

The discovery did not result in an immediate widespread acceptance of ASL as a valid language by the American Deaf community due to internalized oppression and conflicting emotions and opinions about ASL. But over time, with an increasing number of research studies on ASL, more formalized course offerings on ASL, and the rippling effect of Deaf President Now (DPN) in 1988 on the America Deaf community, the respect for ASL has grown within the American Deaf community. Now ASL is one of the most popular foreign languages formally taught in schools, colleges, and universities (see Padden & Humphries, 2005; Rosen, 2010); there are teaching materials for ASL; there are places that regularly evaluate the ASL skills of deaf, hard-of-hearing, and hearing signers; there are professional and academic organizations on teaching, education, and linguistics of ASL. ASL has arrived to an interesting destination as a standard language with prestige (acquired through the standardization with dictionaries, textbooks, classes, and language proficiency evaluation) in the American Deaf community while at the same time being a stigmatized language in mainstream America. However, not all deaf and hard-of-hearing individuals use or even view ASL the same way.

Of all deaf and hard-of-hearing individuals in the United States, a very small percentage is born to deaf or hard-of-hearing parents whose communication preference might be signing, speaking, or both. A large proportion of the population acquired signing systems (ASL, contacting signing, English-based signing, cued speech) in formal education settings. A considerable amount of deaf and hard-of-hearing people who have attended deaf schools (which are the institutions for the deaf and have been long considered as active centers for the transmission and maintenance of ASL) acquired ASL or signing in some form in their young age. The rest have been mainstreamed in restricted or inclusive settings in public or private schools with a variety of communication methods made available by educators and administrators, including English-based communication systems. With declining enrollments at deaf schools, that translates to an increasing number of deaf and hard-of-hearing students whose exposure to ASL is wholly dependent on the kinds of educational settings, parents' wishes, and the presence of a deaf community in town.

In some places and groups in America, English is still seen as the preferred way to be successful in society and ASL, with the number of misconceptions (e.g., 'broken English,' grammarless, an impediment to English skills development), is suggested as a secondary communication method or as something to be avoided entirely. With additional factors such as the onset of deafness and age of ASL acquisition as well as social diversity in terms of race, ethnicity, and socio-economic status, it paints a complicated picture of the perceived status of ASL and English in terms of prestige, identities associated with signing, the purity of ASL, and the extent of English influence in the signing of deaf and hard-of-hearing people.

THE STUDY

This study looks at four different components to help answer the basic research question: 1) subjects' perceptions of signing, 2) effects of social information on the perceptions of signing, 3) evaluation of signing, and 4) description of signing; these four different components helped look at linguistic and social factors. Before the development of the study, a pilot study helped create a spectrum of signing types (e.g., 'Strong ASL,' 'Mostly ASL,' 'Mixed,' and 'Non-ASL') by reviewing sixty fifteen-second signing videos that demonstrated the nature of ASL. These videos were used in the first two components: subjects judged the signing in different videos as 'ASL' or 'not ASL' and then were given social information to see any effect on the perceptions of the signing types. The last two components used eight different one-minute videos videos altogether. The third component was an attitude study with the evaluation scales on different signers and their signing with respect to language and social characteristics. Finally, the fourth component was a collection of the subjects' description of the signing seen in the videos.

SUBJECTS

The subjects were grouped into eight social groups on the basis of three social characteristics: generation (younger and older), race (black and white), and age of ASL acquisition (native and non-native) (Table 1). The reason for grouping the subjects into the social groups was to achieve homogeneity based on social characteristics and use this as a social factor as a predictor for judgments of the signing types in the study components 1 and 2. In study components 3 and 4, the subjects were not grouped based on the social characteristics; instead, social characteristics of the signers in the videos and the description of signing were observed by the subjects.

	White		Black	
	Native	Non-Native	Native	Non-Native
Younger	24 (22 D / 2 HH)	10 (7 D / 3 HH)	5 (4 D / 1 HH)	8 (5 D / 3 HH)
Older	6 (4 D / 2 HH)	7 (6 D / 1 HH)	3 (3 D / 0 HH)	11 (8 D / 3 HH)

Table 1: Deaf (D) and Hard-of-Hearing (HH) subjects (n = 74) in the social groups.

For 'age of acquisition,' 'native ASL' signers are those exposed to ASL at birth and maximally acquire ASL through the typical milestones of language development (Bonvillian, 1999; Petito, 2000; Emmorey, 2002; Wood, 2010). The effects of age of acquisition on signing production skills are discussed in the number of language acquisition studies of sign language and set forth a common assumption that native signers, meaning signers who acquire signed language during this critical period have a better command of language than late learners in some linguistic aspects (ibid.). However, a very small percentage of the U.S. deaf and hard-of-hearing population are born to deaf or hard-of-hearing parents who are skillful ASL signers. That leaves a large percentage of deaf and hard-of-hearing people acquiring other available communication systems (e.g., oral communication, varieties of signed English, cued speech) and, for some, acquiring ASL at later age.

For 'race,' black and white subjects were represented in both native and late signer groups. Race was suggested in Lucas and Valli's 1992 study in which there was a large discrepancy in judgment between a group of white subjects and a group of black subjects with respect to the signing of a black signer in a video. With race as a factor, it must be included in the study.

For 'generation,' younger and older signers were represented in both native and late signer groups as well as in Black and White groups. In the sociolinguistic literature, age of a generation is normally one of the social variables observed in linguistic community studies (Eckert 1997:152). With 'generation,' the emergence of alternative signed communication systems and mainstream programs is a possible source of language perception differences between younger and older groups. This line of reasoning is used in Lucas, et al.'s 2001 study in which three generational age groups (15–25, 26–54, and 55+; along with other social variables) were studied for sociolinguistic variation. Lucas, et al. state that age division is motivated by developments in language policy in deaf education (Lucas, et al, 2001:35). The older group has little or no exposure to mainstreaming education and no prior exposure to the alternative communication systems, while the middle and younger groups have had exposure to various educational programs and communication systems. Another possible effect on language perception difference between younger and older groups is the growth of linguistic research on ASL, linguistic training of ASL, and the cultural pride of ASL. Younger signers may be more aware of and sensitive to linguistic features and structures of ASL than do older signers.

STUDY COMPONENT 1: PERCEPTIONS OF SIGNING

The first part of the study contained five analyses of frequencies of subjects' ASL and Non-ASL responses on all signing types (i.e., 'Strong ASL,' 'Mostly ASL,' 'Mixed,' and 'Non-ASL'). The first two analyses treated the subjects collectively. Based on the first analysis on the relative frequencies of ASL and Non-ASL responses, frequencies of responses differed based on signing types. In the second analysis, the relative frequencies of ASL and Non-ASL responses as a whole were compared with the chance level of 0.05; there was a systematic agreement of the responses from the subjects as whole with the highest proportion of ASL responses for 'Strong ASL,' the second highest for 'Mostly ASL,' the random proportion for 'Mixed' and the lowest proportion for 'Non-ASL.' A further analysis on the difference between 'Strong ASL' and 'Mostly ASL' revealed that the relative frequencies of ASL responses were significantly different.

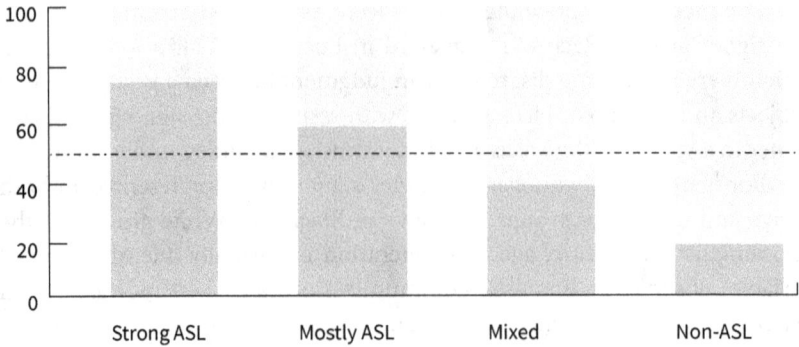

Figure 1: Frequency of ASL (dark gray) and Non-ASL (light gray) responses from all subjects.

The next two analyses treated subjects separately based on the social characteristics (i.e., generation, race, and age of ASL acquisition). The first analysis was on the relative frequencies of ASL and Non-ASL responses to the signing types in each social group; all social groups except the Older Black Non-Native group had the frequencies of responses differed by the signing types. The second analysis focused on the comparison between the chance level of 0.50 and the relative frequencies of ASL and Non-ASL responses. All social groups had higher proportions of ASL responses for 'Strong ASL' and 'Mostly ASL.' For 'Mixed,' the frequencies of ASL responses of a few social groups (Older Black Non-Native, Older White Non-Native, and Younger Black Native) were significantly higher than 0.50 and the frequencies of ASL responses of the other social groups were at the chance level. For 'Non-ASL,' the frequencies of ASL responses of the same few social groups (Older Black Non-Native, Older White Non-Native, and Younger Black Native) were not significantly different from 0.50 and the frequencies of ASL responses of the other social groups were significantly lower than 0.50.

The last analysis was the comparison of the social groups' relative frequencies of ASL and Non-ASL responses for each signing type. The frequencies were not found to be significantly different for 'Strong ASL,' 'Mostly ASL,' and 'Mixed' except for 'Non-ASL' which the difference was significant. Based on the prior analysis in the above paragraph, some social groups (Older Black Non-Native, Older White Non-Native, and Younger Black Native) perceived 'Non-ASL' as a mixture of ASL and English while the other groups perceived as English-based signing.

STUDY COMPONENT 2: EFFECTS OF SOCIAL
INFORMATION ON THE PERCEPTIONS OF SIGNING

This part of the study used the same procedure as in the first component but the presentation of social information of the signers (which was not necessarily true) was included in the second part of the study. It is a study of how a provision of some relevant social information may affect the subjects' perceptions of the signing types, based on the inspiration of the methodology in Niedzielski's study (1996) on the effect of social information on the Michigan subjects' perception of nonstandard vowels in a native Detroit speaker's speech. Niedzielski used two pieces of information, Michigan and Canadian, to influence the subjects' perception of the nonstandard vowels. The study did not focus on the target units as defined as the vowels in the Niedzielski's study, but the aim was the same: to influence the subjects' perception with different pieces of social information. Social features that were culturally relevant to the American Deaf community were introduced here and the features might have a possible influence on a perception of signing types: family hearing status, kind of school setting, and education status.

Family hearing status indicates whether a signer's family is Deaf or hearing. This status is typical in the American Deaf community with common anecdotes and common assumptions held by sign language researchers that considers skillful ASL signers being reared with at least one skillful ASL signer (usually an adult) in their family and signers producing mixed or English-like signing being brought up with no ASL signer in their family.

School settings also signals whether a signer attended a Deaf school or a mainstream program. This status is also typical in the American Deaf community with common anecdotes and common assumptions in sign language research that considers skillful ASL signers as having a significant portion of their primary and secondary education at a special school for the deaf and signers producing mixed or English-like signing having a significant portion of their primary and secondary education in mainstream.

Class divisions could be a factor in the perceptions of signing variation in terms of education attainment in the American Deaf community. The anecdotes in the community are that ASL is said to be perceived as a language used by less educated members of the Deaf community (known as "grassroots") and English-influenced signing is said to be used by higher educated Deaf members (Padden & Humphries 2005:127). For example, grassroots Deaf people are usually working-class, generally uninterested in pursuing higher education, and their signing is generally perceived to be ASL heavy. Another example is that Deaf professionals with college education are perceived to use English-like features in their signing, for example, more fingerspelling of English words and English word order. It may be argued that the signing by professional Deaf people has more to do with register than signing types or with some parts of their social background that influenced their signing.

The study part had three hypotheses which could be tested with a single analysis. The first hypothesis was that 'Strong ASL' and 'Non-ASL' would be less likely to be perceived against their types than 'Mostly ASL' and 'Mixed' because of the respective predominant forms and features in the former signing types. There was no strong support for this hypothesis because there was a few more social information effects occurred for 'Strong ASL' and 'Non-ASL' than for 'Mostly ASL' and 'Mixed.' It did not mean that there were no effects for 'Mostly ASL' and 'Mixed'; there were changes in responses but the direction of changes went both ways between ASL and 'Non-ASL.' With 'Strong ASL' and 'Non-ASL,' a considerable number of subjects made the same responses in the second part of the study as they did in the first part but a few number subjects drastically changed their responses in a single direction from ASL to 'Non-ASL' and thus functioned as outliers in the analyses. The interpretation was that all signing types could be perceived differently due to relevant social information and the changes in responses could go in either direction.

The second hypothesis was that non-culturally deaf-related information ("Hearing Family" and "Mainstream") would exert greater influence on the perception of the signing types with a considerable proportion of ASL forms and features (i.e., 'Strong ASL,' 'Mostly ASL,' and 'Mixed') than would culturally deaf-related information ("Deaf Family" and "Deaf School"). Altogether there were significant and marginal effects of non-culturally deaf-related information on the perceptions of 'Strong ASL,' 'Mixed,' and even 'Non-ASL,' it required a careful interpretation because the number of video samples in the matrix of the signing types and the social information were small; the direction of changes could have gone either way; and there were outliers that skewed the results. The effects were more of a potential that social information could have on the perceptions of the signing types and the potential could be realized with more videos.

The third hypothesis questioned whether high school or college education would be more likely to influence the signing types of relatively equilibrial proportions of ASL and English-based forms and features, 'Mostly ASL' and 'Mixed.' Based on the analysis, there was no effect of high school information on 'Mostly ASL' and 'Mixed' but there was an effect on 'Strong ASL.' The effect was due to a small number of outliers so that skewed the result.

The direction of changes was not the only factor that affected the results. There were also other effects that were not controlled in the second part of the study, for example, the effect of the subjectivity of social information for the subjects, the effect of the social diversity of the subjects, the effect of narrative content produced by the signers in videos, and fatigue effect in two hours of subjects' participation.

STUDY COMPONENT 3: EVALUATION OF SIGNING

The third part of the study was subjects' evaluations of eight signers in videos. The study part contained three analyses: the analysis of the subjects' sign-type responses (i.e., ASL, 'Mixed,' and Signed English) to eight signers; and two analyses of the subjects' evaluative ratings on the signers and their signing in terms of aesthetic, purity, fluidity, leadership, identity, education, and intelligence. The questionnaire asked respondents to identify:

"The signing is pure."	"The signer seems to be a strong Deaf person."
"The signing is beautiful."	"The signer looks hearing."
"The signing is smooth."	"The signer looks educated."
"The signer looks like a leader in the Deaf community."	"The signer looks smart."

The questionnaire followed the method used in language or dialect evaluation in asking people about the aesthetic and properness aspects of a target language or dialect (e.g., Lambert, et al., 1960, 1975; Evans, 2002b) in which subjects answered the questions about correctness, pleasantness, aesthetic, and what linguistic features determine correctness, pleasantness, and aesthetic. The purpose of this kind of questionnaire is to reveal subjects' subjective attitudes about language or dialect in relation to social stereotypes and language ideologies.

The first analysis revealed that three signers were similar in signing and were mostly judged as ASL; the signing of two signers were mostly judged similar as ASL or 'Mixed'; and the other three signers were mostly judged as 'Mixed' or Signed English. The ASL, 'Mixed,' and Signed English responses were treated as an independent variable in the next two analyses of signing evaluations regardless of the association between the signing responses and the signers.

The two analyses were on the responses of agreement, neutral, and disagreement on the language and social evaluation scales related to the perceived signing types, ASL, 'Mixed,' and Signed English. Signing perceived as ASL was evaluated positively on all social and language evaluation scales; signing perceived as 'Mixed' received mixed evaluations from the subjects except for the scale of smoothness, Deaf identity, education and intelligence;

and signing perceived as Signed English evaluated negatively on all social and language evaluation scales except for the scale of smoothness, education, and intelligence.

There were three evaluations that were considerably positive for all signing types: smoothness, education, and intelligence. It was possible that smoothness had two interpretations for the subjects: that the signing was fluent with no hesitation or excessive pauses or that thoughts were expressed clearly with strong points regardless of hesitations. For education and intelligence, there were two possible reasons for most subjects to give positive or neutral evaluations: that education and intelligence had no bearing on forms and features in the signing; or that the subjects were hesitant to reveal their bias against the signers due to the visibility of the signers' identity.

STUDY COMPONENT 4: DESCRIPTION OF SIGNING

The fourth part of the study was a qualitative study of the discussion of comments derived from the interviews with a group of sixteen subjects with diverse background. The comments were organized on each linguistic level from phonological (specific) to discourse (general) and comments that were para-linguistic or non-linguistic were grouped as 'other.' Also, the comments were grouped as 'positive' or 'negative' based on the manner of how the subjects described the forms and features and the adjectives they used in their descriptions.

For ASL, most comments on almost all linguistic levels were positive. There were a few comments about atypical forms or features the subjects described as "errors" (e.g., lack of facial expression, idiosyncratic facial expression, and word choice) or as English (e.g., initialized handshapes, English phrases, and amount of words). Even though ASL was viewed positively, there were a few comments about ASL as not having word order. As for para- and non-linguistic features listed as 'other,' there were some positive comments about clarity of signing, identity (i.e. Deaf identity), composure, personality, and signing style, but there were some negative comments on some of the same features in addition to a few others, for example, "low intelligence," and "grassroots" identity (as to mean working class or vocational trained group).

For 'Mixed,' there were both positive and negative comments on almost linguistic levels. The positive comments were on forms and features that were typical of or standard in ASL and the negative comments were on forms and features that were English-based or were viewed as errors (e.g., "sloppy handshape," "choppy signing," "unusual combination of words," "weak classifiers"). Even with the negativity about English-based forms and features, there were few comments about it having good English order. As for other features that were para- or non-linguistic, the signers were described positively as confident, comfortable, clear, skillful, or negatively as being hearing, unclear, uncomfortable, and possessing sub-standard ASL skills.

For Signed English, most comments were negative on all linguistic levels but there were some positive comments. The positive comments were based on forms and features that were typical of or standard in ASL and the negative comments were about English-based forms and features, errors, and reduced presence of necessary ASL forms and features in signing. As for para- and non-linguistic features, the comments were mostly negative. While there were a few positive comments about the clarity of signing in the English-influenced style preferred by a few subjects, the signers perceived to be using Signed English were viewed to be unclear, unconfident, late-deafened, or affected by a medical condition such as Usher's syndrome.

Following the qualitative analysis of the subjects' description of the linguistic forms and features, a linguistic analysis of ASL-dominant and English-dominant signing was done to uncover the actual linguistic forms and features in term of initialized signs, nonmanual signals, use of classifiers, indicating and locative verbs, and word order. The ASL-dominant signing as shown through the video of Signers 1, 2, and 3 was found to have no initialized signs, a significant amount of nonmanual signals, a productive use of classifiers and dynamic verbs (indicating and locative) in relation to the signing space, and the ASL word order. The findings supported the majority of subjects who perceived the signing of Signers 1, 2, and 3 as ASL. However, a small number of subjects felt that the signing was mixed because they were not satisfied with the use of classifiers and nonmanual signals. The English-dominant signing as shown through the video of Signers 6, 7, and 8 was found to have initialized signs, a reduced amount of nonmanual signals, a lack of classifiers, fewer instances of indicating and locative verbs and the dominant English word order with the function words. A minority of the subjects perceived the signing as Signed English, but a majority of the subjects perceived it as 'Mixed.' Fewer subjects perceived it as ASL. A possible reason for the English-dominant signing to be viewed as 'Mixed' was that it was not strictly English due to the presence of ASL-related nonmanual signals and indicating and locative verbs.

IMPLICATIONS

Each component of the study focused on a particular aspect of the perceptions of and attitudes toward the signing types and had the results that guided the interpretation of the results of the other studies. The components of the studies have produced important implications about the signing perceptions and attitudes toward signing variation.

The first component revealed that most subjects were aware of the standard or typical ASL forms and features as evidenced by the high frequency of ASL responses for 'Strong ASL' and 'Mostly ASL' (which were on the higher end of the signing spectrum). This showed that the subjects had been affected by the process of standardization of ASL in different ways, for example, consistent exposure to the practice of ASL in particular places (i.e., deaf schools, deaf clubs, ASL campus programs), ASL in media (DVDs and internet videos), and contact with ASL teachers with a prescriptive approach to the use of ASL. The subjects were also aware of English-based forms and features based on their low frequency of ASL responses (or inversely, a high frequency of Not ASL responses) for 'Non-ASL' (which was on the lower end of the signing spectrum). As for 'Mixed,' there were approximately equal proportions of ASL and Not ASL responses due to the mixture of ASL and English-based forms and features. The number of responses reflected the nature of the signing types. With 'Strong ASL' and 'Mostly ASL,' the relative frequencies of ASL responses were significantly different for these signing types. This might suggest that there was a systematic difference between them in terms of structure or the usage of particular forms that differed 'Mostly ASL' from 'Strong ASL'; in addition, there was a systematic difference between 'Mostly ASL' and 'Mixed' based on the results. The implication was that there was something systematic about 'Mostly ASL' that distinguished it from 'Strong ASL' and 'Mixed.'

With the subjects as a whole, the signing types were significantly different from each other based on the results but with the social groups, the relative frequencies of ASL responses were not the same for each signing type, even 'Strong ASL' for which all social groups except for Older Black Nonnative had relatively highest proportions of ASL responses. This suggests that the social groups had different standards of ASL that played a role in their perceptions of signing types.

Even with the different standards of ASL, the social groups' relative proportions of ASL responses were the highest for 'Strong ASL.' The implication was that 'Strong ASL' was close to being a typical example of standard ASL. The operative word in the previous statement was "close" because there were a few Not ASL responses for some videos of 'Strong ASL' and they might be made for a reason. It was possible that the choice of Not ASL response was accidental, meaning that a subject meant to select ASL when he or she pressed a button for Not ASL. But it was also possible that the subject meant to say that it was not ASL as to mean "contact signing," "Signed English," or even "error" depending on what forms or features that caught his or her eyes. This presented a reason for doing the fourth part of the study with the investigation of the signers' description of the signing forms and features.

In the fourth component, the description of forms and features of ASL signing type seemed to fit with the standard forms and features of ASL on all linguistic levels, with the avoidance of initialized handshapes, proper use of space, appropriate use of classifiers and facial expressions, typical or vernacular ASL signs, and appropriate discourse markers and signals. A few negative comments were on forms or features that were described as "English" (such as initialized handshapes, English phrases, and amount of words) or "error" (such as odd use of word or classifier, idiosyncratic facial expression, lacking facial expression). With 'Mixed' and Signed English signing types, there were more negative comments about the signing forms and features that were described as "English" or "error." English-based forms and features (that is, initialized handshapes, word order, English mouthing, invented English signs) were noticeable to the subjects and they were rightly judged as "English" but the forms and features that were described as "errors" required a further consideration. Many things could be considered "errors" by the subjects: English-based forms and features, improper phonological parts, less facial expressions, excessive facial expressions, idiosyncratic facial expression, stylistic variation, size and use of signing space, number of pauses, and et cetera. This was beyond the categorization of the signing types. It was another aspect that influenced the subjects' perceptions of the signing types: the correctness of signing forms and features. Some subjects might use it as a guide in determining the signing types while other subjects would treat it as a separate issue. So the implication was that the aspect of correctness of signing overlaid the aspect of the categorization of signing types.

Correctness is one of several aspects studied in language attitude research. This was not directly addressed in the third component of the study with the social and language evaluations of the signing types, but the high favorability of ASL signing type could mean that ASL was a correct signing type with the appropriate ASL forms and features as described in the fourth part of the study and 'Mixed' and Signed English signing types contained a considerable number of errors. A language or dialect that is considered as 'correct' tends to be highly favored on social traits (e.g., leadership, education, attractiveness, and confidence) and the high favorability of ASL in the third part has provided enough support for that. The implication was that there was an ASL ideological standard in the American Deaf community for the signers to consciously or unconsciously observe. However, there were a few subjects (mostly older ones) who commented that ASL did not have word order or that it was "broken English" so they might be more loyal to English than to ASL. Unlike some older subjects, the younger subjects had more opportunities to learn the linguistic nature of ASL and to be inspired by the cultural pride of ASL so that counted as one of the influences on their perceptions of and their attitudes toward ASL. The differences in the signing perceptions and the attitudes with regards to correctness reflected the special position of ASL as being the standard language with prestige in the American Deaf community while at the same time being a stigmatized language in the mainstream America.

Another implication of the study was that there was an association between social identities and signing forms and features. In the fourth component, there were comments about deaf signers who signed ASL were "Deaf" and deaf signers who signed 'Mixed' or Signed English were described as "a mixture of Deaf and hearing" or "hearing." The stereotypical connections between Deaf or hearing identities and signing types were supported by the results in Part 3 with the evaluation scales on Deaf and hearing identities. This should not come as a surprise to anyone who is involved with the American Deaf community and "Deaf" and "hearing" have particular meanings in the community (i.e., "Deaf" is someone who is a skillful ASL signer with the relevant cultural traits and "hearing" is someone who is not as skillful and has less cultural traits). Nonetheless, this is important to consider because there are a number of identities that are relevant in the Deaf community, e.g. hard-of-hearing, late-deafened, mainstream student, cochlear implant users, hearing children of deaf adults (CODA), and hearing siblings of deaf people. These identities are different from the stereotypical "Deaf" and "hearing" identities and the signing may have particular or stereotypical characteristics that reflect the respective identities. Also, a social identity potentially affects the perception of someone's signing as discussed in the second component of the study so any relevant identity in the American Deaf community could have an effect on the perception of signing.

FUTURE DIRECTIONS

One issue that needs to be explored is the relevancy of social identities in the American Deaf community in the studies of social information effect on the perception of signing. The stereotypical identities, Deaf and hearing, have a noticeable effect on a perception of signing, but there is a social diversity in the American Deaf community and social identities may have powerful or negligible effects on the perception of signing, for example, mainstream, grassroots, business professional, academician, ASL teacher, and so on. Even race and ethnicity can have an effect on the perception, for example,

African-American, Hispanic, and Asian. The racial and ethnic groups have different social practices from the mainstream American Deaf community and that can make their signing quantitatively and qualitatively different. As an example, a study on African-American ASL signing, hereby-called Black ASL, has covered different linguistic aspects that make this ASL variant quantitatively and qualitatively different from mainstream ASL based on the social practices and socio-historical foundation of African-American community (McCaskill, et al., 2011). One aspect is a lexical or phrasal borrowing from AAE, (e.g. "dang," "I feel you," "I know that's right," and "girl, please"). In the view of mainstream American Deaf community, these expressions may be English, but in Black ASL, the expressions are acceptable in Black ASL.

Another issue to consider is that there is more than one ASL standard for the American Deaf community. Going back to the previous example of Black ASL, the users of Black ASL may possess a different standard of ASL from the standard upheld by the mainstream American Deaf community based on the social practices. There is regional variation in ASL and that implies there are different regional standards of ASL. Gallaudet and RIT, both with the large populations of deaf and hard-of-hearing students, may have different standards as well, in terms of politics and activism in the standardization of ASL. ASL proficiency interviews are based on a standard of ASL but that brings the question of which ASL standard it refers to and whether social identities or practices play a role in the assessment of deaf, hard-of-hearing, and hearing signers. This is a fascinating albeit complicated issue that warrants further exploration.

At this point in time, ASL has gained a greater acceptance as a language and it is on the way to a complete standardization with the exponential growth of ASL courses, the productive publication of ASL teaching materials and dictionaries, the number of professional and academic organizations on teaching, education, and linguistics of ASL, and the recognition of ASL proficiency evaluations. The findings from the first component of the study show that all subjects were able to detect the linguistic features and forms that are typical of ASL for with the 'Strong ASL' signing, but with the 'Non-ASL' signing, some social groups of subjects perceived the signing as the mixture of ASL and English whereas the other social groups perceived the signing as strong on the English side. The latter social groups (most of them were young or native signers) could be more affected the standardization of ASL based on the extent of their involvement with the American Deaf community, the ASL instruction and use in school, their use of ASL materials and books, their exposure to media in ASL, and their involvement in professional and academic organizations related to ASL. With the standardization of ASL, the latter social groups' discrimination of the ASL and English-based linguistic forms and features was more fine-tuned.

REFERENCES

Bonvillian, J.D. (1999). Sign language development. *The Development of Language.* M. Barrett (ed.) UK: Psychology Press, Taylor & Francis Group.

Eckert, P. (1997). Age as a sociolinguistic variable. *The Handbook of Sociolinguistics.* F. Coulmas (ed.), 151–167. Oxford: Blackwell Publishers.

Emmorey, K. (2002). *Language, Cognition, and the Brain: Insights from Sign Language Research.* Mahwah, NJ: Lawrence Erlbaum Associates, Publishers.

Evans, B.E. (2002). Attitudes of Montreal students towards varieties of French. *Handbook of Perceptual Dialectology, Volume 2.* D. Long (ed), 71–93. Philadelphia, PA: John Benjamins Publishing Company.

Garrett, P. (2010). *Attitudes to Language.* Cambridge: Cambridge University Press.

Hill, J. (2012). *Language Attitudes in the American Deaf Community.* Washington, DC: Gallaudet University Press.

Lambert, W.E., R.C. Hodgson, R.C. Gardner, and S. Fillenbaum. (1960). Evaluation reactions to spoken languages. *Journal of Abnormal and Social Psychology,* 60(1), 44–51.

Lambert, W.E., H. Giles, and O. Picard. (1975). Language attitudes in a French-American community. *International Journal of the Sociology of Language,* 4, 127–152.

Lucas, C. and C. Valli. 1992. Language Contact in the American Deaf Community. San Diego: Academic Press.

Lucas, C., Bayley R., and Valli, C. (2001). *Sociolinguistic Variation in American Sign Language.* Washington, D.C.: Gallaudet University Press.

McCaskill, C, C. Lucas, Bayley, R. and Hill, J. (2011). *The Hidden Treasure of Black ASL: Its History and Structure.* Washington, DC: Gallaudet University Press.

Milroy, J. (2001). Language ideologies and the consequences of standardization. *Journal of Sociolinguistics,* 5(4), 530–555.

Niedzielski, N. (1999). The effect of social information on the perception of sociolinguistic variables. *Journal of Language and Social Psychology,* 18, 62–85.

Padden, C. and Humphries, T. (2005). *Inside Deaf Culture.* Cambridge, Massachusetts: Harvard University Press.

Petitto, L. (2000). The acquisition of natural signed languages: lessons in the nature of human language and its biological foundations. In *Language Acquisition by Eye.* C. Chamberlain, J.P. Morford, and R.I. Mayberry (eds.), 41–50. Mahwah, NJ: Lawrence Erlbaum Associates, Publishers.

Rosen, R. (2010). American Sign Language curricula: a review. *Sign Language Studies,* 10(3), 348-381.

Wood, S. (2010). Acquisition of topicalization in very late learners of Libras. *Deaf Around the World: The Impact of Language.* G. Mathur and D.J. Napoli (eds), 164–183. Oxford: Oxford University Press.

Asian and Hispanic Adult Immigrants' Language Learning Experience: Exploration of ASL in the United States

LEWIS LUMMER. ED.D. AND CYNTHIA PLUE, ED.D.

THIS ARTICLE EXAMINES THE COMPARISON OF TWO RESEARCH STUDIES of Asian and Hispanic Deaf adult immigrant language-learning processes previously documented, identified, and referenced with research findings (Plue, 1997; Plue, 1999; Lummer, 1999, 2011). The researchers explored how learning American Sign Language (ASL) enabled the assimilation of first-generation Deaf adult immigrants into American Deaf culture. These studies of Deaf immigrants from various countries illuminates a unique group of multicultural language learners in the United States (Plue, 2002, 2003).

Seeing these adults acquire ASL during their early entrance into the country was of singular interest to the researchers; these groups quickly learned ASL and their lives appeared to improve and rapidly change around their thriving language development skills. Because their language development skills also doubled as early life experiences here in the United States, these case studies of Hispanic and Asian Deaf immigrants formed the sociolinguistic foundation of the study by introducing and describing the languages and the cultures of Asian and Hispanic Deaf immigrant adults.

When coming to the United States, Deaf immigrant adults constitute a population of unique multilingual and multicultural language learners (Plue, 1997, 1999; 2002, 2003; Lummer, 1999, 2002, 2010). Many have been exposed to two or more languages: 1) the spoken target language of their home country, 2) the native sign language of their home country (e.g., LSM [Mexican Sign Language] or ZGS [Chinese Sign Language]), and 3) ASL in the United States. Similarly, they will have been exposed to two or more cultures: 1) the culture of their home country, 2) the Deaf culture of their home country, 3) the regional culture and language of their home country, 4) the American culture of their new country, and 5) the American Deaf culture of their new country (Lummer, 1999, 2002).

Most Deaf adults struggle with acquiring spoken or written English, an auditory-based language. Yet, ASL, the visually-based language of the American Deaf community, is relatively easy for them to pick up and learn to communicate (Padden & Humphries, 2005). How did these Asian and Hispanic Deaf immigrants do it?

We explored and compared the language histories of a sample of Deaf immigrant adults from our earlier research projects to formulate and build a knowledgebase of how new languages and cultures are learned; we learned that Deaf adult immigrants chiefly acquire ASL by interacting with their peers in cultural learning experiences. This research also shed light on how these interactions may have built on and interacted with prior knowledge and language bases. It also gave us the opportunity to recognize, compare, and document Deaf immigrant demographic data to teach learners to become literate users of all of their languages while living in the United States.

We specifically looked for demographic data associated with immigrant home culture, educational background, first language acquisition ability, and their signed and written language usage. Hispanic Deaf adult immigrant participants identified home as Cuba, Ecuador, El Salvador, Guatemala, Honduras, Mexico, and Panama; Asian Deaf adults identified their home countries as Korea, India, China, Malaysia, Indonesia, and Japan. Some participants self identified multinationally: 'partially Chinese,' 'Spanish,' 'Southeast Asian,' and 'Asian American.'

DEAF IMMIGRANTS' EDUCATIONAL BACKGROUND

Participants also identified various types of academic experience: no formal schooling, homeschooled, or private schooling, either in informal or formal school settings; the highest attained education of the Hispanic Deaf immigrant group was a single bachelor degree. Asian Deaf immigrants came from residential, day school, mainstreamed with support services, and reverse mainstreamed without support services educational backgrounds. The Asian Deaf immigrants in our study obtained two associates, six bachelors, and four masters degrees.

COMPARISONS: PARTICIPANTS' SIGNED LANGUAGE USAGE

The Hispanic Deaf adult immigrants acquired their respective signed languages in their home country before arriving in the United States, and reported usage of Cuban (LSC), Ecuadorian (LSE), El Salvadoran (LESA), Guatemalan (LSG), Honduran (LESHO), Mayan (LMM), Mexican (LSM), Panamanian (LSP), Peruvian (LSP), and Spanish (LSE) Sign Languages. Additionally, Hispanic Deaf adult immigrants had acquired Spanish, Portuguese, and French.

Similarly, the group of Asian Deaf adult immigrants also acquired their signed languages in their home country, reporting usage of British (BSL), Chinese (ZGS; 中国手语), Japanese (JSL; 日本手話), and Filipino (FSL) Sign Languages. One participant acquired both Malay (BIM) and Dutch (NGT) Sign Language; another respondent acquired Japanese and Hawaiian (HSL) Sign Language. These Asian Deaf adult immigrants had already learned Dutch, Chinese, and Spanish.

COMPARISONS: PARTICIPANTS' WRITTEN LANGUAGE USAGE

We noted that Hispanic Deaf participants began acquiring ASL skills between twenty and twenty-eight years old and written English skills between twenty-two and thirty-one years old. At that time of the study, their linguistic skills were comprised chiefly of Spanish, English, Portuguese, and French.

Responses from Deaf Asians demonstrated first language acquisition primarlity in written/signed Dutch, written/signed Malay, ASL, written Chinese, and written/spoken English. Four people acquired ASL between ages of nine and fifteen years; one person learned Signed Exact English at nine years and later learned ASL at fifteen; another learned Pidgin Signed English and later learned ASL at college; and six more people learned ASL at college.

Eight respondents learned written English between age four and ten; three people learned English between sixteen and twenty-one years old. Six respondents did not know any sign language of their home country upon arrival in the United States. At that time of the study, it reported that these individuals listed their language abilities as written Dutch, written English, and ASL; written Chinese and English; ASL and English; and ASL, British Sign Language, written Spanish, and written English.

Acculturation for these two groups of language learners occurred at Deaf clubs, Deaf organizations, academic and social settings, and in Deaf communities. Because of these language learning opportunities, Deaf Hispanics became literate primarily by participating and interacting with others at Deaf clubs, Deaf organizations, and Deaf churches in their home country.

They also learned language while utilizing home signs or contact sign language with Deaf spouses, partners, and friends. Additionally, several immigrants served as language mentors and role models to newcomers, allowing them to secure jobs to earn a decent living.

Deaf Asians indicated that they learned roles of parents, siblings, and leaders by acquiring "receptive/listening" skills, being motivated by encouragement, patience, maintaining an optimistic "can do!" attitude, and demonstrating faithful beliefs through determination and discipline. They also reported they enjoyed reading books and materials and interacting with other Asian Deaf role models. They enjoy being competitive, achieving academic and career goals, and finding a supportive system. They reported that the influence of local, state, regional, national, international, collegiate, and professional Deaf community organizations is highly beneficial. Peers in religious, socio-cultural, educational, and employment settings were also motivational factors; pursuing and obtaining United States citizenship to gain better educational and employment opportunities also incited Deaf Asian immigrants.

Understanding this diversity influences a reframing away from a monocultural lens on Deaf educational practices into a more realistic and modern view of multicultural Deaf education in meeting the needs of diverse, ethnisocial student populations.

Innovative and incidental ASL learning opportunities at Deaf clubs, churches, and social service organizations can lead to redefined strategies of rethinking, reframing, and revamping the cultural lens of Deaf educational practices. Additionally, identifying creative teaching practices learned from Deaf immigrant language ideologies can transform language training programs for ASL and Deaf educators and ASL mentors and trainers as they work with this community of language learners.

Many Deaf community members work in high-demand service professions — healthcare, legal interpreting, social work, and education — that directly serve Deaf immigrant populations. Expanding bilingual language learning programs for these providers can benefit both communities in promoting better quality of life, spiritual health and wellness, and maximizing social, economic, and emotional support to bring parity with hearing peers.

Given the known higher statistics of immigrant populations in larger cities, there is a critical need to promote multicultural and multilingual awareness in larger urban ASL immigrant communities like San Francisco, Los Angeles, Chicago, Houston, Miami, Honolulu, and New York City. The essential needs of language learning communities include peer education, language tutoring, language modeling techniques and methodologies, and sign language assessments. Increased traning in sight translation, interpreting, and mentoring is also an essential part of these community's language needs to make it more visually accessible to both worlds.

RECOMMENDATIONS

Asian and Hispanic Deaf immigrants have various but greater societal support needs, such interpreting, legal, and educational services. Another observation is that there may be an important role for increased advocacy and language support services in these aspects. Strong advocacy may be important to create a positive Deaf culture-friendly society, especially since often Deaf people cannot speak effectively for themselves in the dominant hearing world.

ASL learners feel that they benefit significantly more by interacting with others in cultural, linguistic, and literacy settings where they utilize ASL in order to become literate users of both (or more) languages. This enables immigrant learners to enhance their sociolinguistic abilities and cultivate a better quality of life, a desire to seek better educational and employment opportunities, and enhance language learning experiences in the United States.

Community engagement could be facilitated by creating a welcoming environment, developing reciprocal relationships, and supporting the use of both the home language and ASL in the student's various educational settings. When learners and educators offer a variety of sociolinguistic community engagement opportunities that honor Asian and Hispanic Deaf adult immigrant languages, cultures, norms, and values, immigrant ASL learners and their families can become engaged in ways that feel comfortable, respectful, and meaningful at all levels.

With desired language development as a factor of migration away their home countries' and arrival in the United States as a way to assess their language knowledge and skills, this critical language framework elaborates the continued efforts of their developing reciprocal relationships between language users and language learners to a success in its realms of the sociolinguistic and academic tasks.

In sum, this in-depth discussion led to the foundation of an evolving ASL learning framework aimed at incorporating their language insights with a sociocultural approach to language teaching and learning. The focus of this work has been detailed with descriptive aspects of language learning and sense-making, a process of language development required for learners to engage in language use in community and academic contexts. As multilingual and multicultural learners and teachers are at the center of this endeavor, this demonstrates a critical need to modernize American Deaf education and/or Deaf Studies to enrich and promote sociocultural and sociolinguistic awareness in serving this growing population's needs to their continued language learning discovery path.

REFERENCES

Lummer, L. (1999). Teachers' perceptions of the academic and language needs of deaf immigrant students: An exploratory survey. Unpublished master's thesis, Lamar University, Beaumont, TX.

Lummer, L. (2002, July). Life stories of deaf immigrants living in the United States. Paper presented at the Deaf Way II Conference, Washington, D.C.

Lummer, L. (2010). Contextual issues of deaf Hispanic immigrant adults learning American Sign Language as a new Language, unpublished doctoral dissertation. DeKalb, IL: Northern Illinois University.

Padden, C. & Humphries, T. (2005). *Inside deaf culture*. Cambridge, MA: Harvard University Press.

Plue, C. (1998). An ethnographic study of deaf Filipinos in Los Angeles: Language, culture, identity, and value. In C. Carroll (Ed.), *Deaf Studies V: Toward 2000 Unity Diversity* (pp. 141-156). Washington, DC: Gallaudet University, College of Continuing Education.

Plue, C. (1999). A descriptive study of deaf Asian students at the California and Hawaii schools for the deaf. Unpublished doctoral dissertation. Beaumont, TX: Lamar University.

Plue, C. (2002). Asian Perspectives on Deaf Education. Paper presented at the Deaf Way II Conference, Washington, D.C.

Plue, C. J. (2003). Multicultural Profiles in the Deaf Community. *Multicultural Review*, 12, 3. Asian Perspectives on Deaf Education. Paper presented at the Deaf Way II Conference, Washington, D.C.

Mainstreaming Revisited: Is It Working? Has It Ever Worked?

J. FREEMAN KING, ED.D.

THE READER WILL IMMEDIATELY NOTICE THAT THE REFERENCES USED in this article date back to 1988 and 1989. The reason for this is that the initial red lights raised regarding mainstreaming the deaf child are the red lights still prevalent today. The tragic result is that more than two generations of deaf children have been lost to mainstreaming due to the misinterpretation of "appropriate" and "least restrictive environment" as expressed in the Individuals with Disabilities Education Act (IDEA).

Since the mid-1970s, American education for the child who is deaf has stood at a quagmire in the crossroads regarding what is appropriate and most restrictive. Resultantly, what has transpired, and continues to transpire, has left many deaf children emotionally, socially, linguistically, and educationally impoverished.

The basic tenets of the Individuals with Disabilities Education Act (IDEA) are that the child who has a disability will be educated in the most appropriate and least restrictive environment, and that this environment will lead to socialization of the child with his/her non-disabled peers. Two issues are immediately raised: Should the deaf child be categorized as disabled; and, for the child who is deaf, can socialization ever occur without deep and meaningful communication with peers and teachers?

Has not history taught us that African-American, Hispanic, Oriental, and Deaf children do, in fact, grow up to be African-American, Hispanic, Oriental, and Deaf adults who have and continue to find their niche in American society, often not because of their education, but in spite of it? Has not history taught us that given a truly appropriate education and equal opportunities that children of various cultural heritages can and do find their places as valued, contributing members of American culture? Has not history taught us that continuing to make the same educational-placement mistakes (even though the names of the mistakes have been updated to fit the current socio-political jargon) makes absolutely no sense?

The Least Restrictive Environment clause of IDEA is a controversial, but much promoted component of IDEA, and it should be understood that the primary concern with this aspect of the law is its inappropriate interpretation and application, as applied to the deaf child, not its basic philosophical premise. The law states that the least restrictive environment should be most like a "normal" environment that promotes and enhances socialization skills. However, the misinterpretation of the law, as it applies to the child who is deaf, has placed and continues to place the appropriate and successful education of the deaf child in jeopardy. It is apparent that without communication of a deep and meaningful nature among peers, teachers, and the deaf student, it is impossible for socialization to occur, thus resulting, in fact, in providing the most restrictive environment!

This misinterpretation of "least restrictive" has created a situation in which many deaf children have been, and continue to be, placed in inappropriate mainstream programs within the public schools. Often, these placements have been accomplished disregarding or misunderstanding the child's linguistic preferences, language development needs, identity, and socio-cultural needs. The placement decision of mainstreaming is often made by administrators, special education specialists, audiologists, and speech-language pathologists who do not understand the predisposition of the deaf child to acquire a natural, visual language (even though the deaf child is primarily a visual learner, with or without advanced technological enhancements). Often, the placement team also makes the erroneous assumption that having an interpreter provides for equal language access and remediates the social and emotional needs of the child.

The decision to place the deaf child in the mainstream with an interpreter is often based on the fallacious premise that the interpreter will be the equalizer of communication among the deaf child, their teacher, and their hearing peers. This is not necessarily the case, in that many interpreters are not certified or qualified, and do not possess the skills to truly equalize communication in the classroom environment. It is equally appalling to note that many of the public school districts in the United States that offer educational services for deaf children have historically had and continue to have only one or two deaf students in the entire program. Certainly, the emotional, social, language access, and educational consequences that impact the deaf child as a result of such programs are frightening.

It is evident that most deaf children who are placed in mainstream programs are being educated near hearing children, rather than with them. In these programs, the deaf child is given the worst of both worlds. They are given a limited, partially accessible language, a limited social environment, and resultantly, a limited education. Accepting the premise that many mainstream programs for deaf children are inappropriate, ineffective, and most restrictive, how might these programs be structured so as to be appropriate, effective, and least restrictive? The following suggestions are offered for consideration by the local school district, special education administrators and teachers, audiologists, and speech-language pathologists:

1. The program should include a critical mass of deaf children (at least five per class) in order to provide for socialization, identity development, and language growth and enhancement;
2. Homogeneous grouping possibilities should exist that will facilitate grouping by age, IQ, and linguistic competence;
3. Only teachers who are qualified/certified and have a respect for and understanding of Deaf culture should have deaf students in their classes;
4. Only teachers who can communicate directly and appropriately with deaf students should be utilized in classes with deaf children;
5. Deaf adult role models should be present on a regular basis in the educational process, either as administrators, teachers, or aides;
6. Curriculum that includes Deaf history and Deaf culture should be available in classrooms that have deaf children;
7. Only intelligence, achievement, and other placement tests that have been normed on a deaf population and administered by personnel who can communicate fluently with the deaf child should be used;
8. Interpreters involved in the program should be highly certified and knowledgeable concerning the Deaf culture;
9. The hearing administrators, teachers, and students in the school should be offered continuing opportunities to learn and use American Sign Language.

The most important suggestion that might be entertained by the local school district that attempts to offer an appropriate educational program for deaf children is that the program offer a quality education that will truly prepare the student to compete as an equal in the hearing world. This does not mean or suggest that the adequacy and success of deaf children be measured by how closely they resemble their hearing peers, but that they are educated to become successful Deaf human beings, not imitations of hearing people. The education received should enable them to believe that their deafness is not a pathological condition fostering the attitude of incompleteness. Rather in a quality educational program, the student most respected by his/her teachers and peers should not be the one who is most like the hearing, but the one who is well-educated, successful, and Deaf.

REFERENCES

Commission on Education of the Deaf (1988, February). *Toward Equality: Education of the Deaf,* Washington, DC; U.S. Government Printing Office.

Johnson, R., Liddell, S., & Erting, C. (1989, January). *Unlocking the Curriculum: Principles for Achieving Access in Deaf Education,* Gallaudet Research Institute Working Paper, 89–3, Washington, DC; Gallaudet University.

King, J.F. (1996). *Does Repeating the Mistakes of the Past Protect the Innocent? A Deaf American Monograph,* 61–64, Silver Spring, Maryland; National Association of the Deaf.

King, J.F. (1990). Inappropriate and Most Restrictive: The Dilemma of the Deaf Student in American Education. *Tejas,* 16(1).

Thomas, R. (1989, June). Taking Back Our Rights, a paper presented at the American Society for Deaf Children Annual Conference; Faribault, Minnesota.

Siegel, L. (1989). Educational Isolation of Deaf Children, Newsletter of the Independently Merging Parent Associations of California Together for the Hearing Impaired (IMPACT-HI), 1st Quarter.

Contested Representation: PepsiCo Advertising and the Deaf Community

REBECCA FURLAND

"We would also like to remind you that with the amount of money Pepsi will spend on just one 60-second spot to air during the Super Bowl, you could help an untold number of families obtain hearing aids and other professional services that are costly and in many cases not covered by medical insurance. We would be very willing to work with Pepsi to develop some creative ideas to promote other facets of the deaf community and to highlight positive role models who have met the challenges of this condition and thrived using spoken language." — The Alexander Graham Bell Association for the Deaf and Hard of Hearing (Graham & Youdelman, 2008)

"The NAD applauds PepsiCo for its strong commitment to diversity and creation of this exciting ad in ASL with its employees. This ground-breaking ad will heighten cultural awareness by millions of viewers during Super Bowl Sunday." — The National Association of the Deaf (PR Newswire, 2008)

IN JANUARY OF 2008, EVEN BEFORE IT WOULD APPEAR IN MILLIONS OF homes across America, the hype of the upcoming Super Bowl was widespread (Steinberg, 2011). For members of the deaf community, there was to be one ad that would generate attention, divide members of the viewing public, and serve as catalyst for a fuller analysis of the representation of deaf people in the media. Prior to the airing, news of the commercial, which would showcase deaf actors and play on a story unique to Deaf cultural humor, spread through favorable periodical coverage, such as, "On Sunday, February 3, television viewers will be checking their volume controls when PepsiCo airs a 60-second commercial filmed in American Sign Language" (*Entertainment Newsweekly*, 2008) and "PepsiCo is hoping to make some noise with a Super Bowl ad featuring 60 seconds of silence" (Robinson-Jacobs, 2008) The full significance of PepsiCo's "Bob's House" advertisement was more than just the unique audio feature however. As it garnered attention, the ad revealed polarizing attitudes toward language use and the significance behind representations of deaf people in the media.

The American deaf community is a very diverse group, spanning every ethnicity and culture. "Deafness is democratic in its occurrence. Membership, or 'citizenship' cuts across all boundaries of class, gender, or race" (Wrigley, 1997). Being deaf is a characteristic that brings people together, forms bonds and fosters relationships among the most diverse groups of people.

Furthermore, this membership is not limited to individuals with a 'deaf' auditory status, but rather it encompasses a large group of individuals with varied auditory levels (Woodward & Markowitcz, 1982). While many deaf individuals are bilingual, some prefer the visual kinetic language, ASL, and others the auditory language, English. These language choices are strongly influenced, if not decided for the deaf individual, by his or her parents at an early age. These opposing language and cultural identifications create divides within the deaf community that have been examined in the fields of deaf education, deaf cultural studies, and, as you will see in this paper, in the subject of media representation (cf., Siegel, 2008; Reagan, 2010; Woodward, 1982; Padden & Humphries, 1990). To address this divide within the deaf community, James Woodward (1972) proposed the term Deaf, with a capital 'D,' to be used to indicate an individual who uses ASL as his/her main communication method, is active in the Deaf community, and identifies with Deaf individuals.

Use of the term 'Deaf' differentiates participatory members of the Deaf community from those who are 'deaf' (audiologically deaf) but do not use ASL or associate with Deaf people. This framework will be utilized throughout this paper as it examines representation of Deaf people in mainstream media, views the varied reactions to it from the deaf community (as well as the hearing community), and highlights the importance of positive media representations.

Any discussion of the controversy surrounding "Bob's House" must first begin with the advertisement itself. Commercials, particularly those created to air during the Super Bowl, are generally constructed to do two things: draw attention and elicit feelings of goodwill or a desire to purchase in their viewership. The PepsiCo advertisement was able to do both, and do them well. "Bob's House" was created by one of PepsiCo's employee resource groups, EnAble, that is dedicated to "mak[ing] PepsiCo the employer of choice, partner of choice and brand of choice for people with different abilities" (PepsiCo, 1997). The EnAble network is, in itself, an advertising strategy, attracting viewers of different abilities, but this specific ad is further differentiated from others by its audio track. As noted by the newspaper articles above, "Bob's House" achieves an edge over the competition through the elimination of voice, music, or audio of any kind.

The construction of advertising images is fairly straightforward, for Super Bowl fare. In the silent ad, two middle-aged well-dressed Caucasian Deaf men are driving a shiny yet heavy-duty truck down a street in a residential neighborhood. As they glide past well-manicured lawns, they turn to each other and, using American Sign Language, argue as to the address of "Bob's House." Quickly, after a brief exchange of "I thought, *you* knew"s, it becomes clear that neither can remember the address. The implication here is that the two men are traveling to the house to watch a football game and do not want to waste time driving around aimlessly.

To solve this problem, the driver places the palm of his hand firmly on the horn as they slowly roll down the street. The darkened homes suddenly light up and front doors swing open as hearing households quizzically seek the source of the (seemingly) obnoxious truck horn. Suddenly, the screen fills with the image of a darkened house-front, the only one on the block. The Deaf men knowingly smile as they pull into the driveway of "Bob's House," and our suspicions are further confirmed when the doorbell is pressed and the flashing lights of the notification systems are visible within. Finally, the door opens and the elusive Bob appears with his wife to welcome the men inside, signing "sorry" to the neighbors who now understand the reason for the late-night disruption.

Figure 1: Still image from PepsiCo's "Bob's House" commercial (Super Bowl XLII, 2008).

Though not particularly offensive in form or function, the mere sixty seconds described above managed to elicit an enormous response. Approximately 97.5 million viewers watched the ad during its one and only airing on prime-time national television (Steinberg, 2008; Furland, 2011). At face value, the content of the commercial, while ripe for analysis later in this paper, is relatively straightforward. However, from beginning to end, the production and promotion of this ad were far from typical. In an effort to examine this further, interviews were conducted with PepsiCo employees providing an abundance of information about the production process and company intentions behind the commercial (Furland, 2011).

Clay Broussard, Director for PepsiCo's Customer Supply-Chain, and Andrea Foote, Director for Communications for PepsiCo Beverages America consented to an interview to discuss the "Bob's House" ad. Each of these individuals provides an important and unique perspective with regard to the ad. Broussard developed the idea and fought for its production, a process that involved filming and producing two separate full-length "Bob's House" ads. He even appeared as an actor in the final network advertisement. In her role as Director for Communications, Foote, received and monitored the public's reaction to the advertisement. Their insights with regard to this analysis are invaluable.

To begin, Broussard detailed his involvement as the originator of the idea. This advertisement differed from PepsiCo's usual output because it was generated from within the company. Broussard, an auditorally hearing man, learned ASL and was exposed to Deaf culture by a Deaf religious group. It was as a result of his involvement with the Deaf community that he developed the original idea for the commercial. EnAble helped to develop the concept. The advertisement's target audience was always the general population; however, the inclusion of sign language was also meant to attract the Deaf community and consumers with different abilities, thus reinforcing EnAble's vision (PepsiCo, 2007). Furthermore, because the genesis of the idea came from within the company, but outside the marketing department, a demo version of the advertisement was created with the employees as actors to help gain support for the final production. Broussard explained, "Once we got it to a point where it could be understood, there was an embracing of this [from] top to bottom in the organization" (Furland, 2011).

Leading up to the creation of a demo, his idea was worked into a script, which was then shared with Deaf colleagues and friends. After their feedback was synthesized and armed with a new script and freshly created storyboards, the next step for Broussard was to share this work with an internal focus group. Here it is important to note that the focus group was not composed of Deaf community members, rather, the group was composed of individuals that represent the general population (Furland, 2011). The results of the focus group found that "nearly all the survey responses we [PepsiCo] got were incredibly positive, with less than three percent coming back with anything negative" (Cooper, 2008). The success of this internal focus group fueled the project further, inspiring Broussard and his Deaf colleagues (after approval from their vice president) to create a pilot version of the commercial that could later be presented to the CEOs of PepsiAmericaFoods and PepsiAmericaBeverages. "We were producing it with the idea that it could be put directly on Super Bowl if needed," explained Broussard (Furland, 2011). This polished demo version of "Bob's House" was filmed in Broussard's neighborhood, with Deaf PepsiCo and Frito-Lay employees as actors.

Broussard's proposal moved upward through the chain of command, until finally the pilot version was presented to the CEOs of PepsiAmericaFoods and PepsiAmericaBeverages. In November 2007, it was decided that it could be reproduced professionally and would be done in two months so as to be ready for Super Bowl XLII (Furland, 2011). Here, Foote made an important distinction. She emphasized the unusual nature of this production with respect to time. A typical Super Bowl ad is "a year in the making" beyond the time spent on concept development, product placement, and presentation (Furland, 2011). That an ad, created independently of a marketing department or advertising firm was advanced at this speed and produced for an event as big as the Super Bowl, is definitely uncommon; however, these are only a few of the aspects that make this ad unique.

PepsiCo's ad is differentiated further by its efforts to consult and incorporate a Deaf perspective. After the CEOs greenlighted production of the ad, Mary Beth Scoggins, President of the National Association of the Deaf (NAD), was sought out and consulted. This demonstrates a heightened concern regarding representation in advertising. PepsiCo wanted to ensure that the advertisement was portraying an important Deaf joke and that the characterization of the Deaf individuals was accurate and appropriate.

The correspondence between Scoggins and PepsiCo is significant because it demonstrates that PepsiCo was aware of the value behind inserting a common Deaf cultural joke into mainstream media, and, further, that they were invested in the final product as a positive representation of the Deaf community (Scoggins, n.d.). What was not discussed during the interview is why the NAD, rather than any other deaf organization, was chosen to be the one association trusted to provide feedback on the Deaf representation in the advertisement. PepsiCo's efforts to ensure a positive representation also greatly reflect who they view as the dominate Deaf organization. (The decision to involve the NAD is significant and ultimately fueled the controversial response received by the AGBell Association that will be discussed later in this paper.)

As production moved forward, following the approval of the CEOs of PepsiAmericaFoods and PepsiAmericaBeverages, substantial involvement by deaf individuals can be identified at multiple stages. Additional attention was paid to deaf participation, as the film company utilized deaf individuals to work as part of the film crew for the final production. The ad itself included deaf employees-turned-actors in the demo and final-cut versions of the advertisement. This is noteworthy because it is unusual and demonstrative of PepsiCo's ingenuity and inclusiveness in the creation of this ad. This distinction is significant when we consider the previous dearth of Deaf representation/participation in the media. As disability-theory activists maintain, "nothing about us without us," Deaf people must be involved in the creation and production of their minority's images (Charlton, 2000).

The unique features of the ad that are most discussed and known to the general public are its use of ASL and lack of audio. Foote and Broussard both attest that it was a very conscious decision to produce this advertisement without sound, a decision motivated by the novel nature of an entire advertisment without audio. In the screaming soundscape that is the majority of TV advertising, sixty seconds of silence is certainly a departure! Moreover, this required PepsiCo to communicate with broadcast companies prior to air because typically silence during a television broadcast implies a technological mishap (Furland, 2011). The silence acted as a gimmick to catch the attention of hearing Super Bowl viewers, with the benefit of providing a Deaf audience full access to the entire advertisement (Sands Research, n.d.).

Furland's (2011) study investigates company intentions, including PepsiCo, for the inclusion of Deaf individuals and ASL in its commercials. Several other companies were interviewed and the overall finding was that the inclusion of sign language was not utilized in an effort to target the Deaf market, but rather to emphasize a corresponding adverstising campaign, e.g., Hands Only CPR, and/or to be unique and attract attention from a non-signing audience. Some, but not all, hired deaf culture consultants to offer advice and interpreting services during the production (Furland, 2011). In the majority, ASL was more often treated as a marketing tool, rather than a symbol of representation of an American minority.

The interviews conducted for this study confirm that the PepsiCo "Bob's House" ad was not only completely unique in its lack of audio and use of ASL and captioning for the non-signing audience, but also for its conception and production (cf., Ang, Leong, & Yeo, 1999; Olsen, 1994). The ad spot was not the brainchild of a slick advertising firm, but the spontaneous idea of a mid-level employee. The actors were not professionals, but rather Deaf and hearing employees at PepsiCo and Frito-Lay. There were deaf people behind the lights and cameras working as members of the crew, and at several stages the company paid concerted attention to cultural consultants. Yet the result was a polished, innovative Super Bowl advertisement that, as Foote maintains, "is one of the most viewed Super Bowl ads on YouTube even now" (Furland, 2011).

The inclusion of ASL and lack of soundtrack initially made "Bob's House" memorable, but the story does not end there. For years, companies have produced commercials that utilize ASL and their life has been limited to that of their airtime; companies that have marketed in this way previously are snap.com Search Engine, Wal-Mart, Nabisco, Walt Disney, Kellogg, Kraft, Whiska's, Bayer, Saturn, Mutual of Omaha, PepsiCo, American Heart Association, Kay Jewelers, McDonald's, and Apple (cf., Furland, 2011. Interestingly, PepsiCo's commercial had the shortest on-air lifespan, being shown only once on primetime television in 2008, yet maintains the longest lifespan on the Internet and in social publications (Furland, 2011). Thus, the "Bob's House" production is unique in yet another respect. Although this longevity is due in large part to the novel nature of the "Bob's House" production which was discussed previously, "Bob's House" also sparked a controversy among viewers and was responsible for the first public awareness of deaf representation in advertising.

When one imagines controversy surrounding the appearance of this advertisement on national television, one might expect the conflict to appear between Deaf and hearing groups, and even a cursory glance at American Deaf history would reinforce this assumption. However, the controversy of this commercial hasn't fallen on the boundary between deaf and hearing people, instead it has revealed a much more complicated reading of deaf representation in media.

"Bob's House," which, commendably, involved deaf individuals at every level of production and consulted with the NAD prior to broadcast, was deemed an unfit representation of deaf people by the Alexander Graham Bell Association for the Deaf and Hard of Hearing (AGBell). Thus, despite PepsiCo's efforts to spread a positive Deaf media representation to the largest TV viewing audience, they received a letter of disapproval from AGBell. The letter arrived prior to the commercial's debut, but did not halt the airing. The letter was written, and published publicly on AGBell's website, to loudly voice the following complaint, "Your advertisement perpetuates a common myth that all people who are deaf can only communicate using sign language and are, therefore, isolated from the rest of society" (Graham & Youdelman, 2008) AGBell's response utilizes a rhetoric that reinforces a particular and historically rooted understanding of deaf people — that assimilation into society is, and should be, of highest priority. This response upholds a perspective of deaf people that is antagonistic to that which is associated with the Deaf community and the NAD.

AGBell sent its letter to PepsiCo on January 31, 2008, just three days shy of the national reveal. Due to AGBell's stridency, it did not take long for the complaint to be passed around and to soon become a topic of conversation within the entire deaf community. Just as the AGBell Association was encouraging its members to write personal letters of discontent to PepsiCo, the Deaf Bilingual Coalition (DBC) formulated a note of praise (AGBell, 2008). Sent on February 5th, DBC defused AGBell's reaction, writing,

> "Pepsi's commercial did not just raise awareness about Deaf people's natural way of life; it can actually enhance lives. Because of the unprecedented and highly-viewed commercial, the chances that future parents of Deaf babies will pick up American Sign Language (ASL) increased exponentially."

The letter continued to discredit AGBell's response to PepsiCo:

> "[w]ith the overwhelming majority of AG Bell and Cochlear America's Board members and top executives being non-minority and non-Deaf, the DBC finds AG Bell's characterization of Pepsi supposedly having a "limited" view of Deaf diversity extremely puzzling... The National Association of the Deaf (NAD), with a diverse Board, is the Deaf community's true representative" (DBC, 2008)

The NAD, with its opinion already publicized with the release of the backstage footage, composed a letter to AGBell rather than PepsiCo. The NAD is direct, stating, "[w]e find it deplorable that AGBell continues to perpetuate the myth that the use of ASL isolates deaf people from mainstream society, a stereotype that is far from the truth" (DBC, 2008)

These dichotomous responses make clear the difficulties of representing a minority group appropriately in mainstream media. Within one population, the deaf community, there exist polarized views of the community's goals and practices. Foote contends that PepsiCo was informed of these differing perspectives by the NAD president, Mary Beth Scoggins, prior to filming and as a result, PepsiCo was ready for any and all feedback related to the advertisement (Furland, 2011). In response to these conflicting reactions to the ad's representation, Foote stated, "We were trying to accurately reflect that certain portion of the population which is valid, a part of our consumer base which is ASL users. Obviously there are people who choose not to use ASL and that's fine but I don't think our ad was a statement on that in any way" (Furland, 2011)

With large organizations' opinions made public, one may wonder how the average consumer, both Deaf and hearing, responded and whether or not it was in agreement. The only study to tackle the difference in perception of media representation between hearing and Deaf people, as mentioned above, is in Furland (2011). The heart of this study is the investigation of audience perception of advertisements. It surveys two dichotomous identity groups and compares the results. The hearing focus group was limited to audiologically hearing individuals with very little or no exposure to ASL or the Deaf community, while the Deaf focus group involved individuals with varying audiological levels who used ASL and participated in the Deaf community. While the study covered a broad spectrum of commercials, here we can focus solely on the reactions "Bob's House" elicited.

Though reactions from Deaf and hearing cohorts were certainly different – they were overwhelmingly positive. A Deaf focus group participant, when asked which advertisements were genuine in their inclusion of ASL, wrote that the "Pepsi [advertisement] was. The joke exist[s] in [the] deaf community. For hearing people to incorporate that and use it was cool" (Furland, 2011). When questioned about which ad had the most visual appeal, a different Deaf participant stated, "Pepsi Co. because they used the deaf culture joke as [a] commercial." When asked "Of the commercials just shown to you, which one(s) do you most strongly associate with your own lifestyle and why?" one participant from the Deaf focus group declared, "Pepsi — real life situation, in sign, includes deaf humor — all points that help me relate" (Furland, 2011). Five other Deaf participants responded similarly, indicating that PepsiCo's advertisement was the most (or one of a few) relatable to their lifestyle. Furland's 2011 study results indicate that the "Bob's House" ad appeared in several participant's written responses, the common theme being a connection from the ad's content to Deaf culture. Deaf participants identified the use of ASL, Deaf actors, and the inclusion of Deaf humor as contributing factors that attracted them to TV commercials. These are the same features most often overlooked by hearing respondents.

In the hearing focus group, when asked if the companies were genuine in their use of ASL, one hearing participant wrote, "Yes, They all went out of their way to sign them [their commercial]. Pepsi's may have seemed disingenuine [sic] but it was just showing a humor to the situation" (Furland, 2011). This response not only demonstrates that there is little to no scrutiny in representation, but also that this individual is unfamiliar with the Deaf culture reference and the involved development of this ad. In fact, Furland notes that "none of the hearing focus group participants made reference to this advertisement reflecting a common joke within the Deaf community; therefore, this advertisement was perceived differently based on prior cultural affiliation and knowledge" (Furland, 2011). However, despite these differences, the commercial was undeniably successful in both focus groups as both groups indicated that their likeliness to purchase PepsiCo products after watching the advertisement increased (Furland, 2011). The study suggested no division in opinion where it may be expected, between the Deaf and hearing markets. Instead, the controversial responses highlighted previously sprang from within the American deaf community.

The reason this commercial initiated such a heated debate regarding representation reflects a growing realization and value of "positive" media representation. Minorities, such as the deaf community, are to be found in small numbers throughout the United States. For many Americans, exposure to minority groups such as the Deaf community may be limited; therefore, the person seen on the television screen can easily become a stereotype, by which all members of that minority group are understood. This is exactly why the AGBell organization complained. They feared that post-viewing consumers would (possibly unknowingly) develop an understanding of being deaf that differed from their own. (It is notable to mention that this is the first, very public, response to an ad that involved the Deaf community. This may speak to the quality of production and message included in the ad.). AGBell's letter to PepsiCo was clear on its criticism of the Deaf representation in "Bob's House," however, there was no discussion or suggestions of ways the representation could better reflect AGBell's mission, only that the money used to produce "Bob's House" could be alternately used for assistive hearing technology.

This posits the question of whether they disagreed with the representation for fear of people not knowing some deaf people communicate vocally or whether they would prefer for its rival Deaf organization not be represented. The importance of media representation was realized by the NAD when it reprimanded AGBell for its letter's content while simultaneously applauding PepsiCo's production; for once in advertising history there was a commercial that reflected the Deaf community's view of being deaf and involved deaf people to a great extent in its production. It is important that the Deaf community and its culture are represented positively in the media so that the American public is aware that a proud, linguistically rich, community of Deaf people thrives within America.

The commodification of sign language in advertising is not a new marketing strategy. In the interpretation of these images, cultural affiliation and prior knowledge have a clear and defined influence on a consumer's understanding and opinion of an advertisement (Furland, 2011). For "Bob's House," the different responses illustrated this, but did not illicit concern from the Deaf community because the advertisement, utilizing Deaf individuals in the main signing roles and the production of ASL, as well as the recreation of a Deaf joke, was understood and resonated with them. While it may have been clear that the Deaf audience was not the only target audience for the advertisement, the advertisement's inclusion of ASL was, quite clearly, genuine and not solely for the hearing audience's enjoyment.

Now that it is clear that media representation is important and that there are different definitions of positive representations, an important question arises: what is required for a positive representation of Deaf people? There are currently no set parameters for determining the quality of a Deaf representation. This paper proposes three features: filming technique, linguistic value, and a deep analysis of the implications for inclusion which should be considered when evaluating an advertisement's portrayal of Deaf people. Application of these critical guidelines must be considered, expanded, and applied by academics, especially those involved in that minority for any change to occur in advertisement production and minority image dissemination.

First, filming technique is an invaluable component of media representation, and further examination reveals a good deal about cultural understanding and company intentions. Jennifer Rayman constructed a useful framework for analyzing filmed representations of Deaf people. Acknowledging that the majority of the American audience is not familiar with sign language, Rayman questions the visibility and production of ASL signs with respect to film angles and editing techniques in two TV dramas. Her analysis reveals that several of the television clips she surveyed contained inappropriate representations of ASL. These poorly filmed productions may have a direct influence an audience's perspective of sign language. She declares that "[i]n order to avoid objectification of sign language, extreme close-ups of the hands should be avoided as it de-humanizes sign languages and reduces language to animalistic hand gestures" (Rayman, 2010).

Therefore, the same camera angles and screen frames that emphasize the aesthetics of sign language for the non-signing audience serve to create a barrier to a Deaf audience's ability to understand the signed dialogue. The effects of such representation can be damaging to the minority. If sign language is involved in a production it should be filmed in a medium frame so as to capture the entirety of every sign, allowing it to be easily comprehended by the signing audience, presenting it as a foreign language which only select audience members can understand rather than artistic hand movements.

This framework is easily applied to any filmed production involving sign language. "Bob's house" uses a series of medium shots inside the vehicle capturing the signs while also conveying the feeling of being in a car. The signed conversation can be easily understood by the signing audience and the captions are utilized for the non-signing audience's benefit.

The next criterion that must be examined is the linguistic value of the piece. The content of the signed dialogue must be evaluated. Who is involved in the conversation, how is the Deaf individual expressing him or herself, and how does the dialogue content reflect the minority individual's intellect? All of this information can influence the audience's perception of the individual and thus the minority. In "Bob's House" there are two deaf individuals communicating with each other in ASL. Rather than talking about something that is intimately a "deaf issue," they are discussing directions. This script has a normalizing effect on the deaf experience. Deaf people, just like hearing people, watch football games and are subject to getting lost. However, with the repetitive "I thought you knew"s, a viewer could interpret this as childish. The dialogue could be diversified with comments such as "I told you to look up the directions before we left!" or "You were responsible for the directions; I purchased the Pepsi!" Simple changes like this could better reflect an argument between two mature individuals.

The use of ASL in media advertising is an important measure for positive representation of Deaf people. The perils of inaccurate representation are illuminated by the responses from several hearing focus group members in Furland's (2011) study. Focus groups were asked to evaluate commercials based on the following question: "Of the commercials that involved sign language, do you think the use of sign language was accurate? Why or Why not?" The trend in responses was alarming, yet not unexpected. If you recall the hearing focus group consisting of audiologically hearing individuals had little or no experience with ASL or the Deaf community, it is not surprising that they did not have the knowledge to critically judge ASL discourse beyond providing feedback on the captioning (if that was provided.)

Their responses indicate that media is trusted to provide accurate portrayals of sign language. There is minimal effort made to challenge or critique media images or related implications (Furland, 2011). Thus, with already limited representation and no questioning of any production's intention, one minority group portrayal (whether correct or incorrect) can easily become the signpost and define the minority group as a whole in the minds of many viewers. This serious reality illuminates the perils of media misrepresentation.

> "An unsubstantiated and perhaps unconscious acceptance of media images and messages by many participants emphasizes the need for critical analysis of current representations and increased activism for positive, accurate representations of all minority groups" (Furland, 2011).

Lastly, it is important to scrutinize the intentions behind the inclusion of the Deaf individual/s and sign language. Furland's interviews with advertising agencies and companies is demonstrative that company intentions vary. Some view the Deaf community not as a valued consumer base with a rich minority culture, but rather a positive side effect of this kind of advertising (Furland, 2011). Others realize the importance of representation and seek out appropriate actors and cultural consultants for the production. Interviewing every company to uncover its intentions is improbable and unrealistic; therefore, some questions to foster this kind of analysis include: In what ways does the audience know the actor is deaf? For example, the use of ASL, in a linguistically rich way discussed above, would be more positive than having cameras focus on visible hearing aids or cochlear implants. How is the Deaf individual being portrayed? In need of help or as a 'normal' person just chatting with other Deaf people? Is the Deaf person being portrayed as a member of a linguistic minority or a member of the disability community? Are features of Deaf interactions reflected in the ad? (Bahan, 2010). These are just a few questions to investigate company intentions.

The "Bob's House" advertisement was significant for several reasons. It is true that the inclusion of ASL and lack of audio made "Bob's House" memorable, but PepsiCo was not the pioneer of either of those marketing tactics. Several companies have produced commercials that utilize ASL and others have utilized sound and silence to convey information to the audience, but none have made such a concerted effort on so many levels to include deaf individuals in the production, cultural and linguistic content, or sought a consultation from a prominent Deaf organization. PepsiCo intentionally produced a commercial reflecting American Deaf culture, strategically sought out reliable feedback, and consciously aired the production to the largest viewing audience possible, Super Bowl XLII. These truly unique actions not only sparked a controversy within the deaf community, but are also what makes "Bob's House" noteworthy and fosters discussion years after its one-time television debut, heightening our attention to the features that contribute to a positive representation of Deaf people in mainstream media.

REFERENCES

"AG Bell Speaks Up on Pepsi Super Bowl Commercial," (2008, January 31). http://nc.agbell.org//Page.aspx?pid=370.

Bahan, B. (2009). "Sensory Orientation." Deaf Studies Digital Journal 1. http://dsdj.gallaudet.edu/index.php?view=entry&issue=1&entry_id=48.

Bahan, B. (2010). "Sensory Orientation Part Two." Deaf Studies Digital Journal 2. http://dsdj.gallaudet.edu/index.php?view=entry&issue=3&entry_id=109.

Charlton, J. I. (2000). *Nothing About Us Without Us: Disability Oppression and Empowerment.* New Ed. University of California Press.

Cooper, C. (2008, May) "A Refreshing Sign @ PepsiCo." *Ability Magazine.*

Deaf Bilingual Coalition (2008, May 16). "Pepsi's Commercial: Bob's House." http://www.dbcusa.org/index.php/Letters/Pepsi-s-Commercial-Bob-s-House.html.

Entertainment Newsweekly. (2008, January 28) "PepsiCo, Inc.: PepsiCo Brings Silent Ad to Super Bowl."

Furland, R. (2011). "American Sign Language and the Desire to Buy: A Study of Sign Language in TV Advertisements." Unpublished thesis, Gallaudet University.

Graham, A. T., & Youdelman, K. (2008, January 31). "AG Bell Letter to Pepsi," http://nc.agbell.org/NetCommunity/Page.aspx?pid=804.

Hoon Ang, S., Meng Leong, S., & Yeo, W. (1999, January 1). "When Silence Is Golden: Effects of Silence of Consumer Ad Response." *Advances in Consumer Research* 26, 295–299.

Olsen, D. (1994). "Observations: The Sounds of Silence: Functions and Use of Silence in Television Advertising." *Journal of Advertising Research* September/October, 89–95.

Padden, C. & Humphries, T. (1990). *Deaf in America: Voices from a Culture.* Cambrdge: Harvard University Press.

PepsiCo. (2007). "Talent Sustainability: PepsiCo Annual Report." http://www.pepsico.com/Annual-Reports/2007/purpose-talent.html.

PR Newswire. (2008, January 24). "PepsiCo Brings Silent Ad to Super Bowl: Employees Create and Star in American Sign Language Commercial on Super Bowl Sunday."

Rayman, J. (2010). "The Politics and Practice of Voice: Representing American Sign Language on the Screen in Two Recent Television Crime Dramas." *M/C Journal: A Journal of Media and Culture* 13(3). http://journal.media-culture.org.au/index.php/mcjournal/article/viewArticle/273.

Reagan, T. G. (2010). *Language Policy and Planning for Sign Languages.* Washington, D.C.: Gallaudet University Press.

Robinson-Jacobs, K. (2008, January 25). "Pepsi's Silent Super Bowl Ad Was Plano Man's Idea." *McClatchy-Tribune Business News.*

Sands Research (n.d.). "Pepsi 'Bob' Neuromedia Study." Accessed April 7, 2013. http://www.sandsresearch.com/2008SBMovies.aspx; http://www.sandsresearch.com/PepsiBobNM.aspx.

Siegel, L. (2008). *The Human Right to Language: Communication Access for Deaf Children.* Washington, D.C.: Gallaudet University Press.

Sirvage, R. (2012) "Navigational Proxemics of Walking Signers." Deaf Studies Digital Journal 3. http://dsdj.gallaudet.edu/index.php?view=entry&issue=4&entry_id=169

Steinberg, B. (2011) "Super Bowl Breaks Ratings Records | Special: Super Bowl 2008 — Advertising Age." http://adage.com/article/special-report-super-bowl-2008/super-bowl-breaks-ratings-records/124852/.

Woodward, J. (1982). *How You Gonna Get to Heaven If You Can't Talk With Jesus: On Depathologizing Deafness* (ed.). Silver Spring, MD: TJ Publishers, Inc.

Woodward, J. (1982). "Implications for Sociolinguistic Research Among the Deaf." *Sign Language Studies* 1: 1–7.

Woodward, J. & Markowitcz, H. "Language and the Maintenance of Ethnic Boundaries in the Deaf Community." In J. Woodward (ed.) *How You Gonna Get to Heaven If You Can't Talk With Jesus: On Depathologizing Deafness* (ed.). Silver Spring, MD: TJ Publishers, Inc., 3–9.

Wrigley, O. (1997). The Politics of Deafness. Washington, D.C.: Gallaudet University Press..

Exploring the Concepts of non-Deaf and Deaf Space as Occupied by Deaf and non-Deaf Sign Language Interpreters

NIGEL HOWARD AND LIZ SCULLY

THIS PAPER IS PRESENTED BASED ON THE REFLECTIONS OF A DEAF interpreter and a hearing interpreter whose combined careers equal over forty years of experience. Both work in American Sign Language (ASL) using Deaf communities, one located in eastern and the other in western Canada. Assignments included one-to-one meetings through to large audiences of 3,000 or more occurring in local, national and international settings.

The following discussion looks at Deaf interpreters working among other Deaf people and among those who are not Deaf. The opposite situation of interpreters who are non-Deaf and work among other hearing people as well as working within Deaf settings is also examined. The observations made and the self-reflection carried out was done without judgement. There is no right or wrong, one way better or worse than the other. This paper does not address non-Deaf interpreters who live among Deaf people as partners or family members.

What results is a response to an initial descriptive research question looking for patterns of behaviour and identifying trends. Further discussions are welcomed to validate, expand or refute these observations.

SPACE AND PLACE

Space can be described and measured in terms of the surfaces and physical shapes we see around us. It can also be characterised by a sense of area. The sitting room in your home, the distance between your home and work, and the size of your country are all representations of space.

Geographers have long been archivists of space. There is a branch of geography called human geography. This field looks at how people define and interact with the areas around them. Place is seen as a specific physical area where as space is an abstract, perceived area.

Cultural studies have borrowed the idea of space and applied it to various populations. Sasao and Sue (1993:709) write "an ethnic-cultural community must be viewed more as a social-cognitive-cultural-historical-contextual entity than as one based on physiognomic attributes and/or geographical boundaries per se." Since then Robins and Aksoy (2001) in looking at Turkish-Cypriots in London, England used "mental space as a space both within us and in the external world." They explain how Turkish Cypriot immigrants who lack Turkish language skills as a result of the "monolingual ideology of integrationist education in Britain" has lead to a difficulty in entering "the space of Cypriot or Turkish culture."

Parallels can be made between the Deaf community and other linguistic minorities (Ladd, 2003, Ladd, Gulliver & Batterbury, 2003).

DEAF SPACES

Deaf space transcends nationalistic boundaries such as political borders and even language boundaries as seen at international Deaf events. The inhabitants are those who can access the space through sign language. There are physical aspects such as sight lines, seating configurations and distance communication through cyberspace. Although the concept of "Deaf Nation" has been raised in the past (Ladd, 2003) there is no permanent, physical "Deaf land" one can visit (Mathews, 2006; Lane, Hoffmeister and Bahan, 1996,). Deaf schools do represent Deaf space but their permanence is under threat and many have been closed (Padden and Humphries, 2005:16).

Deaf knowledge makes Deaf space possible and Deaf space makes Deaf knowledge possible (Gulliver, 2005). Deaf space is actually in the minds of Deaf people. Deaf space is perceived by Deaf people as they enter an area and deem it be a Deaf location. It is there they can carry out their ways and foster Deaf knowledge to be utilized and shared (Gulliver, 2006). New people into the Deaf community must learn about these Deaf spaces and Deaf ways.

Ironically, without that knowledge to realise you are walking into Deaf space one might walk right by or through it and be totally oblivious. Such would be the case for members of the general public who were in the vicinity of the Washington convention centre during Deaf Way I and II celebrations or who walked through the Palais des Congres, in Montreal, to get to the underground Metro while the 2003 World Congress of the World Federation of the Deaf (WFD) was happening. This raises the point that such spaces do not belong to Deaf people exclusively. When one, two or thousands of those who are Deaf are no longer present in an environment it goes back to the way it was, simply bricks and mortar.

A Deaf space will be established as created by the Deaf people who are there. Though the space may be recreated if a gathering is repeated it is not exactly the same in each of those manifestations. Deaf spaces are not stagnant environments but are instead a constantly evolving "ecosystem" (Gulliver, 2005). A Deaf seniors citizen group, the weekly Deaf pub goers, Deaflympic athletes, and Deaf film makers all know where and when they will meet again but their Deaf space will not be exactly as it existed previously. Each time it will be created by the new configuration of Deaf participants that are there.

Review of Deaf Spaces
- Stored in Deaf people's mind
- Must be learned by new arrivals
- The Deaf "ecosystem" is constantly changing
- Deaf knowledge makes Deaf space possible
- Deaf space makes Deaf knowledge possible

DEAF INTERPRETERS

Most people are familiar with sign language interpreters who hear. Referring to a Deaf interpreter may be less common. Certainly Deaf people have been interpreting for centuries on an ad hoc basis. An example appears when confronted with someone who has insufficient sign skills. One Deaf person may turn to another and sign "What did they say?" or "I don't understand." That clarification is interpreting. There is a rich history of interpreting by Deaf individuals, only now being researched (Adam and Stone, 2010).

As with interpreters who hear, a Deaf interpreter is someone who receives the information and processes it fully. The Deaf interpreter reconfigures the message into the target language. From the source text the Deaf interpreter must keep in mind the goal of the speaker, message equivalency, linguistic aspects, cultural aspects and pragmatics to reconstruct a signed message that will retain those components.

Deaf interpreters can be seen on stage as a platform interpreter. Monologues, perhaps presentations, are typically received in sign language (from what is sometimes called "a feed," either live or on screen) and put out again in sign language. Deaf interpreters may also provide translations from a print language into a sign language (Stone, 2009).

Deaf interpreters also work in instances where there is a Deaf audience and the sight lines among the participants are not clear. A mirror interpreter takes brief morsels of information, such as a question, and reflects them back to the audience.

Deaf interpreters also provide one to one and small group interpreting with those who may be Deafblind, use an alternate sign language known to the Deaf interpreter, or have non-standard signing.

Preparation for this paper was conducted in sign language following Deaf norms. Live presentations and discussions afterwards were conducted in sign language. Due to both authors being in England at the time, all was conducted in British Sign Language (BSL). It is interesting to note that in BSL the concept of space was one of "elbow room" versus a sign produced off the body, to represent an area "out there."

For this presentation purpose, a hearing academic norm has been adopted and the ideas written in print English. For clarity we provide the following Deaf and hearing perspectives of the terminology used:

Non-Deaf Interpreter = hearing interpreter (H.I.)
• In a mainstream setting = hearing space
• In a predominantly Deaf setting = Deaf space

Deaf Interpreter = Deaf interpreter (D.I.)
• In a mainstream setting = hearing space
• In a predominantly Deaf setting = Deaf space

By exploring interpreters in their own space and interpreters that cross over into the space of the "others," four different conditions result: Deaf interpreters in Deaf spaces and in hearing spaces as well as hearing interpreters in Deaf spaces and hearing spaces. This can be seen in a four-way matrix.

CONCEPT		
	Deaf Space	Hearing Space
Deaf Interpreter		
Hearing Interpreter		

EXTERNAL PERCEPTIONS

External perceptions are how others view the interpreters in each setting:

EXTERNAL PERCEPTION

	Deaf Space	Hearing Space
Deaf Interpreter	Ad Hoc New Profession	New Profession
Hearing Interpreter	Common	Common

As previously mentioned, Deaf people have been interpreting for each other and with those who are not Deaf for generations. That type of interpreting is always there, on standby, and used as needed. Deaf interpreters working formally in Deaf space is a new profession within the Deaf community. It is only in the last ten or fifteen years that Deaf people been compensated with payment to interpret. Where sign language bilingualism exists (for example, ASL and Langue des Sourds du Quebec (LSQ) use in Canada) Deaf interpreter teams are hired to work directly from the signing presenter using one sign language while the interpretation is into another sign language.

The World Congress of the World Federation of the Deaf (WFD) has for many years incorporated Deaf interpreters on stage and they are present in various national delegations. For the first time, at the 2003 World Congress of the WFD during plenary sessions, all platform ASL, LSQ, and International Sign interpreters were Deaf. During breaks Deaf audience members would approach the interpreters and ask if they are Deaf or hearing. When told the interpreter is Deaf many were surprised. Next came congratulations on doing a good job. Although the compliments were welcomed it is interesting to note the lack of expectation that the interpreter would be Deaf. This position had previously been filled by hearing individuals. Such reactions reflected thoughts of "this is my space" and "my kind of interpreter."

It is also interesting to note that feedback from some Deaf people regarding a Deaf interpreter was negative. They felt they did not want, or did not trust that the message was getting through or that the message was literally passing through too many hands before they received it. It would seem even in the Deaf community the profession of Deaf interpreting is not yet fully accepted.

Deaf interpreters increasingly work in non-Deaf spaces such as courtrooms and mental health settings. These Deaf interpreters have been recognised as professionals only in the last five or ten years. Though Deaf people have been going into these settings for longer than that, formal recognition in many cases still does not exist or is rare. Interestingly, many of the on screen (in-vision) interpreters on television in the UK are actually Deaf. Because it is television the average viewer assumes the interpreter is hearing and is surprised to find out otherwise. They don't expect the television interpreter to be Deaf because television has traditionally been a hearing space. When television was invented, it was hearing people who first had full access to it. Yet, it is an audio-visual medium so might it be Deaf space as well, or perhaps shared space? These are further questions to ponder.

Hearing interpreters frequently find themselves working in Deaf spaces. These may range from informational sessions at the local Deaf club where a non-signing guest speaker is brought in through to national and multinational events where sign to voice interpretation is provided for the hearing monolinguals present. In some situations the hearing interpreter provides escort interpreting (spoken in a low voice near the non-signing participants) or interprets through a closed microphone system (where participants must have audio receivers to listen to the interpretation). These techniques are used to maintain the signing environment as intact as possible.

In mainstream settings hearing interpreters are quite common. Much research exists on the training, techniques, attributes and role of non-Deaf interpreters working between Deaf individuals and the general public (Neumann Solow, 1981; Cokely, 1992; Roy, 2000; Napier et al, 2006). This is the image most people are familiar with and the environment in which most hearing interpreters work.

HOME

Interpreters either work within their own environments or in those of the other culture:

HOME

	Deaf Space	Hearing Space
Deaf Interpreter	Own	Frequent visitor
Hearing Interpreter	Foreign visitor	Own

A Deaf interpreter in a Deaf setting is in their home environment. The Deaf interpreter feels very connected to the Deaf audience because they are alike. Should there be an interpreting error on the part of a Deaf interpreter the Deaf audience is likely to be more forgiving. Some, of course, will be critical but Deaf audience members generally wish to promote the idea of Deaf interpreters and enjoy the feeling of kinship with the service provider.

When a Deaf interpreter goes into hearing space they are similar to a frequent visitor. The term "frequent" is used because as a Deaf person that interpreter has to deal with the hearing ways of the general public on a daily basis. As a Deaf person the Deaf interpreter is used to being inundated by hearing people around them. Deaf interpreters can leave the hearing world, but takes a conscious effort.

The hearing interpreter in Deaf space is like a foreigner, arranging to go where Deaf people are. They would not ordinarily come upon groups of Deaf people unless they went to where they are located. A hearing interpreter has the choice to enter the Deaf world and choose when to leave. They may not encounter a Deaf person again unless they make the effort to.

Hearing interpreters in hearing space are at home. They feel very comfortable with the familiarity of the environment and the expectations of their role, the protocols and processes of interpreting in that setting.

POWER BASE

Another aspect to look at is the power base or hegemony (centre of control) in a given environment:

POWER BASE		
	Deaf Space	Hearing Space
Deaf Interpreter	Deaf	Hearing/Deaf; not naturally shared
Hearing Interpreter	Deaf; closer monitoring	(very) hearing oblivious

When there is a Deaf interpreter in Deaf space, the power base is Deaf-centred. The Deaf interpreter and participants make sure the environment, the lighting, and sight lines are good and that the interpretation is working. If communication breaks down, things stop and are clarified or rectified until all can follow again. This is a Deaf cultural norm. The interpreting process has almost an organic fit as Deaf-to-Deaf the message gets imparted.

If a Deaf interpreter is in a hearing environment it means they are usually with a hearing interpreter. Perhaps a Deaf person might solo interpret during a hospital visit, for example, but such ad hoc interpretation is not included in the discussion here. Sharing interpreter space with someone other than another hearing interpreter is new for many hearing interpreter.

Many aspects of Deaf and hearing interpreters working together have not yet been researched. Working together is something that the hearing and Deaf colleagues need to learn how to do. Power sharing does not happen naturally and must be negotiated between the Deaf and hearing interpreters. There is the possibility on the part of the naïve general public to try and give more power to the hearing rather than the Deaf member(s) of the interpreting team.

When a hearing interpreter goes into Deaf space the Deaf people present tend to closely monitor the performance of the interpreter. This is likely due to a matter of trust. Often it is the Deaf participants rather than the hearing interpreter(s) who will stop an event if communication is unclear due to visibility conditions or interpretation. When an interpreter co-ordinator is present we see increasingly that role is filled by a Deaf person. Beyond simply ensuring that the interpretation process is running smoothly, the Deaf inhabitants want to make sure that the foreigner (hearing interpreter) in their midst follows the appropriate protocols and is respectful of the Deaf space.

Mainstream events often give little thought to interpretation. Hearing interpreters when in hearing space are may be oblivious to the subtleties of the differences between Deaf and hearing people. Hearing people, in general, tend not to give Deaf people a second thought.

The following two examples illustrate this point. An interpreter on a multi-day assignment had a hair appointment on the evening of the first day. The next day she returned to the assignment and her previously waist long hair was now cut quite short. The change in the appearance of the interpreter was very jarring to the Deaf audience. The interpreter had no expectation of this effect. In another example an interpreter had what can be classified as a truly "hearing accident" as they answered a telephone and mistakenly hit their cheekbone instead of raising the phone to their ear. The resulting yellowish bruise was very distracting to Deaf people. Because there was no swelling, the interpreter miscalculated the importance of the visual impact.

MESSAGE OWNERSHIP

Upon receipt of the source message the interpreter possesses it prior to reconstructing it into a format that is best received by the audience. The degree of ownership of that message as it passes through the interpreter can vary:

MESSAGE OWNERSHIP

	Deaf Space	Hearing Space
Deaf Interpreter	Strong possession	Strong possession
Hearing Interpreter	Minimal	Detachment

To a Deaf interpreter in Deaf space, the task is not just a job. There is a strong sense of message ownership and need to get the interpretation right. The message is taken on by the Deaf interpreter and then becomes theirs to give to the Deaf participants.

A Deaf interpreter in hearing space faces a Deaf consumer with this same sense of ownership. In the situation there may be only one other Deaf person along with the Deaf interpreter(s) in the midst of hearing people. A Deaf interpreter well understands what the Deaf consumer may be feeling. Because of a sense of empathy, there is also a sense of urgency and importance put onto the message by the Deaf interpreter.

Hearing interpreters in Deaf space know it's not their space. They are not Deaf. It is the rights, the health, the children, the issues, the politics and the lives of Deaf people that exist in Deaf space, not those of the hearing interpreter. When the interpreting is finished the hearing interpreter leaves and returns to their hearing world. Certainly there is an attachment to Deaf people but a hearing interpreter is somewhat detached from the information. There is the challenge and commitment within the non-Deaf interpreter to provide the best interpretation they can. There may be empathy and support, even understanding from the hearing interpreters towards the Deaf consumers, but in the end it is still a job.

The gift of doing the best job possible can be seen in an example of the interpretation of the funeral of a young Deaf man known to the hearing interpreter. Concurrently, the interpreter had feelings of sadness and thoughts of message equivalency as their mind never stopped working. As the deceased's life was recounted the Deaf people present would weep in unison. Although it was very sad, it was also an indicator of a successful interpretation. The emotional tears marked "message received." In a way one might think this is a horrific attitude to have at a funeral but the hearing interpreter felt a responsibility to the message and the Deaf mourners. The hearing interpreter's detachment from the message made the interpretation possible.

Hearing interpreters in hearing space are reminded even more so that their interpretation is a job. They arrive, share the message and leave. The Deaf and hearing participants got the information they needed and afterwards everyone goes home. The hearing interpreter remains in their hearing world and may never see the other hearing participants again.

EFFICIENCY

Different environments call for different skills. The efficiency of the Deaf and non-Deaf interpreter is effected by their working in either Deaf space or hearing space:

CONCEPT

	Deaf Space	Hearing Space
Deaf Interpreter		
Hearing Interpreter		

A Deaf interpreter in Deaf space can be very efficient. They know who the audience is and how to get the message across. As they receive the message they make the proper linguistic and cultural adjustments and there is a strong liaison between them and the audience.

A Deaf interpreter in hearing space is also efficient, but it comes with less ease. There is more work to be done on the part of the Deaf interpreter. They usually work as part of a team and must accommodate to having a hearing colleague who has learned to one degree or another how to work with a Deaf interpreter.

A hearing interpreter in Deaf space can function well, though efficiency does not come easily to a hearing interpreter. They must purposefully learn Deaf ways. A non-Deaf interpreter who is not a native signer (not born into a Deaf family) is dealing with the complications of working with their second language.

A hearing interpreter in hearing space is quite efficient. They are quite familiar with the milieu and the cultural demands of the environment. This space uses their first language so efficiency is high. As mentioned, working with sign language as their second language means efficiency in that task will vary with their second language skills.

The interpreting task involves more than simple message relay. There are also the human elements to service delivery:

WORK SOCIALISATION

	Deaf Space	Hearing Space
Deaf Interpreter	Socialise with Deaf participant(s)	Socialise with Deaf consumer(s)
Hearing Interpreter	Own group*	Socialise with hearing/Deaf participant(s)

(*a single hearing interpreter in Deaf space may become assimilated)

For a Deaf interpreter in Deaf space, their work is not simply a job done that begins and ends abruptly. A Deaf interpreter in Deaf space will have a strong tie with the Deaf audience. Before and after their assignment they will be chatting with the Deaf participants. There is little separation from the other Deaf people present. A role is taken on for a specific time then, when not in that role, the Deaf interpreter becomes a fellow Deaf person. For this reason the matrix refers to socialising with Deaf "participants."

A Deaf interpreter in hearing space is probably outnumbered by those present who can hear. They may socialize with the Deaf consumer(s) but on a more limited basis. Professional distance will be maintained throughout their time in the hearing setting. They will ensure that the message is well received but the feeling of being "on duty" leads to the matrix description of socialising with "consumer(s)."

Hearing interpreters in Deaf space tend to stay together. This is seen before and after sessions, during breaks, and over meal times. Often the interpreters will "go off" to some place or be huddled in a corner or around a small coffee table. They may split up to interpret separate sessions but will congregate again at the first chance they get. Partially this is an element of the preparation process. Perhaps subconsciously they do it as any foreign people might when they meet others of their own kind when away from home. The matrix has an asterisk (*) for non-Deaf interpreters in Deaf space because when there is only one hearing interpreter in Deaf space, depending on the duration of their presence among a Deaf group, they tend to be assimilated. Examples include while providing escort interpreting or working as a committee member in the organization of a Deaf event. It may be forgotten that in fact the interpreter is from the hearing world.

Hearing interpreters in hearing space do socialize somewhat with the Deaf people who are present. What is interesting is that they also socialize with hearing people that they may not previously know at all. This is seen at coffee breaks, in buffet lines, and other pauses before, during or briefly after assignments. Hearing interpreters also socialise with each other. Deaf participants may choose to also socialise with each other. The two groups, Deaf participants and non-Deaf interpreters may socialise increasingly during breaks or meal time depending on the length of the assignment. If there is only one or very few Deaf participants they may socialise with the interpreters from the beginning.

EXPECTATIONS

Perhaps it is not surprising that given the different perspectives, languages and cultures involved, the expectations of the parties present in interpreted events within Deaf and non-Deaf spaces are different:

EXPECTATIONS

	Deaf Space	Hearing Space
Deaf Interpreter	Monitor but more forgiving	H: "fix it" D: advocacy/ally
Hearing Interpreter	Cultural sensitivity	"Just do it"

Regarding a Deaf interpreter in a Deaf environment the audience is more tolerant of errors but they do monitor the interpretation. As Deaf interpreters become more commonplace, the demands of Deaf audience members are rising. So too, the demands for better working conditions, are rising among Deaf interpreters.

Deaf interpreters in hearing space are met with an expectation that they will come in and fix things. Often the communication has broken down before a Deaf interpreter is brought into a hearing situation. It may be with a sense of relief that the hearing people involved expect the Deaf interpreter to not only facilitate communication but also solve the problem no matter what the issue, thus allowing the hearing parties involved to divest themselves of such responsibilities. This expectation is misplaced and not part of the Deaf interpreter's role.

In a hearing setting the Deaf individual may also think at last there is an interpreter here who can help fix things or that the Deaf interpreter is there as their personal ally who will help them get through this situation together as a team. They may look to the Deaf interpreter as someone who will counsel them or at least advise them as to how to behave in or handle the hearing situation. There isn't really a clear cut boundary between the Deaf interpreter and the Deaf consumer, especially if they are the only two Deaf people in the hearing environment.

It is important that the Deaf interpreter be aware of all these expectations from the Deaf and non-deaf people involved in the interpreted situation. To rescue the situation or even the Deaf person is quite a heavy expectation. This, too, is another area of research to be done.

A hearing interpreter in Deaf space has an expectation on them to adopt Deaf ways. They are expected to be non-judgmental of the Deaf environment and respectful of Deaf decisions. When cross-cultural conflicts happen the phrase "should have known better" is often applied by Deaf individuals towards hearing interpreters. There is also the expectation that the actual interpretation provided will be of the highest quality. If it is not, then the hearing interpreter is perceived as being at fault for accepting the assignment.

The expectation of a hearing interpreter in hearing space is that the interpreter should be efficient and not cause any problems. They are expected to know their job and just do it. The public image of hearing interpreters is that they can instantly provide seemingly effortless interpretations. Hearing people who have their fleeting encounters with Deaf people interpreted assume everything is going well. Deaf people who grab an interpreter for brief, spontaneous interpreting (for example at a cocktail party or to make a phone call) are showing their implicit trust in the accuracy of the hearing interpreter.

THE FUTURE

We need more information. We need to clarify the role of a Deaf interpreter be it in Deaf space or in non-Deaf space. What, too, of the role of hearing interpreters in Deaf and in hearing space? Are the roles the same or are they different?

As the profession of Deaf interpreter grows will it be like that of the profession among hearing interpreters? Do Deaf people want it to follow the same path? Could it, or will the path of Deaf interpreters naturally be completely different?

Are the signs to depict an interpreter who is Deaf and one that is not Deaf the same or different? Among many hearing interpreters the term "interpreters who are Deaf" is used to reflect an equal possibility of an interpreter being Deaf or hearing. The ASL sign INTERPRETER has a connotation that the person referred to is hearing otherwise the sign DEAF INTERPRETER is used.

Will the number of young hearing people learning to sign change the face of Deaf-hearing interactions and the role of interpreters? What about interpreter space as physical space or even psychological space? It is interesting to contemplate in which directions these developments will go.

CONCLUSION

The cultural content of Deaf space can be attained through sign language. New members of the Deaf community must enter Deaf space and access it through sign language in order to gain the knowledge both held and grown within that space.

If one further accepts the idea that Deaf space appears and disappears therefore is held in the minds of Deaf people, and those who successfully associate with them, then going to where Deaf people are is the only way to access their language and knowledge. This has great implications for sign language students, interpreters, those who wish to research the Deaf community and members of the Deaf community itself. It raises questions of hearing participation in the Deaf community.

The idea of spaces as borrowed from human geography and various social sciences is useful when looking at the Deaf world in contact with the rest of society. By contrasting the experiences of Deaf interpreters and hearing interpreters in their own space and that of each other's we begin to see similarities and differences.

It is the position of this paper that further discussion of interpreters and space will add to the understanding of the interpreting profession. It is hoped that this paper has sparked enthusiasm for the topic and an interest to investigate it further.

REFERENCES

Cokely, D. (ed.). (1992). *Sign language interpreters and interpreting.* Burtonsville: Linstok Press.

Gulliver, M. (2006). The Deaf Geography: Spatialising Deaf Knowledge. Postgraduate Seminar Presentation, Centre for Deaf Studies, University of Bristol, 5 June 2006, Publication pending.

Gulliver, M. (2005). *Deaf Geographies: Spaces of Ownership and Other Real and Imaginary Places.* Centre for Deaf Studies, University of Bristol, Unpublished monograph.

Ladd, P. (2003). *Understanding Deaf Culture*. Clevedon: Multilingual Matters.

Ladd, P., Gulliver, M. & Batterbury, S. (2003). *Reassessing Minority Language Empowerment From a deaf Perspective: The Other 32 Languages*. Presentation, Mercator First International Symposium on Minority Languages and Research — European Minority Languages and Research: Shaping an Agenda for a Global Age, Aberystwyth.

Lane, H., Hoffmeister, R., & Bahan, B. (1996). *A Journey into the DEAF-WORLD*. San Diego, Calf.: DawnSign Press.

Napier, J., McKee, R. & Goswell, D. (eds.) (2006). *Sign Language Interpreting*, Sydney: The Federation Press.

Neumann Solow, S. (1981). *Sign language interpreting: A basic resource book*. Silver Spring: National Association of the Deaf.

Mathews, E. (2006). *Place, Space and Identity — Using Geography in Deaf Studies*. Postgraduate Seminar Presentation, Centre for Deaf Studies, University of Bristol, 5 June 2006, Publication pending.

Padden, C. & Humphries, T. (2005). *Inside Deaf Culture*. Cambridge: Harvard University Press.

Robins, K. & Aksoy, A. (2001). From spaces of identity to mental spaces: lessons from Turkish-Cypriot cultural experience in Britain, *Journal of Ethnic and Migration Studies*, 27(4), pp. 685–711.

Roy, C. (2000). *Innovative Practices for Teaching Sign Language Interpreters*. Washington, D.C.: Gallaudet University Press.

Sasao, T. & Sue, S. (1993). Toward a Culturally Anchored Ecological Framework of Research in Ethnic-Cultural Communities, *American Journal of Community Psychology*, 21(6), pp. 705–722.

Preparing Deaf-Friendly Teachers in a Diverse Setting

DAVID H. SMITH, PH.D. AND BRYAN BERRETT, ED.D.

PRIOR TO 1970, DEAF EDUCATION TEACHER TRAINING PROGRAMS WERE focused on providing their candidates with auditory/oral training as that was the predominant approach for most of the 20th century. However, the atmosphere began to change during the 1960s, due in large part to the Babbidge Report on the dismal state of deaf education (Babbidge, 1965), national outcry in educational, cultural, and civil rights settings, and William Stokoe's ground-breaking linguistic research on sign language (Baynton, 1996)

Feeling the criticism and pressure to turn away from pure oralist approaches, many educational programs began to use manual approaches (Van Cleve, 1993). Several manual systems were invented that attempted to fit ASL signs into an English syntax. The idea was that these would help deaf children see a visible form of English (Lane, Hoffmeister, Bahan, 1996). As naive as these early attempts may have been, they did afford sign language exposure in additional schools and classrooms. Eventually, with increased understanding and research, natural ASL began to make its way into the educational forum, most notably as the bilingual-bicultural approach spurred by the works of Francois Grosjean, Harlan Lane, Michael Strong, and others as well as the series of National Symposiums on Sign Language Research and Education (first one in 1977) sponsored by the NAD.

Add to these, the increased advocacy of Deaf individuals for improved education programs, and the inclusion of Deaf history and culture, the reverberations of the Deaf President Now protest in 1988, and changes in the law such as the Individuals with Disabilities Education Act and Americans with Disabilities Act (Simms & Thumann, 2007).

As a result of the changes occurring in classrooms and societal view-points on what it is like to be Deaf, programs that prepare teachers needed to adjust their standards accordingly (Nover, 1995; Simms & Thumann, 2007). This was evident by the growing number of courses in ASL and Deaf culture in many of these programs (Jones & Ewing, 2002). The accrediting organization for US teacher preparation programs is the Council on Education of the Deaf (CED), organized in 1960, it is comprised of representatives from several organizations including the Alexander Graham Bell Association for the Deaf (AG Bell), the Association of College Educators-Deaf and Hard of Hearing (ACEDHH), the Conference of American Instructors of the Deaf (CAID), the Conference of Educational Administrators Serving the Deaf (CEASD), and the National Association of the Deaf (NAD).

It needs to be noted that NAD did not become a member until 1994 (Nover, 1995). Programs that wish to obtain accreditation are required to show proof that their graduates have been given knowledge and/or skills in a variety of areas related to educating deaf children (Council on Education of the Deaf, 2003). Prior to the 1990s, there were few if any standards on ASL or knowledge of Deaf culture. While there was resistance in some quarters, most notably from AG Bell, this change in the standards did begin to take place in 1993. (Nover, 1995).

By 2003, there were CED standards in place for teacher candidate knowledge and skill in topics such as cultural dimensions of Deafness and Deaf Education, language development, use, assessment and intervention for both English and ASL, educational design and practices of Comprehensive, Oral/Aural and Bi/Bi programming, demonstrating understanding of and proficiency in the language(s) needed to instruct D/HH children, Deaf cultural factors that may influence classroom management, processes for establishing ongoing interactions with peers, D/HH role models and local, state, regional and national D/HH communities, actively seek and demonstrate the ability to interact with adults in the Deaf community to maintain/improve ASL, English signs or cues as consistent with program philosophy (Council on Education of the Deaf, 2003).

However, these just touch on the overall skills and knowledge of ASL and the Deaf community and in some cases are ambiguous as in the case of the last standard cited above. Most programs are comprehensive in their philosophy, while a few identify as bilingual ASL/English programs or auditory/oral. The reasons most frequently given for comprehensive philosophies is the need for flexibility of the graduates to work in a variety of environments that range from residential schools to self-contained classrooms to itinerant teaching with a variety of communication needs (Jones & Ewing, 2002).

Another topic that came to the fore in the past two decades is the growing number of deaf students who are from a variety of cultural backgrounds. Luckner (2010) has identified cultural identity as a topic that teachers of the deaf need to understand, the cultural identity of deaf individuals often includes additional layers not only related to how they perceive themselves as Deaf or not, but also race, ethnicity, language, and religion. As an example, in the western and southwestern U.S., the number of students from Latino and other backgrounds has actually outnumbered those who are white. Several studies as summarized by Moores (2001), have shown repeatedly over the years that the majority of teachers of children who are D/HH are white, hearing, and female. These studies also indicate that only 5% to 10% of these teachers are members of an ethnic minority, and that only 15% of all teachers classify themselves as deaf. Andrews & Jordan (1993) found that minority and/or deaf teachers of deaf and hard of hearing students tend to work at residential schools for the deaf.

They also found that the highest concentrations of Hispanic deaf and hard of hearing students were in New York, Florida, and California while Texas and New Mexico had the highest concentrations of Hispanic teachers of deaf and hard of hearing students. California State University Fresno is right in the thick of a very culturally diverse environment and is an example of a program that has evolved since its founding right at the beginning of the ASL and Deaf-oriented reform in Deaf Education.

DEAF EDUCATION AT FRESNO STATE

California State University Fresno is located in Central California, right in the middle of one of the most abundant agricultural regions in the world that served as the backdrop for John Steinbeck's novel *Grapes of Wrath*. It is one of twenty-seven campuses of the California state system, distinguished in part by its extraordinarily large service area in the geographical center of California as well as its high percentage of rural, underserved students, significant percentages of whom attended high schools with Hispanic student enrollments of between 70% and 99%. Fresno State has more Hispanic students than the three other public universities between Los Angeles and Sacramento combined.

Moreover, no other university in California enrolls as many rural Hispanic students, an overwhelming percentage of whom are educationally underserved and economically disadvantaged. The California Post Secondary Education Commission has called the Hispanic populations in the region, now numbering into the hundreds of thousands, the "neediest of California's needy."

Fresno State enrolls 22,098 students and 82% of students at Fresno State come from the immediate surrounding region. The ethnic minority undergraduate enrollment includes Hispanic (35%), Asian (15%), African American (6%) and American Indian (1%). Unlike most other CSU campuses, Fresno State is designated a "regional" university with unique outreach goals for underserved students in a rural region whose geographical area the size of Connecticut, Massachusetts, and New Jersey combined (Institutional Research, Assessment and Planning, 2007).

The Deaf Education program at Fresno State has been in existence since 1969 right at the time of the philosophical shift in deaf education from auditory/oral to comprehensive or bilingual philosophies. The program began with several students in Fall 1969 as part of the Department of Communicative Disorders, which also included majors in Speech Pathology and Audiology. In September 1970, the first program director was hired. At that time, there were about ten student majors in the program. One full-time faculty position was added in Fall 1971, and another in Fall 1972 to bring the full-time Deaf Education faculty to a total of three positions. Part-time faculty have been added as needed. The Deaf Education program received its first Council on Education of the Deaf (CED) accreditation approval in Fall 1972.

In 1979, Dr. Paul Ogden, a Deaf tenure track faculty member began working at Fresno State. At that time, he was one of the very few, if not the only Deaf faculty member with a Ph.D. degree teaching in a deaf education program outside of Gallaudet College. A second Deaf faculty member, Dr. David Smith, joined the program from 2003 to 2012. When qualified instructors were available, the instructors for ASL and Deaf-related courses have usually been Deaf. Student enrollment gre from ten in 1970 to approximately 95 undergraduate and graduate students in 2012. An average of six to eight teachers complete their California Deaf and Hard of Hearing teaching credentials at Fresno State annually. The latter statistic speaks for the rigor of the Deaf Education program, which requires at least six years to complete. In Fall 1997, the department then added a new undergraduate option in Sign Language Studies. Beginning in Fall 2000, the Sign Language Studies option was removed when the university approved the Sign Language Interpreting program developed by Dr. Ogden and a faculty member and community interpreter Dr. Bryan Berrett.

History of ASL and Deaf Studies Courses

At its inception, like most others in existence, the Fresno State program was more auditory/oral in focus, however some notable changes took place within a few years. First was the hiring of a Deaf instructor, Reno Colletti, a graduate of California School for the Deaf at Berkeley, to teach a course in

"Manual Communication for the Deaf" listed in the 1971–72 campus catalog. The first listing for an American Sign Language course was for the 1977–78 academic year also taught by Mr. Colletti. The "Manual Communication" course then focused on manual English systems separately from ASL. This course evolved into "Sign Language for Classroom Use" in 1988–89. This solitary ASL course remained until "American Sign Language II" started in 1992–93. Deaf Culture first made its appearance in the 1991–92 academic year taught by Dr. Ogden and was approved by the university as an upper division general education course in 1999.

The ASL 3 and ASL 4 courses began in 2001–02 at the same time that Deaf and hearing faculty members attended a one-week colloquium spearheaded by Carolyn Stem and other Deaf ASL instructors in California. The purpose was to identify ways to incorporate each of the standards of foreign language learning developed in 1996 by American Council on the Teaching of Foreign Languages (ACTFL). A course titled "Hard of Hearing and Deaf" which focused more on issues related to the latter started in 2004. "Linguistics of ASL" was added in 2007–08. "Deaf Literature," developed and taught by Dr. Smith made its debut during the 2008–09 academic year (http://www.csufresno.edu/catoffice/archives/oldcourses/Default.html). As we just saw, ASL got off to an early start and basically stalled at one course for nearly three decades before a rapid expansion to nine ASL and Deaf-related courses over the past decade.

Program Philosophy and ASL

Since the early 1970s, the Fresno State program has had a comprehensive (covering all approaches to deaf education, from auditory/oral to bilingual) philosophy. Most of the program graduates work in variety of environments with D/HH students who vary in hearing loss, communication styles, and whose cultural orientation ranged from fully hearing to Deaf. Less than 10% of graduates work at residential schools although the Director of Instruction at both state schools in California (Fremont and Riverside) are Fresno State graduates. While there has never been a debate on whether to pursue a bilingual ASL/English philosophy there has been a consistent push over the last fifteen years to increase student exposure to ASL, Deaf Culture, and interaction with the Deaf community. The goal has been if they do not work in a Deaf environment such as residential schools, then they would at least be advocates and allies of the Deaf (Ladd, 2003) and have good ASL skills.

Increasing ASL Exposure for Students

In regards to ASL skills, Fresno State has obviously been playing catch up during the past decade with other programs like California State University

Northridge (CSUN), which has had both Deaf Education and Deaf Studies programs for at least three decades now. Recently, both residential schools in California have established minimum ASL skill standards for student teaching interns. This has added impetus for our students to improve their ASL skills. Additionally, with the advent of the Interpreting program in 2000, there is an increased awareness among the student cohort of the need for collaborating on learning and improving their conversational repertoire in ASL.

One of the important issues that needed to be addressed was increasing exposure to the Deaf community, which is a critical component of language learning. The American Council on the Teaching of Foreign Languages (ACTFL) stresses the importance of exposure to cultures and communities as part of language curriculum (ACTFL, 2006) These ACTFL standards have also been adopted by American Sign Language Teachers Association (ASLTA), which is currently working on a final draft (ASLTA, 2011). Thus all of the courses have a graded requirement that students will attend activities within the Deaf community or perform service related activities.

Service-learning courses are another way we have addressed the issue of encouraging community involvement and cultural immersion. Fresno State has a rich history of incorporating community engagement into the academic experiences of their students, faculty, and staff campus-wide. There is even an endowed center, the Jan and Bud Richter Center for Community Engagement and Service-Learning. For the past two years the campus as a whole has exceeded one million service hours annually in the community. (Fresno State, 2012). The university has designated two courses, "ASL 4" and "Sign Language for Professionals" as approved service-learning courses, which means students are required to do a minimum of 20 hours of service activities in the community.

Specifically, they are asked to work with community-based organizations (CBO) such as deaf agencies, clubs, churches, or schools. There are numerous reflection activities throughout the semester associated with their service-learning assignments and they typically are required to write a reflective summary of their experiences. In addition, students must write a letter of appreciation to the CBO and provide a copy to their professor. Many students have reported positive experiences in spite of their initial feelings of trepidation at meeting and communicating with Deaf people.

THE DEAF EDUCATION PERSONNEL PREPARATION PROGRAM

In 2008, the Fresno State Deaf Education program was awarded an $800,000 personnel preparation grant from the Office of Special Education Programs (OSEP Grant #H325080408) at the U.S. Department of Education. While the main purpose of the grant, which we gave the acronym DEPP, was to provide training and stipends to twenty scholars who met program admissions standards, so that they would receive a teaching credential in California, it also sought to increase cultural awareness, skills, and knowledge, not only for the Deaf community and ASL but also for the increasing diversity of students from various ethnic and cultural backgrounds that is particularly endemic to western states. Another objective was to provide retention and recruiting activities for scholars to help them get a better understanding of the profession and become ambassadors for deaf education by encouraging other students to consider a career in this field. This grant is now nearing completion and has provided teaching certification to twenty scholars.

Program Evaluation

One of the requirements of the grant, like all current Federal grantees, is to evaluate effectiveness in meeting the stated goals and objectives. Obviously, the grant met its main goal of training twenty new qualified teachers of the deaf in a profession that is desperately in need of more teachers. We evaluated other factors besides program completion including recruiting, retention, student performance on state and federally mandated teacher skill assessments, research skills of scholars, attainment of ASL skills, employment as teachers (the Federal government has a service requirement for scholars of two years in special education settings per year of support), and dissemination of program results via presentations and publication.

Results for attainment of ASL Skills and Attitudes

While we have successfully met the other objectives, for the purpose of this publication, we will focus on ASL skills and attitude attainment in relation to American Council on the Teaching of Foreign Languages (ACTFL) standards for language acquisition embedded within the five Cs (communication, cultures, connections, comparisons, and communities). Quantitative results of a pre/post survey of eight DEPP students' self-perceptions are reported in fourteen areas of ASL grammatical features identified by the North Carolina America Sign Language Teachers Association (NCASLTA) (table 1).

Results for Student Retention

After being awarded the DEPP grant, Fresno State has developed a series of compulsory one-unit retention courses; to date, there have been seven courses offered. In terms of retention, the courses have provided mentoring with some of our students of diverse and at-risk backgrounds. It has also provided a safe forum for discussing different issues such as prejudice, family problems, school issues, and challenges facing deaf educators. For each of the retention courses students learning activities are designed around the ACTFL standards for the five Cs. The results of a qualitative inquiry into these experiences is reported below.

RESEARCH OVERVIEW

This is a mixed-methods design using multiple data collection approaches and is the first of multiple studies to explore the impact of the Deaf Education Personnel Preparation Project (DEPP). As part of the research protocols, potential risks associated with participation in the study were outlined, and the university and individuals participating gave consent prior to participation and data collection. The present study includes quantitative responses of eight DEPP students of self-perceptions of their ASL skills. Qualitative data was gathered in a random sample from each of the required one-unit retention courses. The research questions were developed to provide in-depth descriptive information to allow the researchers a greater understanding of the impact of the DEPP grant project in relation to ACTFL standards. Following are the specific research questions used to achieve the general purposes of this study:

1. What is the perception of the DEPP scholars of their signing skills?
2. What is the impact of the one-unit courses that DEPP scholars are required to enroll in each semester in relation to ACTFL standards?
3. What do the DEPP scholars cite as motivational factors to participate in the project?

As a condition of the DEPP grant for the scholars, participation is required in topic courses. Ultimately, the goals for this paper are to explore how the curriculum changes within a university deaf education program combined with a DEPP federal grant can influence the linguistic and cultural knowledge of students wanting to become deaf educators.

GRANT SUMMARY

At the time of this publication $268,830 has been provided to thirty-three DEPP scholars. A total of eleven students have earned a bachelors and/or a masters degree in deaf education. As of the end of our third year, there is a statistically significant placement rate in Deaf and hard of hearing classrooms. Four DEPP scholars are teaching Deaf children full-time in a special day class with an emphasis on American Sign Language; three are serving as itinerant teachers working with hard of hearing children from birth to high school; one is teaching full time in a special day class with an emphasis on oral education; one is teaching 51% of their time in a special day class and teaching American Sign Language at the local high school the remainder of the time; and one is teaching full time at a residential school for the Deaf in outside of California; one student is no longer part of the DEPP program and is pursuing their degree in another field due to poor performance as it relates to our standards of ASL fluency. Over 90% of these eleven DEPP graduates have demonstrated fluency by achieving a score of three out of five on the NCASLTA proficiency assessment. There are currently nineteen DEPP students in the program who have passed the California Subject Examination for Teachers (CSET) in either the Multiple Subjects (elementary) or Single Subject (secondary) area.

QUANTITATIVE FINDINGS

Quantitative data was gathered from DEPP performance measures and survey data collected from students. The ASL attitudes survey was piloted on 131 ASL students from seven colleges and universities; 101 of the survey responses were completed. The instrument was revised to a twenty-eight-item survey with a Cronbach's alpha of .91 indicating validity and reliability. Reported in this study are the results of eight DEPP scholars who completed a pre-survey, participated in a cultural immersion topics course, and then completed the post five-point likert scale survey.

The survey instrument focused on fourteen areas of ASL grammatical competence, as related to the North Carolina America Sign Language Teachers Association (NCASLTA). In each of the fourteen questions, the pre/post survey data indicated that students self perceptions of their signing skills improved. (Statistical significance of $p<.05$ was found on two of the fourteen questions using the Wilcoxon signed ranks test.) However, the mean decreased on each of the questions showing that students were more likely to strongly agree or agree to each of the survey questions after their participation in the retention course. Outlined below (Figure 1) are the results of pre/post self reported ASL grammatical skills involving the use of body shifts to compare and contrast different things; the use of indexing and space to locate and refer to people or places not present; the use of eye gaze as a grammatical marker; the use of facial expression and sign movement modification to show degree, size, and manner; the use of sign verb movement for directionality for location and pronoun incorporation.

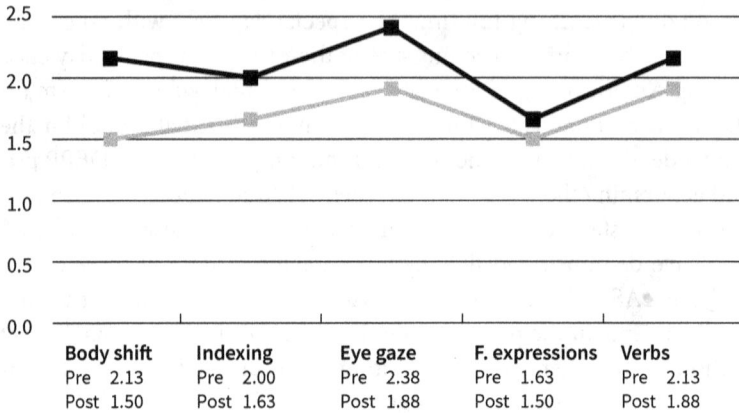

Figure 1. Pre-/post- self reported ASL grammatical skills. ■ Pre; ▨ Post.

Each of the eight DEPP students are currently enrolled in or have completed ASL four. Each question showed an increase in the pre/post survey results. Below are grammatical spatial features (Figure 2) that include:

- "I am able to describe the size, shape and location of an object"
- "I use classifiers to describe actions of people and how something is used or functions."
- "I use negation effectively."
- "I use repeated sign verb movement for repeated action."
- "I use repetition of sign noun movements and vertical and horizontal sweep for plurals."

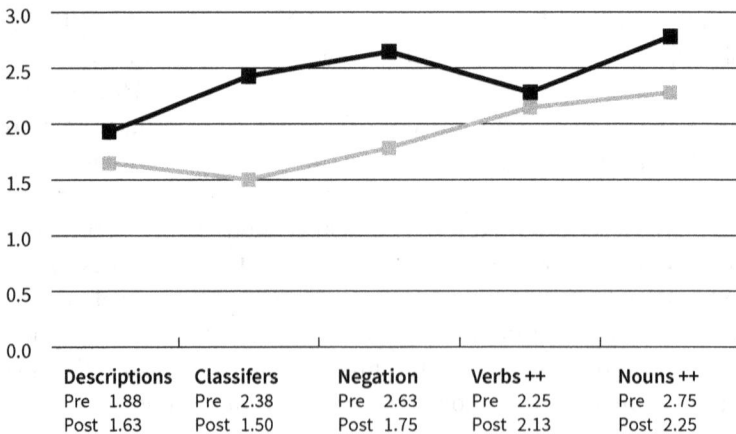

Figure 2. Pre-/post- self reported ASL grammatical spatial features. ■ Pre; ▨ Post.

There was a 2:1 ratio of students to Deaf language mentors at the cultural immersion weekend. This allowed each mentor to facilitate language production (Figure 3) and cultural exposure and interaction for the following:

- "I use number incorporation for people, age, and time."
- "I use listing on my non-dominant hand and body shifts for connecting a story line or ideas."
- "I use sign word order for topic comment and object-subject-verb."
- "I use non-manual expressions in my conversations."

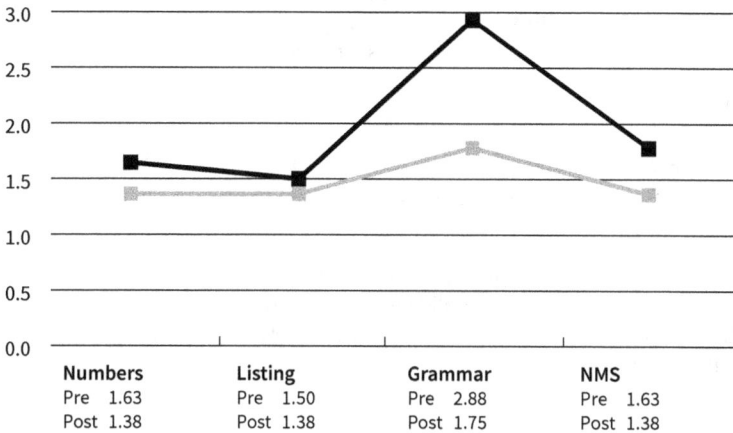

	Numbers	Listing	Grammar	NMS
Pre	1.63	1.50	2.88	1.63
Post	1.38	1.38	1.75	1.38

Figure 3. Pre-/post- self reported ASL language production skills. ■ Pre; ▨ Post.

Each of the eight DEPP scholars was linguistically challenged while interacting with the Deaf language mentors and commented on their increased comprehension and communication skills. Below are the qualitative findings of students from the one-unit retention courses they are required to take each semester.

QUALITATIVE FINDINGS

In an effort to appropriately characterize the qualitative data from each DEPP scholars' comments, ACTFL standards were used to develop a coding rubric. The researchers used the five Cs (communication, cultures, connections, comparisons, and communities) as themes to code and analyzed the data. Data was randomly selected from each of the one-unit retention courses and statements were studied then identified as a specific theme or themes. After one researcher completed the coding of statements and theme identification, a second researcher repeated the process. When discrepancies arose, the researchers dialogued by email or video-phone until there was a resolution.

Communication

All second language learners are initially challenged to express themselves
effectively in their L2. Research shows that frequent exposure and interaction with native L1 users increases the language competences by the second
language learner. One student commented on the immersion one-unit class
indicating that it

> [G]reatly increased my signing skills and confidence in my signing. I feel a
> lot more comfortable signing with Deaf adults and hearing signers that are
> more advanced than me. I also feel that the weekend has given me more
> personal experience with the Deaf community values, rather than purely
> classroom lecture information. I will cherish the connections and friendship
> I made this weekend for the rest of my life.

Clearly this individual effectively engaged in an ongoing dialogue about
a variety of topics. Another student indicated that the experience was

> [L]ife changing. It was more than I could have ever expected. It was a
> wonderful experience. Meeting and interacting with Deaf individuals and
> my peers made me feel more confident and comfortable with my signing
> skill. The experience really helped me grow into a better signer and I would
> definitely do it again.

Culture

Understanding and respecting the collectivist nature of Deaf culture is
invaluable for a deaf educator. One student commented that their experience in a one unit retention course "Helped me learn new vocabulary,
allowed me to participate in deaf cultural events, and improved my ASL fluency." As indicated by this student, culture and language are inseparable in
the Deaf community.

Connections

An important component of the ACTFL standards is for second language learning to occur in environments that allow individuals to have an
opportunity to connect content knowledge and language. Another student
attended the state wide CalEd conference indicated that they gained insights
about empowering deaf or hard of hearing students:

> I learned that one of the difficulties these individuals face during this transi-
> tion is their reading levels. On average, deaf individuals have reading levels
> that are lower than what is age appropriate…It concerns me that if students'
> education is only focused on life skills, we send the message that they will
> not go to college and thus they do not need preparation in that area.

Content knowledge shared by current practitioners allowed this student who was taking a one unit course on building a learning community to identify the importance of connections:

> After participating in this meeting, I became very motivated and excited for the semester. This is my second semester in the deaf education graduate program and I have felt very disconnected from the department because of all of the credential courses that have been consuming my time. At this meeting, I learned about all of the things that we will be able to participate in and get reconnected to the Deaf community and meet professionals that are currently working in the field.

Comparison

Deaf educators must be able to provide appropriate language modeling for their students. The ability to provide comparisons using demonstrative language in a way that allows for comprehension of subject matter is challenging for many hearing deaf educators. A student who took "professional roles in deaf education," a one unit course stated that:

> The information presented is important because the teachers of the deaf are able to teach language in context. Additionally, just because a student is deaf does not mean they are incapable, they should be taught skills to become independent. All professionals in deaf education should be striving for the same goals, encouraging and expecting their students to do well." This was the students reflection after a two hour observation of a deaf education preschool classroom.

Communities

Hearing students are frequently counseled to "get involved in the Deaf community." One student reported on their activities attending a meeting with one of the local school districts where they interacted with D/HH teachers and administrators. "The importance of building a rapport with the school and the families that itinerate work with is critical. The relationship built between the iterant and their students is often very important. The itinerant serves as a teacher and an advocate." The deaf education curriculum at Fresno State requires service-learning hours which is an invaluable tool that provides students an opportunity to apply classroom concepts in real world applications.

LIMITATIONS

A limitation of this study is the sample size of the population; only eight students completed the pre- and post- survey instrument. Ideally, each of the eight students providing quantitative data would have completed the SLPI that would have allowed the researchers to correlate perceived grammatical

Variable	Pre Mean (SD)	Post Mean (SD)	P-value
I use body shifts to compare and contrast different things.	2.13 (.835)	1.50 (.535)	.414
I use indexing and space to locate and refer to people or places not present.	2.00 (.962)	1.63 (.518)	.414
I use eye gaze as a grammatical marker.	2.38 (1.061)	1.88 (.991)	.102
I use facial expression and sign movement modification to show degree, size, and manner.	1.63 (.518)	1.50 (.535)	.567
I use sign verb movement for directionality for location and pronoun incorporation.	2.13 (.991)	1.88 (.835)	.705
I am able to describe the size, shape and location of an object.	1.88 (3.54)	1.63 (.518)	.317
I use classifiers to describe actions of people and how something is used or functions.	2.38 (1.061)	1.50 (.535)	.66
I use negation effectively.	2.63 (1.061	1.75 (.707)	.038
I use repeated sign verb movement for repeated action.	2.25 (1.035)	2.13 (1.126)	.564
I use repetition of sign noun movements and vertical and horizontal sweep for plurals.	2.75 (1.035)	2.25 (1.035)	.180
I use number incorporation for people, age, and time.	1.63 (.744)	1.38 (.518)	.414
I use listing on my non-dominant hand and body shifts for connecting a story line or ideas.	1.50 (.535)	1.38 (.518)	.564
I use sign word order for topic comment and object-subject-verb.	2.88 (1.356)	1.75 (.707)	.037
I use non-manual expressions in my conversations.	1.63 (.518)	1.38 (.518)	.705

Table 1. Results of DEPP scholar (n = 8) pre-, course exposure, and post- survey of self-perceptions of language learning and skill improvement.

skills in ASL and actual results provided by independent evaluators such as the NCASLTA. The DEPP grant also required professional development, mentoring, service-learning hours, and mandatory tutoring with Deaf language models. Each of the language models are native ASL signers and were selected by faculty or suggested to faculty my Deaf community leaders. While the Deaf language models are an invaluable component of the success of each DEPP student, that data is not reported in this paper and would have been an additional method of triangulating the data.

CONCLUSION

As Michael Fullan, a noted expert on educational change stated, changing an educational culture or a set of behaviors passed down over generations is challenging. He wrote that one of the best places to begin is in teacher education programs and especially with the faculty at these programs. As the faculty go, so do the teacher candidates (Fullan, 1993). The faculty at Fresno State are committed to the improvement of the ASL skills and development as allies of Deaf community in our teacher candidates. Even in the face of the current resurgence of audism by the medical and oral/auditory professions, the belief is there that we can and will overcome the lingering effects and reputation of the past as "Good teachers, lousy ASL."

REFERENCES

ACTFL, American Council on Teaching of Foriegn Language. (2006). *Standards for foreign language learning in the 21st century.* Lawrence, KS: Allen Press.

ASLTA. (2011). *History of the American Sign Language Teachers Association.* Retrieved from http://www.aslta.org/node/185.

Babbidge, H. (1965). *Education of the Deaf in the United States: Report of the Advisory Committee on Education of the Deaf.* US Government Printing Office, Washington, DC.

Baynton, D. C. (1996). *Forbidden signs: American culture and the campaign against sign language.* Chicago: University of Chicago Press.

Council on the Education of the Deaf (2003). *Standards for Programs Preparing Teachers of Students Who Are Deaf or Hard of Hearing.* Retrieved April 10, 2012 http://www.deafed.net/activities/ManualOneRevised.htm.

Fullan, M. (1993). *Change forces: Probing the depths of educational reform.* Levittown, PA: Falmer Press.

Jones, T. W., & Ewing, K. M. (2002). An Analysis of Teacher Preparation in Deaf Education: Programs Approved by the Council on Education of the Deaf. *American Annals of the Deaf,* 147(5), 71–78.

Ladd, P., Gulliver, M., & Batterbury, S. (2003). Reassessing minority language empowerment from a Deaf perspective: The other 32 languages. *Deaf Worlds,* 19(2), 6–32.

Lane, Harlan L., Hoffmeister, Robert, & Bahan, Benjamin J. (1996). *A journey into the DEAF-WORLD.* San Diego, Calif.: DawnSignPress.

Nover, S. (1995). Politics and language: American Sign Language and English in deaf education. In C. Lucas (ed.), *Sociolinguistics in deaf communities* (pp. 109–163): Gallaudet University Press.

Simms, L., & Thumann, H. (2007). In search of a new, linguistically and culturally sensitive paradigm in deaf education. *American Annals of the Deaf,* 152(3), 302.

Van Cleve, John V. (1993). *Deaf history unveiled: Interpretations from the new scholarship.* Washington, D.C.: Gallaudet University Press.

Service Learning: Deaf Studies in the Community

SHERYL B. COOPER, PH.D. AND JODY H. CRIPPS, PH.D.

THIS PAPER DISCUSSES THE FOUNDATIONS OF SERVICE LEARNING IN Deaf Studies on college campuses. Deaf Studies includes the study of deaf people, signed language and the cultural behaviors and idiosyncrasies of this population and those affiliated with them through the considerations of sociological, anthropological, and ethnographic perspectives (Marschark & Humphries, 2010). Beginning with the fundamental concept of learning through civic engagement, the authors review the literature and note that some research exists regarding service learning in deaf-related fields such as interpreting and deaf education. However, there is a lack of research and implementation in the specific area of service learning in Deaf Studies.

This paper will introduce a Deaf Studies program with a service learning component. The university's mission statement encourages community involvement, identifying itself as a metropolitan institution serving a diverse population through economic development, social progress, and community and business outreach. This has led to institutional support for civic engagement in the form of service learning, a teaching method that engages the community. Service learning in Deaf Studies has led to strong reciprocal partnerships with a variety of community partners, and an increase in student enthusiasm for this type of learning. This process has included four categories of challenges that are discussed along with suggested solutions. As part of the overall look at service learning in Deaf Studies, a research study was conducted to determine the students' attitudinal changes while taking this course, with a goal of identifying ways to improve the quality of the course. The Deaf Studies' service learning course maintains the goals of involving students in reciprocal civic engagement experiences by preparing them to become active global citizens (Jacoby and Associates, 2009) and teaching them to advocate together with deaf people who use American Sign Language (ASL).

CIVIC ENGAGEMENT AND SERVICE-LEARNING IN ACADEMIC SETTINGS

Responding to society's most pressing issues and preparing graduates for responsible citizenship has always been a core goal of American colleges and universities. In the twenty-first century, a concept called "civic engagement" was introduced to the academic environment that changed the ways Americans have involved themselves in civic and political activities (Jacoby, 2009). During that time, Americans joined organizations and associations and sent donations to service groups run by professionals. Over the past few decades, the American style of responsible citizenship has changed from membership to advocacy (Skocpol, 1999). More recently, experts in higher education have noted that colleges and universities were investing innovative efforts to bolster the civic services and duties of their institutions (Gibson, 2006). Civic engagement has been defined as

> "acting upon a heightened sense of responsibility to one's communities. This includes a wide range of activities, including developing civic sensitivity, participation in building civil society, and benefiting the common good. [It] encompasses notions of global citizenship and interdependence. Through civic engagement, individuals — as citizens of their communities, their nations, and the world — are empowered as agents of positive social change for a more democratic world" (Coalition for Civic Engagement and Leadership, 2005, as cited in Jacoby, 2009, p. 9).

The university highlighted in this paper is one of many American universities promoting strong relationships between the university and the community. Programs and courses in the university utilizing a philosophy of civic engagement foster opportunities to enrich the academic and life experiences of students while enriching the quality of the community. Utilizing a variety of supports from the university, students in the Deaf Studies program have made significant contributions to their local, national, and global communities while enhancing their own academic experiences and lives and developing their own understanding of, and commitments to, social welfare.

Underlying the civic engagement movement, an innovative type of teaching called service learning has been developed to provide a specific link between colleges and the needs of the community (McEwen, 1996). In the spirit of civic engagement, Jacoby (1996) defined service learning as

"... a form of experiential education in which students engage in activities that address human and community needs together with structured opportunities intentionally designed to promote student learning and development. Reflection and reciprocity are key concepts of [S]ervice-[L]earning" (p. 5).

Reflection targets what students learn about the social issues behind the needs of the community. It includes the in-depth understanding of the historical, sociological, cultural, economic, and political issues that need to be addressed. The second concept, reciprocity, involves the learning process for the service providers (e.g., students and employers) and the person or group being served (e.g., individual community members). In this case, students, community partners, and community members learn from each other to develop relationships where everyone is expected to change as a result of the learning process involved (Jacoby, 1996; Karasik, 1993; Kendall, 1990).

Berman (2006) identifies many benefits to utilizing service learning as a method of teaching and learning. As a result of students' responsible independent actions, they have the opportunity to increase their levels of self-confidence and self-esteem. The community experience helps students to open up to new people and new experiences, and allows students the opportunity to grow as communicators, leaders, and teammates. From their community experiences, students are able to develop an awareness and acceptance of others from different ethnic, national, and economic backgrounds. These hands-on experiences help students to become more empathetic and less judgmental, and enable them to accept their own locus of control, becoming less likely to blame other or make excuses for shortcomings. Overall, service learning opportunities enable students to grow through their experiences (Berman, 2006).

The authors believe that service learning is, in fact, an excellent match for education in the field of Deaf Studies. Related fields have already shown the efficacy of implementing service learning in their curricula. From the perspective of educating sign language interpreters, Monikowski and Peterson (2005) point out that academia often creates a chasm between the classroom experience and cultural, experiential, and linguistic immersion into the deaf community. To that end, Shaw and Roberson (2009) theorized that Interpreter Education programs would be strengthened and students would receive a more comprehensive education through collaborative learning through immersion in the deaf community. Similarly, Shaw and Jolley (2007) purported that students in Interpreter Education programs benefit from service learning projects working with the deafblind community. Likewise, Hansmann and colleagues (Hansmann, Saladin, & Quintero, 2011; Hansmann, Saladin, Shefcik, & Garza-Gutierrez, 2009) showed the value of

using service learning as part of a capstone experience in an undergraduate
Deaf Rehabilitation program. Service learning in the field of ASL instruction is discussed in Reading and Padgett (2011) and Reading and Carlstrand
(2007). In these articles, service learning is viewed as an opportunity for students to learn from deaf signers. However, there is no known research on
service learning in the Deaf Studies field. For this reason, further investigation is needed.

Deaf Studies students will ultimately pursue careers in a variety of disciplines such as teaching, counseling, social work, rehabilitation, and research,
requiring knowledge of deaf-related topics. Careers in any of the above fields
will require the ability to integrate knowledge of the experiences of deaf people with the ability to explain it to those unfamiliar with ASL and the cultural
aspects of the deaf community. Professionals and future professionals in any
discipline working with the deaf community often find themselves not only
providing services to the consumers they serve, but educating their family,
friends, and colleagues about the unique needs of the deaf community. This
need for multi-directional learning and teaching methods requires students
of Deaf Studies to learn from both faculty and individuals in the deaf community. Simultaneously, deaf individuals in the community can learn from
Deaf Studies students while participating in a variety of community programs (see Cripps & Cooper, 2012). This cycle provides an insightful starting
point for students of Deaf Studies to ameliorate social welfare issues through
hands-on action with this microcosm of American society.

SERVICE-LEARNING IN DEAF STUDIES

The university discussed here is privileged to be one of the few universities
in the United States offering a Bachelor's degree in Deaf Studies. In this role,
the program attempts to meet the needs of the students, while implementing the mission of the university to serve the community. The faculty of the
Deaf Studies program recognized strong correlations between the university's mission and the program's goals. As the program aged, the objectives
matured, and the need to implement opportunities for civic engagement
also became more relevant. Preliminary lessons learned from service learning experiences provide the foundation for ongoing curricular revisions that
will take the program forward in new directions.

OBJECTIVES AND PHILOSOPHY

Several goals for implementing a service learning course in the Deaf Studies program were developed. The original goal was for students to enhance

their signed language skills through personal interactions with deaf people. This would be achieved by exposing students to deaf people in the community, allowing them to develop relationships that facilitated meaningful conversations, and encouraging improvement in signed language skills through ongoing feedback from the community members. A second goal was to develop students' intercultural sensitivity and competence. It was anticipated that the overall experience would enable students to develop an interactive and trusting relationship with individual members of the community and dispel the myths, negative perceptions, and inaccurate stereotypes (Dunlop & Webster, 2009) about signed languages and deaf people while enabling students to enhance their communication skills. The faculty saw potential for the enhancement of students' awareness about deaf people and their lives through real-time exposure and interaction. Students could apply cultural concepts learned in the classroom to their on-site experiences, and subsequently engage in personal in-depth reflection about deaf people in American society.

The third goal for specifically selecting the service learning format was to incorporate signed language and deaf-related educational objectives with meaningful service to the community, including a dual focus on academic learning and authentic volunteer projects. It was expected that these projects, which were based on the academic learning from the classroom, would strengthen students' thinking skills in developing empathy, personal ethics, and the habit of advocating for and within the community. Among other benefits, it was anticipated that service learning would assist students in understanding their connectedness to the role of service provider through hands-on experience (Berman, 2006). The "flip side" of this benefit would be for individuals in the deaf community, who would receive services such as interpretation of the contexts of complicated written and telephone communication that have traditionally been missing in the provision of any type of services to deaf people. While this might only be the first step in a series leading to independence, individualized support such as the plan outlined above can provide a critical foundation for the understanding of all service-delivery systems. After implementing the actions required to achieve these goals, the Deaf Studies students were predicted to become advocates for deaf people who sign.

HISTORY AND STRUCTURE OF
SERVICE LEARNING IN DEAF STUDIES

Implementing a new type of learning experience is a long and dynamic process, as faculty become aware of the strengths and weaknesses of a new pedagogy. Service learning in Deaf Studies at a Mid-Atlantic university has undergone tremendous change since its initial implementation in 1992. In the 1990s, Deaf Studies was an individualized, student-designed Interdisciplinary Studies major. One course most students included in their self-designed programs was an Independent Study, designed to provide them with a "hands-on" experience volunteering for agencies serving deaf people. In 2000, Deaf Studies became an approved major at the university. At that time, the loosely-structured independent study described above became a formalized internship course.

Over the years in the program, the concept of service learning spread across the university's campus, and the Deaf Studies program coordinator realized that the internship experience was very similar to service learning although not labeled as such. As the program matured, the faculty noticed the need for a "pre-internship" experience to precede the capstone internship experience, so that students' first immersion experience in the Deaf community was not also their last. A formally structured service learning course was an area lacking in the Deaf Studies program.

In 2008, the Deaf Studies faculty proposed two courses utilizing the service learning format as a way to (1) expand and strengthen the Deaf Studies program, (2) provide students with a structured opportunity to bridge the gap between their academic learning and their knowledge of the community, and (3) develop personal relationships with deaf people and their community which would lead to greater comfort in future interactions. Two service learning courses, entitled "Social Services in the Deaf Community" and "service learning in Deaf Studies" were added to the Deaf Studies curriculum. The differences between these courses include the structure of the course and the area of focus. The "service learning in Deaf Studies" course was designed as "independent study"-style course where individual Deaf Studies students have the opportunity to select off-campus sites that match their career interests.

For example, a student interested in working with legislation for deaf people would be placed in Governor's Office of Deaf and Hard of Hearing, and a student planning on a career in social work might be placed in a community rehabilitation program. This course requires 90 hours on-site in an agency serving deaf individuals under the supervision of a qualified supervisor, with periodic meetings with the instructor and no classroom component. In addition to this, each student keeps a journal documenting insights and reflections and obtains regular feedback from the professor.

A more structured and traditional approach was developed with the "Social Services in the Deaf Community" course. Unlike the aforementioned course, this course utilizes a pedagogical classroom setting with up to 40 students. The academic component of this course includes lectures and activities focusing on a variety of social welfare issues, followed by the opportunity to apply these concepts on-site at a variety of non-profit and governmental agencies. In 2008, 2009, and 2010, students were placed in these agencies, working together in pairs, for 15 hours during a 15-week semester. Table 1 provides a list of the community partners. Pairs of students were placed in one of two types of social service agencies: deaf-related sites where they would experience working with deaf people first-hand, or a non-deaf-related agency with little to no knowledge or awareness about deaf people and their needs. This was necessary due to the limited number of agencies serving deaf people who were willing to accept students for this short-term project.

At the sites without dedicated programs for deaf people, students had the opportunity to educate staff members about deaf people and their needs (i.e., creating a signed language-friendly environment, or teaching signed language to staff and consumers). Becoming advocates for signed language, many students found themselves teaching staff members and consumers beginning ASL. However, students recognized that their ASL lessons were rudimentary and they should refer staff members to take ASL courses in college and universities and to interact with deaf people who sign in order to advance their signing skills.

Deaf-Related Agencies	Non-Deaf-Related Agencies
• Humanim	• County Department of Social Services
• Governor's Office of the Deaf and Hard of Hearing	• Volunteer Fire Department
• Deaf Shalom Zone	• County Health Department
• Deaf AIDS Project	• Boys & Girls Club
• Deaf Services	• Hearts & Ears
• Community Support Services for the Deaf	• University Disability Support Services
• Deafblind Camp	• ARC
• People Encouraging People	• Genesis
	• Movable Feast
	• Talmar, Inc.

Table 1: Agencies engaged in the "Social Service in the Deaf Community" course

CURRICULUM REVISIONS

As part of an ongoing process, "Social Services in the Deaf Community" is constantly being revised to improve the quality of the course. Areas such as placement arrangements and sites have been reviewed every semester for effectiveness and efficiency. No textbooks could be found that integrated information regarding provision of social services to the deaf community. A variety of techniques were tried, beginning with the use of a general textbook on social welfare issues (Zastrow, 2008) supplemented with lectures by the instructor on the impact of these issues on the deaf community. More recently, another technique was tried, using a teacher-made packet of articles laying the foundations for each social welfare issue and providing articles showing the impact on the deaf community.

Year	Placement	Data
2008	Pairs of students placed in sixteen agencies: eight provide service to deaf, eight provide service to hearing (approx.)	None collected
2009	Pairs of students placed in sixteen agencies: eight provide service to deaf, eight provide service to hearing (approx.)	None collected
2010	Pairs of students placed in sixteen agencies: eight provide service to deaf, eight provide service to hearing (approx.)	Pre- and post- service learning survey completed by students. Feedback obtained from community partners
2011	Students spend seven weeks providing direct services to deaf consumers within one agency; seven weeks preparing first responders	Pre- and post- service learning survey completed by students and community partners

Table 2: Revisions made to "Social Services in the Deaf Community" course design

Table 2 shows the site and data collection revisions that have been made since Fall 2008. It compares certain aspects of course implementation: the year, the off-campus placement model, and the type of data collected for research purposes. The first column indicates the year that the course was undertaken. The second column shows the evolving structure of the placement arrangements. There were several reasons for the change in placement structure between 2010 and 2011. One reason for the initial dichotomy of placements was the reality that it was difficult to locate enough agencies providing specialized social services to the deaf community who were willing to do the extra work to take on student volunteers. A decision was made to utilize some agencies without specialized services for deaf people since there were other benefits of these sites. Students would still have the opportunities to learn about organizational structure of social service agencies, budgeting, staffing, and the process of service provision.

The decision to utilize agencies without specialized services for deaf people resulted in opportunities to spread deaf/signed language awareness to a new group of agencies with the goal of developing open-minded attitudes toward deaf people and the use of signed language. This initiated the multi-directional goal of providing opportunities for students to learn from their agencies, and for the agency staff members to learn from the students. This could be a focus for fruitful future investigation.

In Fall 2011, the student placement model was changed from one 15-hour experience during the second half of the semester to two 10-hour placements comprising the first and second halves of the semester. During the first half, students provided volunteer social welfare-type services to deaf people in the community and during the second half, students were assigned to agencies where they were expected to assess the needs of the agency regarding Deaf Awareness, provide training in this area, and assess the effectiveness of the training. The reason for the change to this format was to allow all students to have opportunities to learn about (1) the type of needs of members of the deaf community, and (2) the service-delivery system for provision of services to deaf people, and subsequently to have the opportunity to teach about deaf people and signed language, rather than some students having one experience, and other students having a different experience.

The third column shows that data was collected regarding students' perceptions of the impact of service learning in 2010 and 2011. Students completed the same questionnaire before and after their service learning experiences, which sought evidence of any change in their attitudes toward service learning. Anecdotal feedback was also collected from the supervisors representing the community partners regarding the students' contributions and learning experiences. Both the data from the students and the feedback from the supervisors supported the expectation that the service learning experiences were worthwhile and beneficial to all constituencies involved. The implementation of service learning in Deaf Studies is an area ripe for investigation.

CURRENT SERVICE-LEARNING
INVESTIGATIONS IN DEAF STUDIES

At the present time, the authors are engaged in several research projects in this area. One project involves the analysis of meeting the challenges of implementing service learning in a Deaf Studies program. Another project involves analyzing the process of reciprocity in service learning in Deaf Studies. Finally, a third project involves collecting data to investigate if service learning in Deaf Studies promotes altruistic behaviors and attitudes with charitable and/or social justice perspectives among students.

Meeting the Challenges of Service Learning

Cripps and Cooper (2012) acknowledge that there are challenges for all new service learning courses, as well as issues specific to service learning in the field of Deaf Studies. Cripps and Cooper provide suggestions for other Deaf Studies programs to address the four general challenges associated with the pedagogy of service learning, which are:

1. increased need for institutional support
2. significant time required to learn new pedagogy
3. increased logistical complexity of incorporating partners into the teaching process
4. anxiety associated with less control over curriculum (Morton, 1996).

Because service learning is new to the field of Deaf Studies, some unique and additional challenges were anticipated. Students entering this course in its first semester were unprepared for specific scheduling time and transportation needs for off-campus responsibilities. Since this was the first time the course was offered, there was no student pipeline of information to prepare them psychologically. Also, no textbooks could be found specifically designed to address the social welfare needs of deaf people who sign. These challenges were met by adding verbiage to the university's catalog explaining the off-campus component, and by developing a packet of articles for the students to purchase at the university bookstore.

To meet the challenge of obtaining institutional support, the faculty member teaching this class participated in a year-long on-campus program which assisted faculty incorporating service learning into their courses, and to provide resources including discussion opportunities, guest speakers for service learning workshops, ideas, formats, rubrics, a bibliography of suggested readings, and templates for faculty new to service learning. These supports allowed for maintaining a high level of faculty motivation to ensure the success of service learning experiences. The faculty member was also able to obtain grant money from the university to pay for bus transportation for field trips during the semester. The faculty support program was also able to provide standardized instruments to measure change in attitudes based on service learning experiences, and assistance with data entry and analysis. All of these resources supported the university's emphasis on civic engagement as part of its larger mission.

Revising a course from didactic teaching to service learning requires an investment of faculty time for planning and logistics. Through all stages of the conceptualizing and implementation, the faculty member must balance the learning and service objectives, integrating the goal of developing students' critical thinking skills into the curriculum (Morton, 1996). The initial development of materials required a significant investment of time, but tasks were made easier by adapting templates for various documents, and borrowing thought questions for student journals from existing materials on service learning. As mentioned previously, the faculty member created a course packet of readings to be used as a textbook, which included the most relevant and seminal articles as required student readings.

The faculty member contacted sites already in use as internship sites to establish off-campus placements. When keeping track of each student's placement and service project became time-consuming and logistically complex, a new placement design was created with one agency as the sole point of contact. It became obvious that students who had more personal contact with deaf consumers were considered to have richer experiences. To provide equally rich deaf-related experiences for all students, and limit the amount of administrative time needed to create placements, the faculty member worked with one social service agency to identify individuals and families with social service needs. Using a single agency to match students with local deaf consumers significantly reduced the amount of time needed to arrange the logistical complexity of this course and alleviated the concern from community partners wanting more guidance regarding students' duties and projects.

Implementing a new course is bound to produce anxiety for the faculty member. Challenges include creating a rubric for reflective journals focusing on growth and reflection, and predicting and attempting to allay student concerns. To address student questions regarding the service learning process, the faculty member provided explanations in the syllabus and presentations to the class early in the semester about the definition and goals of service learning. The faculty member also included explanatory text in the university catalog course. Assignments, rubrics, and fictitious examples were posted on the course's website, which alleviated much anxiety for the students. The faculty member utilized class time to explain in detail the objectives and expectations of this type of course, and worked with students both in- and out-of-class to provide emotional support for their anxieties about working in the deaf community. Because much of the actual learning in service learning takes place outside of the classroom, faculty members often feel a loss of control of student learning. Faculty members depend heavily on student journals to learn about students' insightful moments. Rubrics were developed to provide guidance for students and to make measurement of student progress clear.

When the faculty member does not have control of what the students are doing on their sites, and what instruction or supervision is provided off-campus, they experience a loss of control. When students were placed with many different organizations, the faculty member could not check up on each site regularly. The revised course design utilizing one coordinating organization reduced stress for the faculty member by easing administrative needs. A sense of trust was accomplished through regular meetings, emails, and phone calls, sometimes involving a series of people. With most work taking place off-campus, there is the freedom for some students to falsify paperwork by fabricating journal entries or adjusting time sheets, taking advantage of the independence of the service learning experience. The faculty member must carefully review paperwork for peculiarities indicative of falsification, stay in regular contact with the community partners, and take punitive measures if needed.

Reciprocity in Service Learning
Cripps and Cooper (2012) described how the service learning partnership involves several individuals and organizations working together toward common goals. University representatives (including faculty, administration, and students), rehabilitation agencies, and members of the deaf community must all be committed to the success of the program, and be willing to work together. Figure 1 describes the relationships among the constituencies involved, and ongoing communication is critical.

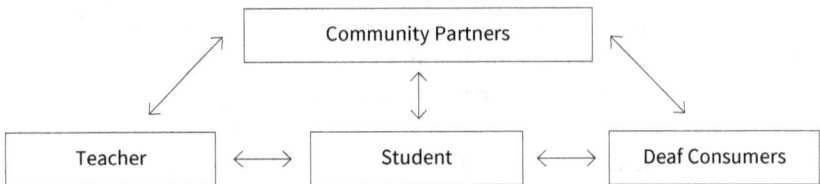

Figure 1: Model of the Student-Centered Service Learning

The faculty member begins by contacting community partners to identify appropriate placements while students provide input to the faculty member regarding their time and geographical preferences. After the placements are made, the faculty member meets with the students in class weekly to check on progress and to discuss reflections on their experiences. The faculty member coordinates all paperwork. The faculty member contacts the community partner regularly to keep abreast of any issues that might come up regarding the overall experience.

Community partners work closely with the faculty member to design experiences that will be beneficial to the agency, the consumers, and the students. They identify needs of the consumers, communicate these needs to the students, provide guidance and supervision to the students, and report back to the faculty member regarding progress and any concerns which might arise. Additionally, community partners check in regularly with the consumers to ensure that the service learning experiences are going well for them.

Deaf consumers receive explanations from the community partner about the service learning project, and then receive services from the students. In most situations, as relationships develop, the consumers begin to provide informal feedback to the students on their signed language communication skills. Finally, the students play a central role in this reciprocal learning process. They are learners and teachers, interacting with all constituencies. Students learn and receive guidance from faculty members and community partners, simultaneously giving to the deaf community and receiving back from them. This student-centered model provides benefits for all involved. Cripps and Cooper identified the need for further investigation involving reciprocity with the community-at-large as part of civic engagement.

SURVEY ON ATTITUDE TOWARDS
SERVICE LEARNING IN DEAF STUDIES

Cooper, Cripps, and Reisman (2013) conducted a study to ascertain the impact of service learning on the development of altruism among college Deaf Studies students. Schwartz and Howard (1982) defined the concept of altruism as helping with a self-based locus of normative motivation. In other words, altruism is motivated by internal personal norms, generated by one's own internal values, rather than helping which is motivated by external social norms. For example, students may be willing to go into the community to help because they know it is expected of them, but they may not possess the internal feelings of altruism that would motivate them to do these same actions if they were not required. Altruistic behavior describes "how aware individuals are of the needs of others and to what degree they want to help others" (Shiarella, McCarthy & Tucker, 2000, p. 287).

More specifically, Kahne and Westheimer identified two categories of altruism, "charity" and "change," which represent very different perspectives. "Charity" emphasizes character-building and a kind of compensatory justice where those who have help those who do not have. However, altruism can also aim for social change and development of civic responsibility, emphasizing the mutual responsibility and interdependence of rights and responsibilities, focusing on enlightened self-interest, connecting students to the community in a way that creates a shared sense of purpose in working toward social justice.

Charitable and change-related altruism do not inherently conflict; in fact, while aiming to achieve social change and social justice, it is possible for philanthropic and charitable change to occur. Some scholars (e.g., Kahne & Westheimer, 1996; Marullo & Edwards, 2000) suggest that service learning experiences perceived as acts of charity can, over time, facilitate the politicization of students and help them to become promoters of a more just society.

The methodology for this study was a survey questionnaire administered to a group of Deaf Studies students before and after their service learning experiences. The goal was to determine if there were changes in the students' attitudes toward service learning as a result of the actual experience. In 2010, there were twenty-eight students in the class. Twenty-seven completed the pre-survey, and twenty-six completed the post-survey, therefore the results of this study are based on twenty-six matched pairs. Twelve of these students were between the ages of 18–20 and another eight were aged 21–22. The remaining six students were between the ages of 23–29. There were twenty-three females and three males. The student self-identified their ethnic backgrounds as Caucasian (n=21), African American (n=5). More than half of the students identified as Juniors (n=16). There were eight seniors and two sophomores.

Significant change was noted in students' responses to twenty of the fourty-six statements. The statements that reflected the change included:

1. "Community groups need our help."
2. "Volunteer work at community agencies helps solve social problems."
3. "College student volunteers can help improve the local community."
4. "Volunteering in community projects can greatly enhance the community's resources."
5. "The more people who help, the better things will get."
6. "Contributing my skills will make the world a better place."
7. "My contributions to the community will make a real difference."
8. "I can make a difference in the community."
9. "I am responsible for doing something about improving the community."
10. "I feel an obligation to contribute to the community."
11. "It is important to me to gain an increased sense of responsibility from participating in community service."
12. "It is my responsibility to take real measures to help others in need."
13. "It is important to me to have a sense of contribution and helpfulness through participating in community service."
14. "Our community needs good volunteers."
15. "All communities need good volunteers."
16. "Without community service, today's disadvantaged citizens have no hope."
17. "Community service is a crucial component of the solution to community problems."

18. "Lack of community service will cause severe damage to our society."
19. "Community service is necessary to making our communities better."
20. "I want to do this service learning activity."

The responses were categorized according to eight stages identified by Shiarella, et al. (2000) that outline the development of altruism. Findings indicated that overall, the service learning experience had significant impact on the attitudes of the students in both charitable and social justice areas. Responses in five out of the eight stages showed increased awareness of the target issues. The most significant changes were in the area of "Seriousness," the reassessment and redefinition of the reality and the seriousness of the need and responsibility to respond. The second-most significant changes were in the area of "Ability," the recognition of one's own ability to do something and provide help. The third-most significant changes were in the area of "Connectedness," the feeling of a sense of responsibility to become involved with the community or people in need. Significant changes were in the areas of "Actions," the perception that there are actions that can relieve the needs, and "Norms," feeling a personal or situational moral obligation to help.

Through this process, students showed an increased sensitivity to social welfare issues and the need to respond to them. Students acknowledged that they have the ability to make the world a better place and that their actions can make a difference in the world and in the lives of others. Additional research would be beneficial to support these initial findings. Suggestions include focusing on other types of attitude change affected by service learning and utilizing a larger number of participants.

SUMMARY AND CONCLUSION

Overall, service learning seems to be a good fit with the field of Deaf Studies. Incorporating relationships with off-campus organizations provides both the immediate benefits of the service learning experience, as well as future networking opportunities for graduates. Service learning in Deaf Studies allows the university to partner with community agencies as part of a model of civic engagement that benefits both students and the deaf community. Service learning can engage students in the community in beneficial ways. Students have the opportunity to build relationships and become aware of resources in the community, bolstering their skills and confidence. This non-traditional approach to learning is a reality-based pedagogy, including work in the community and meaningful field visits, provides a change from typical classroom settings. It can poignantly help students apply their knowledge in the areas of signed language and Deaf Studies. Their experiences in the community can lead to increased career networking and a smoother transition into the work force.

Based on four semesters of service learning, with feedback from students and community partners, it appears that service learning is a promising tool for sharing deaf- and signed-language-awareness between the university and the deaf community. Some suggestions for addressing the challenges of this pedagogy and course implementation in Deaf Studies have been proposed. This model has deepened relationships with community partners and given students meaningful opportunities. Incorporation of the suggestions provided in this paper regarding service learning in Deaf Studies can provide the missing link between students' classroom learning and true understanding of signed language used by deaf people and issues faced by deaf people.

The potential impact of this type of learning can be far-reaching. By adding a curricular component where Deaf Studies students provide training to the community-at-large, awareness of and sensitivity to deaf people who use signed language can be significantly increased. Additionally, a variety of student skills can be developed, such as critical thinking, the ability to give professional-level presentations, and the ability to manage discussions on potentially controversial topics.

The minimal body of research that exists on service learning has been positive. However, more research is needed in ASL- and deaf-related service learning, utilizing larger populations, and including additional studies on attitude change affected by service learning. Studies similar to the one discussed in this paper need to be done using validated instruments such as the Community Service Self-Efficacy Scale (Reeb, 2006) and the Service Learning Benefit Scale (SELEB; Toncar et. al., 2006), examining the benefits of service learning on students' self-efficacy. Specific research is needed in Deaf Studies to investigate the impact of service learning on all of the constituencies involved, and to measure the impact of the experience on student attitudes toward community service and experiential learning, consumer attitudes toward receiving services, and community agencies' attitudes toward receiving training on signed language and deaf awareness.

Achievement of the mission of institutions of higher education and academia regarding civic engagement can occur through reciprocal and structured experiences such as service learning. The involvement of dedicated partners in the community, pro-active faculty members with institutional support, and motivated students can create mutually beneficial experiences. Academic programs in Deaf Studies should consider maximizing community resources and offering their services to their local, national, and global community to improve the quality of life for deaf people while attaining institutional goals of civic engagement.

ACKNOWLEDGEMENTS

The authors acknowledge the significant contributions of Dr. Diana Emanuel, Dr. Samuel Supalla, and Joel Reisman to earlier drafts of this paper.

REFERENCES

Berman, S. (2006). *Service-Learning: A guide to planning, implementing, and assessing student projects, 2nd ed.* Thousand Oaks, CA: Corwin Press.

Cooper, S. B., Cripps, J. H., & Reisman, J. I. (Winter, 2013). Service-Learning in Deaf Studies: Impact on Altruism and Social Justice. *American Annals of the Deaf.*

Cripps, J. H. & Cooper, S. B. (Fall, 2012). Service-Learning in Deaf Studies: Integrating academia and the deaf community. *The Journal for Professionals Networking for Excellence in Service Delivery with Individuals who are Deaf and Hard of Hearing.*

Dunlop, M. R. & Webster, N. (2009). Enhancing intercultural competence through civic engagement. In B. Jacoby & Associates (Eds.), *Civic engagement in higher education: Concepts and practices* (pp. 140–153). San Francisco, CA: Jossey-Bass.

Gibson, C. M. (2006). *New times demand new scholarship: Research universities and civic engagement.* Medford, MA: Tufts University and Campus Compact.

Hansmann, S., Saladin, S., & Quintero, J. F. (2011). Development of social learning program for students in undergraduate deaf rehabilitation program. *The Journal for Professionals Networking for Excellence in Service Delivery with Individuals who are Deaf and Hard of Hearing,* 44(3), 106–115.

Hansmann, S., Saladin, S., Shefcik, T., & Garza-Gutierrez, M. (2009). Development of an undergraduate concentration in services to individuals who are deaf or hard of hearing. *The Journal for Professionals Networking for Excellence in Service Delivery with Individuals who are Deaf and Hard of Hearing,* 42(3), 167–184.

Jacoby, B. (2009). Civic engagement in today's higher education: An overview. In B. Jacoby & Associates (Eds.), *Civic engagement in higher education: Concepts and practices* (pp. 5–30). San Francisco, CA: Jossey-Bass.

Jacoby, B. (1996). Service-Learning in today's higher education. In B. Jacoby & Associates (Eds.), *Service-Learning in higher education: Concepts and practices,* (pp. 3–25). San Francisco, CA: Jossey-Bass.

Jacoby, B. & Associates. (2009). Introduction. In B. Jacoby & Associates (Eds.), *Civic engagement in higher education: Concepts and practices* (pp. 1–4). San Francisco, CA: Jossey-Bass.

Kahne, J. & Westheimer, J. (1999). In the service of what? The politics of service learning. In J. Claus & C. Ogden (Eds.), *Service learning for youth empowerment and social change* (pp. 25–42). New York: Peter Lang.

Karasik, J. (1993). Not only bowls of delicious soup: Youth service today. In S. Sagawa and S. Halperin (eds.), *Visions of service: The future of the national and community service act* (pp. 47–48). Washington D.C.: National Women's Law Center and American Youth Policy Forum.

Kendall, J. C. (1990). Combining service and learning: An introduction. In J. C. Kendall (Ed.), *Combining service and learning: A resource book for community and public service, Vol. 1.* (pp. 1–36). Raleigh, NC: National Society for Experiential Education.

Marschark, M. & Humphries, T. (2010). Deaf studies by any other name? *Journal of Deaf Studies and Deaf Education*, 15(1), 1–2.

Marullo, S. & Edwards, B. (2000). From charity to justice: The potential of university-community collaboration for social change. *American Behavioral Scientist*, 43(5), 895–912.

McEwen, M. K. (1996). Enhancing student learning and development through Service-Learning. In B. Jacoby & Associates (eds.), *Service-Learning in higher education: Concepts and practices* (pp. 53–91). San Francisco, CA: Jossey-Bass.

Morton, K. (1996). Issues related to integrating Service-Learning into the curriculum. In B. Jacoby & Associates (eds.), *Service-Learning in higher education: Concepts and practices* (pp. 276–296). San Francisco, CA: Jossey-Bass.

Monikowski, C. & Peterson, R. (2005). Service-Learning in interpreting education. In M. Marschark, R. Peterson, & E. A. Winston (Eds.), *Interpreting education: From research to practice* (pp. 188–220). New York: Oxford University Press.

Reading, S. & Carlstrand, G. (2007). Service-learning across language and culture. *Academic Exchange Quarterly*, 11, 123–128.

Reading, S. & Padgett, R. J. (2011). Communication connections: Service Learning and American Sign Language. *American Journal of Audiology*, 20, S197–S202.

Reeb, R. N. (2006). The Community Service Self-Efficacy Scale: Further evidence of reliability and validity. *Journal of Prevention & Intervention in the Community*, 32(1/2), 97–113.

Schwartz, S. H., & Howard, J. A. (1982). Helping and cooperation: A self-based motivational model. In V. J. Derlaga & J. Grzelak (eds.), *Cooperation and helping behavior: Theories and research* (pp. 327–352). New York: Academic Press.

Shiarella, A. H., McCarthy, A. M., & Tucker, M. L. (2000). Development and construct validity of scores on the Community Service Attitudes Scale. *Educational and Psychological Measurement*, 60(2), 286–300.

Shaw, S. & Jolley, C. S. (2007). Assessment of Service-Learning in the deaf-blind community. *Association of Experiential Education*, 30(2), 134–152.

Shaw, S. & Roberson, L. (2009). Service-Learning: Recentering the deaf community in interpreter education. *American Annals of the Deaf*, 154(3), 277–283.

Skocpol, T. (1999). Advocates without members: The recent transformation of American civic life. In T. Skocpol & M. Fiorina (Eds.), *Civic engagement in American democracy* (pp. 461–509). Washington, DC: Brookings Institution Press.

Toncar, M. F., Reid, J. S., Burns, D. J., Anderson, C. E., & Nguyen, H. P. (2006). Uniform assessment of the benefits of Service-Learning: The development, evaluation, and implementation of the SELEB Scale. *The Journal of Marketing Theory and Practice*, 14(3), 223–238.

Zastrow, C. (2008). *Introduction to social work and social welfare: Empowering people, 10th ed.* Belmont, CA: Brooks/Cole.

Restructuring Deaf Art through the Lens of Contemporary Art

TABITHA JACQUES

THIS PROPOSAL COMES FROM AN ACADEMIC VIEWPOINT OF AN ART historian. Deaf Studies has seen an incredible boom in academic research and publications within the last twenty years, but there is a very small percentage of research dedicated to deaf art. This paper seeks to give deaf art some kind of structure, classifying by genre, era, and movement. This paper will not be able to discuss all the classifications in depth, but hopes to at least give justification of its place. The justification of each category will help readers have a better conceptual understanding and distinction of art made during a specific time in history, and its stylistic tendencies.

Before I begin with my proposal of restructuring deaf art history, I'd like to visit art history and its timeline and the classifications used to help distinguish one art period/movement from another. For example, Modern Art began in the late 1800s as a rejection of past genres and traditions of art. Modern Art sought to experiment and portray a subject that was not confined within straight lines or traditionally used colors. Artists created works from the perspective of seeing the world through new and fresh eyes. Modern Art's place in history was such an important one because it responded to various historical events that took place in Europe and America. More could be said of Modern Art, but the reader will have to deviate from this article, and read the numerous books that have been published on the subject.

My point is that Modern Art had its place in the classification of art history and the art period had its own set of classifications. That art period spawned Impressionism, Cubism, and Abstract Expressionism; they were related, and yet also independent of each other, falling under the umbrella of

Modern Art. The same system will apply under deaf art as I elaborate later in this article.

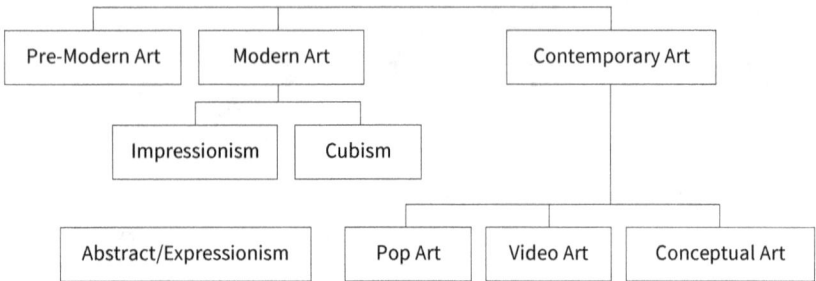

Figure 1: Simplified art history timeline

As you can see, the classification system has its own subcategories and the system reflects the complexities of various movements. the timeline is not comprehensive, and merely serves as an example of how I would restructure deaf art history classification. During my years of observation and research, I realized that even deaf art history has its own classification system. However, no formal attempt has been made at documenting the system. De'VIA is a classification of its own, but has always been used as an umbrella term to describe the deaf experience made by any artist who creates works of art that discusses the subject. This is an accurate classification, but I am hesitant to use it as an umbrella term because the art materials used by artists have evolved, and even contemporary deaf artists who express their deaf experience in more abstract ways have rejected the label of De'VIA.

As a general principle, art has been a reaction to a historical event or a shift in how society perceive traditions and cultural norms. This reaction or shift creates a new classification within art history. This new classification may be a new art form, new way of using art materials, or even a new genre of art. Going back to the example of modern art, artists changed how people viewed art by creating works that went against cultural norms and rules of art that was accepted before modern art came into the scene. I am interested in restructuring deaf art as to reflect the changes within the deaf community and its culture.

CURRENT TYPOLOGY

At the moment, the breakdown of deaf art history is into two categories: Deaf Art and Deaf View Image Art (De'VIA). My proposal is to break down into two major classifications with at least three to four sub-categories. This is in no way covers the breadth or depth of deaf art history. This is to at least give a general idea of the variations of deaf art and to start a dialogue within the deaf studies and the art history fields.

Before I begin my proposed classification system, I'd like to talk about the types of labels that deaf people may or may not assign to themselves. There's a wide range of types of deafness, which includes, but is not limited to: Deaf, deaf, Hard of Hearing, DeafBlind, DeafDisabled, Late-Deafened, person with hearing loss, and more. This presentation was originally given in 2012, but over the last five years, many new ways of identifying one's self has come up. One major terminology of identification is *intersectionality*. Intersectionality includes identification with race, gender, or gender within a system of oppression or discrimination. Intersectionality is a term broadly used by the hearing world, but is also a topic heavily researched within the deaf community as a system of identification.

This complex system within the deaf community is very hard to break down, and varies from individual to individual depending on their family background, school choice, socioeconomic class, and many other variables. The classification of deaf art history should also reflect this variation. However, because there is so little research in deaf art history, the general acceptance is deaf art and De'VIA as two forms of classification. My proposed classification system will increase the number of categories to reflect the variations of artists' deafness, identification systems, and choice in subject matter and art mediums. Certain art classifications may even reflect monumental historical events within the deaf community.

Currently, deaf art is described as art made by deaf people, but subject matter does not focus on the deaf experience. This allows for a larger number of artworks to be placed in this category, but is so broad and does not explore complexities of the deaf artist and his/her works.

De'VIA, the second category within the current typology was a hugely monumental movement that was officially recorded in 1989, but already had traces of the movement starting in the 1970s. De'VIA, or Deaf View Image Art, was founded by a group of deaf artists right before the historical event of Deaf Way I. The De'VIA movement had more structure as a category and probably was the first formal attempt at a typology. Subject matter focused specifically on the deaf experience, and artworks suddenly became a source of inspiration and understanding amongst many deaf people who also shared similar experiences. Betty G. Miller was considered to be the Mother of De'VIA. She held her first exhibition in the 1970s and her artworks portrayed the common deaf experience of growing up lonely and frustrated in a hearing family, being forced to speak and lip read, being slapped on the hands because sign language was not allowed in the classroom, and so on.

De'VIA has specific characteristics found in artworks: bright and bold colors, enlarged eyes and hands, smaller or nonexistent ears and lips. Artists who associated themselves with De'VIA other than Miller were Ann Silver, Chuck Baird, Paul Johnston, Guy Wonder, Susan Dupor, Harry Williams, and many more.

One of the biggest reasons why De'VIA was a reflection of a historical time in deaf history is because of the civil rights movement for people with disabilities, Deaf President Now, and the passing of the American Disabilities Act, which gave more deaf people access to communication, to take claim in themselves as citizens and human beings. For the first time in history, perhaps, deaf people felt that they could proclaim their pride in their deafness and their culture. Deaf people were also willing to discuss their feelings of oppression in a world of auditory-led stimulation.

RESTRUCTURING DEAF ART

This is a proposed system of classification within deaf art history that I have created. I've broken down the system into two major art classifications: Folk Art and Fine Arts. Folk art may or may not have a classification system within itself, but I've not had the opportunity to research this area as intensively as I have with Fine Arts.

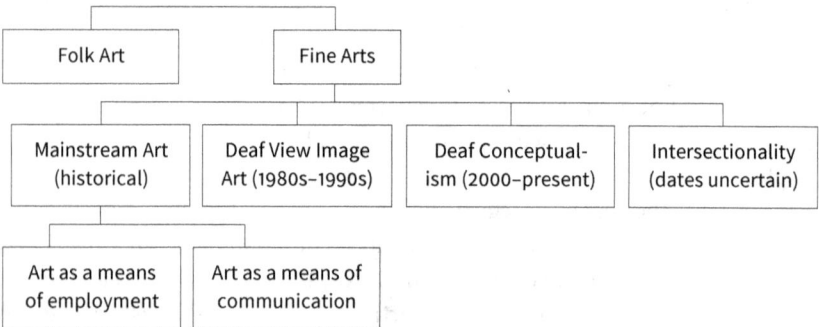

Figure 2: Proposed restructured deaf art history timeline

Folk Art

Folk Art, which is defined as "artistic works, as paintings, sculpture, basketry, and utensils, produced typically in cultural isolation by untrained often anonymous artists or by artisans of varying degrees of skill and marked by such attributes as highly decorative design, bright bold colors, flattened perspective, strong forms in simple arrangements, and immediacy of meaning." People often see these types of art at deaf expos and festivals, church revivals, and/or deaf clubs where an artist would sell hand-sewn "I love you" hand-shape pillows used to decorate the home. Folk art is found everywhere in the Deaf community and there are numerous examples that can be discussed within this category, but is not my focus in this article.

Fine Arts

The second category focuses on fine arts, and this is where the classification system becomes more complex. Fine Arts is described as an artist who has had formal training in the arts, or is an artist who has been recognized by the art world.

Mainstream Art

The first sub-category is Mainstream Art. Within the Mainstream Art classification, you have two types of art: art as a way of making a living, and art as a means of communication. This usually describes the deaf artist's purpose of creating artworks. This time period could cover hundreds of years. Technically, it still covers even the present as there are many deaf artists out in the world who do not disclose their deafness, but create beautiful and meaningful works of art. There are many deaf artists who have been isolated by their families and create works of art that communicate their needs, feelings, and thoughts. Examples of artists include Hendrick Avercamp, James Castle, Granville Redmond, Cadwallader Washburn, Helen Dyer, and Jean Hanau. These artists do not really imply anything about their deafness in their works. Subject matter focuses more on what they saw within their surroundings. Avercamp and Castle both painted everyday life. So too did Redmond, an impressionist painter, who painted landscapes, seascapes, and other every-day scenes of nature.

For many centuries, talented fine artists who were deaf were a part of art history, but recognized as deaf. Since the rise of deaf studies, more effort has been placed on identifying deaf people in the mainstream world. Most of the time, artists who were deaf had very little record of their deafness, unless it was disclosed through hand written letters or other forms of documentation. One such artist was Hendrick Avercamp. He was a talented Dutch artist in the seventeenth century specializing in detailed oil paintings of everyday life in the Netherlands. Very little documentation is made about his deafness other than his nickname, "de Stomme van Kampen" (the Mute of Kampen). Avercamp made a living from his paintings as did many other European and American artists. This category needs a name to reflect art as a means of employment.

James Castle, on the other hand, used art as a means of communication. His works are primitive, but also very detailed about what he saw in his everyday life. Many artists prior to the 1970s most likely created artworks as a means of communication with their family or friends. Language played a barrier for many deaf artists, and they used visual literacy to convey their thoughts and feelings. This type of category needs a name.

DE'VIA AND ARTIVISM

The next classification within Fine Arts would be De'VIA, of which I have already elaborated previously in "Current Typology."

Many deaf people have considered De'VIA to be encompassing of all artworks that talk about the deaf experience. I, however, think that De'VIA was a period in history from the late 1970s to the late 1990s and early 2000s. To reiterate, De'VIA was a result of historical events. A second wave of De'VIA began in early 2000 and still continues to the present. This second wave may be better identified as a new category called *Artivism*, which means being an activist through art. Artivists became more interested in creating works for a cause, to educate the public about the anger and frustration of being oppressed. The artists became more vocal about showing how oppression of deaf people still continues regardless of how progressive our society has become. Their art speaks to the public of how laws for deaf people have passed, how communication access for deaf people have improved through the use of technology, and yet, the public still views deaf people as abnormal. When a hearing parent has a deaf child, his/her first reaction is to make sure the child is as normal as possible, which means choosing an avenue where the child is immediately trained to listen, and speak, rather than learning language and/or accomplishing educational milestones as hearing children would.

Subject matter in Artivism tends to focus on resistance against oppression. For example, Nancy Rourke, a prolific artist, has created many beautiful paintings that speak volumes of language deprivation, oralism, Alexander Graham Bell as an individual, and as an organization, and how those efforts have gravely affected a deaf child's education and his/her ability to flourish as a human being. She also celebrates deaf leaders who have pushed for the legalization and recognition of American Sign Language, deaf rights, and other efforts that improve the quality of a deaf person's life. Artivism, like De'VIA, is structured and has specific characteristics. Identifying characteristics are relied on motifs. Every object that is painted in the artwork is a symbol. For example, a butterfly symbolizes Deafhood, identity, and happiness, whereas a puppet symbolizes colonialism, submissiveness, and audism. These symbols were taken from the De'VIA curriculum wordpress site. Other artists who also are part of Artivism are Ellen Mansfield, Patti Durr, David Call, and Laurie Monahan. Rourke also leads a month-long challenge where she encourages artists to create an artwork related to a motif. Due to access to technology and the internet, a mass of deaf people suddenly could learn about Artivism, and collectively create art pieces that actively speak to the public about the oppression of deaf people. This is a valuable art movement, and I believe should have its own place within deaf art history that is separate from De'VIA.

DEAF CONCEPTUALISM

I've been discussing several types of classifications that are somewhat familiar within deaf studies, but Conceptual art is a new category within contemporary art, which began in the late 1950s to the present. I see an emerging trend with contemporary deaf artists focusing on conceptual art, which I call Deaf Conceptualism. Deaf artists of that genre have not come together to discuss a category that best defines their work as a collective. Deaf conceptual artists often reject the label of De'VIA for a number of reasons. One is because they feel that their art does not blatantly talk about the deaf experience, their art doesn't talk about oppression or marginalization. Instead, their work is more subtle, more theoretical, and in some ways, even more interactive with the public about their experience. Their art invites the public to see the world from their eyes. Their artwork may be understood and appreciated by hearing people, but viewing/experiencing art works may be exclusive of their deaf peers. This generation of artists may even be more interested in talking about other parts of their identities such as race, gender, sexual orientation, and even the type of hearing loss they have. They are interested in discussing bodily or social experience through video, performance, installation, and even sound art. The documentation process for deaf conceptualism is far harder to capture than it would be with artworks of other genres. The artworks created are more dynamic, experiential, and temporal. Artists from this typology are more likely to be hard of hearing, or less likely to celebrate deaf pride as artists from De'VIA or Artivism. Example of deaf conceptual artists are Joseph Grigley, Christine Sun Kim, Jeff Mansfield, and Aaron Williamson.

INTERSECTIONALITY ART

There's also a growing trend of deaf artists of color claiming a place of their own in deaf art history. Black deaf artists are creating works of art that talks about being black and deaf. Takiyah Harris is one artist who heavily researches on the history of black deaf people, and incorporates them in her artworks. There are also Latinx, Jewish, and Queer deaf artists who are coming into the spotlight, and they deserve a category of their own because their works cannot be lumped together within other categories from the same period. Each deaf cultural group have their own ways of creating art, focusing on specific subject matter that is reflective of their cultural beliefs and norms. For now, I'm proposing the category be called Intersectionality Art, but a deeper and more complex classification system needs to be created and applied within that category.

CONTINUED RESEARCH

What I've been discussing through this article is only the beginning. There is so much more research needed. I need to sit down with artists individually, and as groups, to begin to understand the historical significance and to better explain characteristics of each category, and how it parallels with art history as a whole. The next phase of my research is to explore artists in the field of deaf conceptualism, and discuss their works, and why they are such valuable contributions to deaf art history. The same kind of research needs to be applied to Deaf Artists of Color and intersectionality art. I am also interested in doing a more interdisciplinary approach in explaining each typology, looking at the effects of history, societal expectations, technological advancements, ideologies of the deaf community, and more. I want to push for deaf art history to have its own place within art history, just as women's studies, African American studies, Native American studies and more. They have their own place in Art History, and with this research, so too can Deaf Art history.

We are at a very crucial part of our deaf history. We are claiming — and reclaming — our history and incorporating it in academia. Deaf Studies have already began their place in academia, but other aspects of the studies need theirs too: Deaf literature, Deaf art, Deaf theatre, and Deaf film. There is already and will be even more of a creative production within the arts field. This is a collective consciousness of the deaf community to be recognized for our place in the world. We earned our place as citizens and humans in the late 1980s early 1990s, and now it is our time to earn our place as artists and creative spokespeople of our community within the world at large. Timing is often everything, and I think right now, is our time.

De'VIA and Deaf Jewish Art

MARK ZAUROV

WITHIN THE WESTERN RANKING SYSTEM FOR "CULTURE," A CONSTANT canon of classic works of art testifies of "high culture." Whenever the artistic production of minorities enters the canon, the works tend to serve as identity formation. Deaf Visual Art (De'VIA) is a manifesto about locating aspects of Deaf culture and signed languages within the works of visual art.

Is visual Deaf Art becoming part of the canon, and what about Deaf Jewish art? This presentation examines the biographies and works of artists such as Richard Lieberman, Rudolf Franz Hartogh, David Bloch, Hans Bloch, Julius Hans Spiegel, Elisabeth Seligmann, survivors of the Holocaust and artists who left a wealth of works exposing particular features they have in common. Do we encounter a new artistic direction in these works to be defined as modern or post-modern Deaf Jewish art?

The Jewish non-deaf artist Max Liebermann (1847–1935) exposes his Jewish identity in "Selbstbildnis mit Küchenstilleben" ("Self Portrait With Kitchen Still Life," 1873). In this still life, there is not only a self-portrait of the artist as cook but also a *kashrut* letter symbolizing that the food depicted is kosher.

By comparison, the 1845 work "Card-sharpeners" by the Deaf non-Jewish artist Feliks Peczarski (1804/5–1862) depicts the subject with extremely pronounced facial expressions, a striking representation of the *deaf* visual experience. Respective cultural affiliations can be represented in subject or style or both.

The Deaf Jewish artist Richard Libermann (b. 1900) attended the Royal Deaf-mute Institute Munich and studied at the Academy of Fine Arts in

Munich and converted to Catholicism in 1923. Under the national social-
ists, he was not allowed to paint, but in 1936, took a teaching position at the
Jewish school Herrlingen led by Hugo Rosenthal. During the *Reichskristall-
nacht* in 1938, he was taken by the Gestapo to Dachau and, although fortu-
nately, released one month later, all of his works were confiscated and sold
at auction by the Nazis. In 1940, together with his father and siblings, Libermann was taken to Gurs. He and his family managed to be transferred to
Noé where their father died. In 1943 they were rescued and remained hidden
in the French monastery St. Just-St. Rambert near Lyon. After the war, they
remained there until Libermann's death in 1966.

Liebermann strongly identified as both a deaf person *and* a Jew. His
works, however, show very little if any trace of his respective cultural affiliations, as in the portrait of the school director of the Royal Deaf-mute School.
Liebermann artistically translated his personal suffering in the camps into
Christian iconography, as in "Camp Noé." In this work, Liebermann identified with Christ on the cross, murdered because he also was a Jew.

Liebermann was an important part of an exhibition of deaf-mute artists
in Schleswig in 1925. Among these deaf-mute contemporaries were Rudolf
Franz Hartogh, Hans Bloch, Julius Spiegel, Elisabeth Seligmann and Hans
Arnheim. These artists' works were also exhibited in Berlin (1930) and Hamburg (1927, the 200th anniversary of Samuel Heinicke's death).

DEAF JEWISH ARTISTS

Rudolf Franz Hartogh (1889–1960) studied under the supervision of Lovis
Corinth and worked for Walter Gropius in the Dessau Bauhaus. His work
was influenced by both the Impressionists and later the Expressionists. Hartogh survived both the Farge (near Bremen) and Theresienstadt camps. His
1929 portrait "A Jewish Deaf-mute Artist," is the only visual document of
his colleague Elizabeth Seligmann (no photographs of her exist) and is the
singular work which depicts Deaf Jewish identity. His 1954 drawing "Camp
Farge," is a rare document of his memory of the camp. His 1950 painting
"Red Houses" depicts one or two isolated houses without doors surrounded
by trees without leaves. How would you interpret this negative symbolism of
community and communication, knowing the artist was deaf?

Elisabeth Seligmann (1893–1947) is, to date, the only known Deaf Jewish
German woman artist from this timeframe. Baptized as Protestants by her
parents Emil Seligmann and Isabel Hahn, she also had a deaf brother (Edu-
ard) among her seven siblings. During her childhood she was educated at
home and sometimes with other local deaf individuals. She was a member of the Hamburg Artists and Imperial Chambers of Fine Artists and was

expelled during the Nazi regime. In 1941, she fled to Ecuador to live with her brother Carl. Sadly, her work is also lost to history.

Hans Arnheim (1881–1942) was a sculptor who won the Michael Baer-Prize of the City of Berlin which lead to a journey to Rome (1909/10). One of his works bears the title "The Deaf-Mute," a crouching nude, knees pulled in, head pulled in and covered by hands, which can be seen at the Deaf school in Leipzig. Other artworks depict landscapes of bridges and houses and churches. He was deported to and died at Theresienstadt in 1942.

Hans Bloch (1885–1961) was a sculptor and studied in several academies in Germany, Switzerland, and Italy. He was one of the original founders of and exhibitors at the Association for Deaf Artists in Germany. Banned from his profession under the Nazis, and sent to forced labor at a Berlin train station between 1943–1945, most of his artworks are Madonnas and portraits of prominent persons of Berlin's high society. He converted away from Judaism in the 1920s and survived because of his "mixed marriage." He sculpted a bust of his Deaf Jewish colleague, Julius Spiegel, and after the war, continued his strong friendship with Spiegel via letters and gifts.

Julius Spiegel (1891–1974) was a painter and dancer, well-known as the "Fisherman of Capri" (Zaurov, 2009). He graduated from the Royal Prussian school for Deaf in Berlin and then studied painting in the Academies of Fine Art in Berlin and Munich between 1913–1918. After living in Rome for five years, Spiegel relocated to the island of Capri, returning to Berlin from time to time to work in several varietés and theaters. Spiegel was rather assimilated and converted to Christianity in the 1920s in Rome. He began a dancing career in his thirties, a departure from his formal training as a painter. His modern solo dance adapted religious dances of southern and eastern Asia, known for covering his face with the masks he passionately collected. Spiegel's creativity evolved through his performance art rather than his visual art though "A Capri Lane" (1929) is representative in its lack of any allusions to Jewish or Deaf culture.

During the war, Spiegel was taken to the Italian internment camp Ferramonti; though liberated by the Allies, Spiegel seemed suspicious to the Americans afterwards and was briefly kept in an internment camp. Spiegel could sign but preferred the community of European artists and gays to the Jewish and Deaf communities. He never returned to Germany but was instead visited by Deaf German and Israelite tourists. After the war, he was too old to relaunch his dance career and reinvented a second career as the Fisherman of Capri. Famous actors of the time appeared with him in several newspapers and magazines.

David Bloch (1910–2002) graduated from the deaf school in Munich and became a porcelain painter. At the beginning of the war, he was interred at

Dachau, but after four weeks he escaped to Shanghai. There, Bloch depicted scenes of daily Chinese life. In 1980, he turned his attention towards his personal emotional experiences of the Holocaust; in 1997, Bloch was recognized by the German Deaf community for his work. His paintings are a unique delivery of the horror in the concentration camp seen through the eyes of a deaf person.

In the diptych "My Biography," Bloch visually narrates his life in a flow of small, dated scenes. He starts with the individually traumatic train trip as a baby after his parents' early death on his way to an orphanage ("1910"), goes on with the collectively traumatic experience of oral education ("1915–23"), his years of studying ("1923–25"), and work as a porcelain-painter ("1927–30"). "1930–36" shows him painting, and "1936–38" shows him working in the department store Salinger, whilst above him the Nazis rage burning books, setting synagogues on fire, and marching. In the same narrative structure Bloch continues his biography in the second tableau, starting with the concentration camp: prisoners stand in a row, commanded by a Nazi; children are led to the crematorium, the angel of death hovering above.

Bloch also depicts his camp number and narrates his escape to Shanghai. The final triumphant scene shows his new home, a house, in New York City, above which a bridge displays the word *pax* ("peace"), the World Trade Center towers, and the Statue of Liberty. The flame she keeps burning is contested by a hand embodying the ASL-sign "I love you." Bloch's "My Biography" is a very clear statement of De'VIA art, putting forth Deaf specific subjects as well as styles: narrativity, wordplay (*weiss* [white] and *Waise* [orphan] in German are homophones for a Deaf person), the use of space and mapping (globes), and the use of specific signs. Above all, Jewish identity is very present in the paintings.

Maurice Minkowski (1881–1930) studied in the Cracow Academy of Fine Arts where Leon Rosenblum and Zygmunt Nadel also studied and was well known through exhibitions in Warsaw, Paris, Antwerp, London, Düsseldorf, and Buenos Aires. The 1911 exhibition of Jewish artists in Berlin showed his works, an inspriration of the noted Jewish modernist Marc Chagall. Minkowski's paintings are found in world-class collections in London, Tel Aviv, New York, San Francisco and Buenos Aires. Minkowski witnessed and captured the 1905 pogrom (massacre) in Bialystock (http://www.the-jewishmuseum.org/198680about) in his work. "Pogrom" (c. 1910) is an oil panel showing a wild crowd fleeing from a village set on fire, discernable on the horizon of flames and smoke. In the center, a woman stands dressed in white, her hands folded in front of her chest. The woman (and another less discerned woman's face in the crowd behind her), audaciously and directly stare into the viewer's soul. Minkowski concentrated on women and children within the crowd of Jewish victims. Although it would be easy to grasp the allegory of suffering and innocence in the center figure, the stunning communication in this painting triggered by the eye gaze can also be interpreted as Deaf. The presence of the other Deaf face in the crowd behind the center figure especially reinforces this interpretation. Minkowski's subjects are mostly Jewish, he was fully socialized within the Jewish community, yet he was active in the international Deaf community as well. He helped to found a Jewish Deaf association in Poland and was a member of the American Society of Deaf Artists.

Leon Rosenblum (1884–1944) attended the Jewish Deaf-Mute Institute in Vienna until he returned to Cracow at 16 years of age. He was accepted into the Academy of Fine Arts there because of his extraordinary sculpting talent and studied under Florian Zinken, Jan Stanislawski, and Witschalka-vazkii. He was awarded a bronze and three silver medals during his art education. Several of his paintings are installed a Cracow synagogue and his name is relevant art historical literature. He was famous for his intimate and melancholic style, his landscapes and night scenes of Cracow. There is a Yiddish article mentioning his artworks of Jewish Life like the Hassidic "Dance of Havdala" (hassidim are religious East-European Jews). He was deported to and died at Auschwitz in 1944.

Zygmunt Nadel (1854–1926) lived in Lemberg, Munich, and Cracow and also attended the Jewish Deaf-Mute Institute in Vienna. Nadel typically portrayed Jewish subjects. In relevant literature, Nadel is mentioned together with the prominent Jewish Polish painters of his time.

Alexei Svetlov (1964–) is a contemporary artist living in Stockholm. He studied at the Academy of Fine Arts in St. Petersburg and his works have been exhibited extensively in Scandinavia and Russia, the recipient of international grants and awards. One of the first Deaf Jewish post-modern artists, David Bloch's late oeuvre and influence is seen in Svetlov. His "Flying House, St. Petersburg" (2011) is one of a series of flying houses, uprooted and ephemeral dwellings hovering above European cities. The metaphor can be clearly related to the Jewish ghetto experience, the forced displacement, diaspora, and the Holocaust. At the same time, this metaphor is strikingly spatial, more easily understood with its implications if rendered in sign. Svetlov's subjects are wide-range, he paints figuratively and compiles dense and complex imagery that cannot be accounted for through an understanding of Deaf culture and Jewish experience only.

In contrast to Svetlov, the works of the Israeli Uzi Buzgalo (1956–) are dominantly informed by the artist's conflict between Deaf and Jew. He attended the Jerusalem School for the Deaf and was sent to the Jerusalem Arts Museum at age eleven years. From 1973 to 1975, Buzgalo studied lithography and sculpture at the Art Museum of Tel-Aviv and continued his studies of art in the residency program Ein Hod in Israel. He relocated to the United States (Washington D. C. and Boulder, Colorado) between 1986 and 2012. Currently, Buzgalo lives in Reshion Lezion, Israel. His painting "The Deaf Club is Our Synagogue" (2002) is a cityscape under the night sky (Zaurov, 2009). The architectural synagogue remains in the background, whereas the foreground is dominated by a rather simple but inviting, illuminated building with an open door and a large window. The deaf club, as the title suggests, turned into a synagogue, is a space in which both identities can proliferate; through the window we see intermingling human silhouettes signing ecstatically in golden light. This light also emanates from a central female figure, referred to by Buzgalo as "floating messenger." On her left bosom, the red ILY handshape "represents," according to Buzgalo, "the fact that Sign Language constitutes [its] own language and culture, and keeps them congregating on Sabbath evenings" (Buzgalo, 2009).

Buzgalo is also a performing artist, a member of the professional dance company Kol Demama (sound-silence) internationally known for its Deaf and hearing dancers. He developed stage designs translating music into visual patterns. Buzgalo openly develops a Deaf style and imagery: "The beauty of signed languages shape[s] my art style, which is a composition of colors and hands with stories of similar experiences, a way of artistically depicting the language and culture of deaf people" (http://www.rit.edu/~420www/dada.htm). He is also active in shaping De'VIA discourse ("My thoughts about De'VIA motifs"). His works are represented in collections in Israel, Switzerland, Germany, Belgium, and the United States.

CONCLUSION

With an overabundance of history and surviving works as backdrop, it is inconceiveable to deny the existence of modern Deaf Jewish art in Germany prior to the Holocaust. After the war, the Jewish experience of recurring extinction and the marginalization Deaf culture gained sharper contours, at once in competition and support with itself. Recurring imagery is evident in the choice of paintings compared here: cityscapes and displacement (Hartogh's "Red Houses," Minkowski's burning village and refugees, Svetlov's "Flying Houses" and Buzgalo's "Deaf Club/Synagogue") and female signing heralds (David Bloch's "Lady of ASL-Liberty," Minkowsky's white woman with her eye gaze, folding hands in front of her chest and Buzgalo's "messenger" with her ASL-heart). There is still so much more to discover.

REFERENCES

Buzgalo, U. (2009). My artworks as a deaf israeli. In M. Zaurov & K.B. Günther (eds.), *Overcoming the Past, Determining its Consequences and Finding Solutions for the Present, A Contribution for Deaf Studies and Sign Language Education: Proceedings of the 6th Deaf History International Conference July 31–August 04, 2006* at the Humbold University, Berlin. Signum: Seedorf, 61–69.

Zaurov, Mark (2009). Deaf Holokaust. In M. Zaurov & K.B. Günther (eds.), *Overcoming the Past, Determining its Consequences and Finding Solutions for the Present, A Contribution for Deaf Studies and Sign Language Education: Proceedings of the 6th Deaf History International Conference July 31–August 04, 2006* at the Humbold University, Berlin. Signum: Seedorf, 173–197.

http://www.thejewishmuseum.org/198680about

http://www.rit.edu/~420www/dada.htm

Deaf Students: A Linguistic Minority in Higher Education

CAROL SANDERSON-MACNICHOLL

AN HISTORICAL OVERVIEW IS NECESSARY TO UNDERSTAND THE CONTEXT of my personal experience as a linguistic minority graduate student. I am one of a few Deaf students who have enrolled in the Masters of Education (M.Ed.) Educational Leadership and Policy (ELP) program at the University of Utah. Despite my language and culture challenges, I decided to enroll in the ELP program. Often during the program, I wanted to give up, but my support system believed in me, which caused me to believe in myself. I would not have been able to persist in the graduate program if it was not for my support system, the staff at the Women's Resource Center, The Writing Center, The Center for Disability Services, The Student Affairs Council, my friends, professors, and cohort members, and Ph.D. students in the program.

We have laughed and talked together. My favorite quote is an African proverb, "It takes a village to raise a child" by Igbo and Yoruba (quotes.net, website). I have always felt that I was raised by the village. I was raised in a boarding school for the Deaf (where school is taught in American Sign Language (ASL), attended several different higher education institutions, and have been surrounded by great mentors, teachers, leaders, and friends; they are my village. I see these educational institutions as the village and practitioners helping students along their educational journeys.

As I go through my journey from a graduate student to a future student affairs practitioner, I want to educate student affairs practitioners about Deaf students and my experiences. The learning outcomes of the ELP program state students will be: (a) change agents committed to implementing social justice ideas into their practice; (b) experienced practitioners and educational leaders; (c) aware and sensitive of themselves and others; (d) student affairs scholars; and (e) reflective and critical thinking skills (www.utah. edu). These skills are crucial for student affairs practitioners as they prepare to work with Deaf students.

My journey as graduate student has caused me to explore Deaf student issues from identity development to graduation rates. As a result of the lack of literature about Deaf students in higher education, I will share my experiences throughout the paper. For this paper, I use a capital "D" for Deaf instead of a lower case "d" to make the word "deaf" a proper noun to connote respect for a specific group of people who use American Sign Language (ASL) as their primary language of communication and are involved in the Deaf community (Lane, p. xi). The capital "H" for "Hearing" refers to mainstreamed society which is primarily comprised of people who can hear and a lower case "h" for "hearing" meaning audiological ability (Senghas & Monagahan, p. 72).

STATEMENT OF THE PROBLEM

Student affairs practitioners often forget about Deaf students and their unique needs. Nichols and Quaye (2009) explain that

> students with disabilities [and Deaf students] encounter specific barriers that impede their academic and social engagement; however their needs are often overlooked in comparison to other student populations. These students are sometimes thought of as a 'forgotten minority' of student affairs practice in higher education (as cited S. R. Harper & S. J. Quaye, p. 263).

Deaf students are a linguistic minority because they have their own language, American Sign Language (ASL), and their own culture (Lane, 1992). Lane (1992) maintains that "in the revolution of thought, deafness-as-disability is increasingly replaced by Deaf as linguistic minority" (p. xv).

The paper will entail three sections. First, academic classes influencing the topic; then, second, a literature review of the Deaf Identity Development, Critical Race Theory, and retention is presented. Lastly, I will touch on best practices for the ELP program and student affairs practitioners working with Deaf students.

ACADEMIC CLASSES/THEORIES

As a Deaf person, my classes ELP 6580 "Multiculturalism & Diversity in Higher Education," ELP 7620 "College Student Development Theory," and ELP 6560 "College Student Retention Theory" have led me to be curious about Deaf students, even though there is lack of discussion about Deaf students in the classroom. To counter the lack of discussion, I tried to add my experience as a Deaf person when the circumstances permitted.

Multiculturalism and Diversity Theory

In ELP 6580 "Multiculturalism & Diversity in Higher Education," I learned about racism but, interestingly, not about *audism*. Solórzano (1997) and Solórzano, Ceja, and Yosso (2000) define that racism occurs when people act or talk in a manner that implies that they are looking down on people because of their skin color and that racism exists when the system is oppressive at all levels, individual, institutional, and metaphysical.

Humphries (1975) "offers this dictionary-like definition: Audism [is] the notion that one is superior based on one's ability to hear or behave in the manner of one who hears" (Bauman, 2004, 240). *Audism* is the term that is used to refer to the systematic oppression of Deaf people on individual, institutional, and metaphysical levels. Often, people hear the terms "racism," "sexism," "ableism," but not "audism," which is what Deaf students face in higher education institutions and in society in general.

Throughout history, Hearing people have discriminated against Deaf people; to wit, marginalizing the right to own property and to have children based on their hearing ability (Lane, 1992). It is a sign of oppression; therefore, audism is framed for the individual and system because the system is based on a Hearing environment (Humphries, 1975, in Bauman, 2004). Furthermore, some Hearing people think Deaf people cannot do the same things as they do like drive a car, operate a machine, or talk on the phone. Some Hearing people's minds are framed to be oppressive toward Deaf people without thinking about it. Humphries (1975) in Bauman (2004) talks about if the educational institutions were based on a visual-centered paradigm and how that would change the physical space, curriculum, assessment, and campus environment for Deaf students: deaf students would experience equal access with Hearing peers.

STUDENT DEVELOPMENT THEORY

In ELP 7620, "College Student Development Theory," the concepts of Asian American Identity, bicultural models, Black Identity Theory, Chickering's Seven Vectors of Student Development, Chickering and Reisser's Theory of Development, and Critical Race Theory (CRT) were all discussed. My teacher allowed me to research Deaf Identity Development (Glickman, 1993) and teach it to the class. Deaf students' development is different than Hearing students' development because of their language and culture. (A

discussion of Deaf Identity Development (Glickman, 1993) is in the literature review section.) Chickering's Seven Vectors of Student Development
(Chickering, 1969) discusses competence, emotions, moving through auton-
omy toward interdependence, mature interpersonal relationships, identity,
purpose, and integrity (Evans et al., 2009). Deaf students go through some
type of development during higher education. Since Deaf students are a linguistic minority group, they have different ways of how to communicate and
navigate in higher education.

RETENTION THEORY

ELP 6560 "College Student Retention Theory" examined Astin's Theory of
Involvement, Schlossberg's Transition Theory, and Tinto's model of college
student persistence/withdrawal. Astin's Theory of Involvement posits that
when students are involved with activities on campus, they are more likely
to graduate. Schlossberg's Transition Theory talks about moving in, moving
through, and moving out with rating of transition for three Ss: situation, self,
and support. Students decide the seriousness of a situation, apply experiential coping skills, and then look for support from other people, agencies, and
financial capability. Tinto's model of college student persistence/withdrawal
states about student's integration into the social and academic system of the
institutions which can impact retention and graduation.

For higher education, becoming involved with activities on campus,
healthy transition, support system, and social and academic engagement are
crucial for retention. Deaf students in social and academic settings need have
people to share their culture with and use ASL as communication which can
impact their persistence in higher education. In mainstreamed institutions,
Deaf students typically communicate through ASL interpreters if Hearing
persons they interact with do not know ASL; interpreters relay the information from English to ASL and vice versa. Some Deaf students use Real Time
Captioning which converts sounds to text. Often there are low numbers of
Deaf students in mainstreamed institutions, but rarely there are a sufficient
number of Deaf students to have social and academic engagement where
they can use ASL. Although Deaf students themselves and faculty, staff, and
students who know ASL can provide support, how many people on campus
must use ASL for Deaf students to feel they belong on campus? If there are
only few people using ASL on campus, Deaf students face less social and academic integration from Tinto's model.

For example, Gallaudet University is the only self-proclaimed university in the world where, through classes to residential halls, ASL is the primary language. (California State University at Northridge (CSUN) and the

National Technical Institute for the Deaf (NTID) at the Rochester Institute of Technology do offer some partial direct communication access for their classes and programs.)

Personally, I have experienced loneliness in the classroom because no one knew enough of my language to converse with me; I mostly talked with the interpreters. I received few gestures or communication from my peers, but saw other students easily interacting with each other. The feeling of belonging is the key to persistence, and I did not experience a sense of belonging in my classes with Hearing students (Weidman, 1989). As mentioned earlier, what about retention for Deaf students?

Retention and graduation is important in higher education. Deaf students are at risk for not persisting through college as noted earlier, but many mainstream institutions do not keep records of the Deaf student graduation rates, so the scope of the problem is unknown. In the state of Utah, several institutions (Dixie State University, Westminster College, Utah Valley University, Salt Lake Community College [SLCC]) do not keep data on the retention rates of Deaf students (Acosta, Kinner, DeWitt, Wahabu, personal communication, March 2011). However, SLCC reports that in the past, graduation rates are lower for Deaf students (personal communication, Jodi Kinner, March 2011). This is a shocking fact because there is no accountability for mainstream institutions except for Gallaudet University, NTID, and CSUN that are required to report institutional graduation rates due to receiving federal funding (www.gallaudet.edu, www.ntid.rit.edu, www.csun.edu). Both communication access for social and academic engagement and low retention rates are red flags for institutions to pay attention to the needs of Deaf Students as linguistic minority group. The next section, the literature review, will continue to integrate the classroom concepts while expanding on the concepts and theories of the leading literature.

REVIEW OF RELATED LITERATURE

Deaf Identity Development

An ethnic or cultural identity model can provide an understanding of individual differences (Torres, 2010). Student affairs practitioners can best understand the background of students with cultural differences, sexual orientations, and major and minor groups by using ethnic or cultural identity models. The Deaf Identity Development Scale (DIDS) by Glickman (1993) defines four identity stages: hearing, marginal, immersion, and bicultural. First is the dominant (hearing) stage. Deaf students stay with dominant (hearing) culture's attitudes and beliefs about Deaf students. Second, culturally marginal Deaf students shift their attitudes and beliefs between the deaf and hearing worlds; their relationship is both to deaf and hearing worlds. Third, immersion identity focuses on only the Deaf-only world. Fourth, bicultural deaf people have accepted their Deaf pride into both Deaf and hearing world. The DIDS was developed in both English and ASL to measure Deaf cultural identity. I consider myself a bicultural Deaf person because I can navigate in both worlds as long there is no oppression or communication barriers. Smith (1996) states that practitioners and students can have communication gaps due to varying backgrounds such as racial, ethnic or social groups, and the lack of knowledge about differences and similarities in identity development where one's social group identity impacts interaction. If Deaf students are not comfortable with their identity, how can they focus on their academics if student affairs practitioners do not know the stages of Deaf Identity Development?

Deaf people do not consider themselves disabled (Lane, 1992). Now over twenty years old, the Americans with Disabilities Act (ADA) mandates that public places provide equal access by providing accommodations. For example, if a Deaf student wants to interview for a job on campus and he or she requests ASL interpreters, the institution must provide the accommodation. Though colleges and universities have centers for people with disabilities to provide accommodations, Deaf students might not feel comfortable walking into an office that has labeled them a "student with a disability." Some Deaf people view the word "disability" as having a negative connotation. Interviewed during the 1988 'Deaf President Now' protest, a student observed that "[t]here is more of an ethnic difference than a handicap difference between us and hearing people" (Lane, xii).

Lane (1992) elaborated that having an identity comes from social norms. It is important that there is correct amount of critical mass of Deaf faculty, Deaf staff, and Deaf students on campus for the development of identity. Collegiate Deaf Studies programs (Lane, 1992) often have Deaf faculty members, Deaf staff, and Deaf students and Hearing students who know ASL for social norms. Only a few universities have an undergraduate Deaf Studies major: Utah Valley University; California State University, Northridge; California State University, Sacramento; Gallaudet University; and Lamar University. "Deaf Studies in the United States was born out of a movement in the 1960s and 1970s when linguistic scholars struggled to prove that ASL is a language and that Deaf people have culture, history, and educational practices that are important to learn about" (Myers and Fernades, p. 30). Some Deaf Studies courses offered at these universities include "American Deaf Culture," "Deaf History," "ASL/English Interpreting," "ASL Literature," "Pre-Deaf Education," "Deaf Community Services," and "Deaf Cultural Studies."

Of course, American Sign Language classes are part of the curriculum of these programs. ASL is connected to Deaf student's development and identity. ASL is a spatial language and is similar to spoken languages in that it has its own phonology, morphology, semantics, syntax, and pragmatics (Lane, 1992). ASL is an important sociocultural study of Deaf people (Senghas & Monaghan, 2002). ASL plays an important role in access and interaction on campuses not only for Deaf students but for Hearing students as well. This makes campuses more linguistically accessible. "Spanish, French, and German lead as the three most studied languages, followed by American Sign Language (ASL), fourth ... since 2006" (Furman, Goldberg, & Lusin, 2010, 3). ASL is recognized as a foreign language in many universities and colleges (including my institution, The University of Utah) and can be used as foreign language credit as part of an institution's general education requirements. Some ASL and Deaf studies teachers are required to be members of American Sign Language Teachers Association (ASLTA). This organization has its own membership requirements, professional development, and workshop series.

Critical Race Theory
Critical Race Theory (CRT) (Yosso, 2002) is an application of critical theory, which provides analysis of race, law, and power. CRT views education as a tool to eliminate all forms of subordination and empowers underrepresented groups to help change society. Also, one of the CRT tenets focuses on curriculum with a focus on the commitment to social justice to omit oppression like that from audists, as well as empowering Deaf students (Solórzano, 1997, 1998). Critical Race Theory discusses different lenses of cultural capital; Yosso (2005) explained that capital is obtained from cultural wealth, upon which I elaborate in this section. Cultural wealth is aspirational, cultural, navigational, social, linguistic, resistant, and familial and focuses on elements that help people understand culture meaning (culture, knowledge, skills, abilities, and contacts with marginalized groups). By using CRT, I wanted to examine if Deaf students have cultural capital in educational institutions and in the community.

- *Aspirational capital* means one is capable to have hope for the future with the realization that there will be stumbling blocks. Deaf students value the Deaf community because Deaf leaders give back to their community. Deaf adults are role models to Deaf children (Lane, 1992) and Deaf students. Deaf children and students learn how to navigate in the world from Deaf adults.
- *Navigational capital* informs how Deaf people navigate in the world. Deaf students who see Deaf adults complete their education and hold jobs in a Deaf, hearing, or bi-cultural environment help them develop

aspirational capital. Gallaudet University has a far-reaching impact on
the Deaf population because of its rich history, future, community, and
legacy; Deaf students could often be considered as having familial capital. The needs and demographics of college students have changed but
most universities and colleges are still set up for White students to succeed (Taylor, 2000). Institutions need to be considerate of cultural capitals available to Deaf students who are a linguistic minority group. In
my classes, my cohort evolved to learn about Deaf culture, how to use
the interpreter, and how to communicate with me. Milem, Chang, and
Antonio (2005) posit that if universities are inclusive and make space
more friendly to diverse populations, it will benefit the entire institutional community.

- *Linguistic capital* overlaps with other types of cultural capital. For
  example, Deaf students can communicate with each other through
  ASL without any communication barriers or through ASL interpreters when communicating with Hearing people. For instance, my parents learned American Sign Language to communicate with me, and I
  had Deaf adult role models at the residential school I attended. I was in
  a Deaf space most of my younger years. Deaf space is where Deaf students meet. I noticed that my self-esteem is higher when I have more
  access to cultural capitals. In a classroom environment with more people who know ASL, I feel more comfortable to talk. Yosso et al. (2006)
  mentioned the American Council on Education (ACE) and talked
  about white space but not Deaf space on campuses. Institutions must
  consider deaf space as a way for Deaf students to feel more comfortable, explore culture, and use ASL on campuses, which could help with
  retention. Senghas and Monoghan mentioned that there has been a
  long history of Deaf place, i.e. clubs (2002, p.79). During my employment at the Center for Disabilities office, I meet with Deaf students
  and often they expressed loneliness, the need for other Deaf students
  to socialize with, frustration with hearing professors, and the reality of
  Deaf-friendly campus. I recall few students who would just stop by regularly to chat with me pretty much about anything.
- *Resistant capital* is a measure of the ability to cope any difficult situations. Students who have resistant capital are more likely to cope with
  audism. Then, familial capital means common knowledge with shared
  culture. Deaf students whose parents are Hearing will learn Hearing
  culture from their Hearing parents. On the other hand, if Deaf students are bicultural, they will have both Deaf and Hearing, which creates two families.
- *Cultural capital* stems from cultural wealth acquired within the com-

munity; Deaf people develop their Deaf identity from interacting with other Deaf people, despite the fact that nine out of ten deaf children have hearing parents (Woodcock, Rohan, & Cambell, 2007; Lane, 1992; Glickman, 1993). Deaf students as a linguistic minority group share common a language and culture, and Deaf role models are found in the Deaf community. Nine out of ten people in the American Deaf community, for example, marry other Deaf people (Lane, 1992).

Within the framework of Deaf Identity Development and CRT, education is a way to minimize oppression and empower people with knowledge about their actions. If Hearing people do not have experiences of working with Deaf Students or knowledge about Deaf people, they are likely to become audist. Smith et al. (2006) discussed that people of color, faculty and students alike, often have lower self-esteem and social withdrawal. A faculty member of color stated that there is a need to be cognizant of the needs and interests of minorities, acknowledgment of racism (and I add audism), eliminate inequality of sexism, (and I add, not put Deaf under disability) (Anonymous, personal communication, November, 2011). Also, I refer to audism as a form of a racist psychological disorder that must be minimized. Student affairs practitioners need to be aware of emotions caused by audism and be prepared to provide coping strategies to Deaf students.

In examining communication between Deaf and Hearing people, it is helpful to study stages in the development of a supervisory relationship: induction, acclimation, application, and closure (Cooper, Saunders, Winston Jr., Hirt, Creamer, & Janosik, 2002). However, I felt it could also apply to the internship stages of Deaf students when they first meet their Hearing teacher, students, peers, boss, or colleagues. *Induction* refers to becoming acquainted with the environment that an intern (or student) must experience acclimation. *Acclimation* means knowing the way around the environment; in application this means understanding the history of the site, knowing participants' personalities, and seeing the site's weaknesses and strengths. These stages help us to overcome any fears including communication barriers which affect relationship focus on relationship. *Closure* refers to knowing what needs to be learned in terms of a relationship and self (Cooper, Saunders, Winston Jr., Hirt, Creamer, & Janosik, 2002).

Again with CRT, Yosso (2002) recommended that people should broadly educated about intercultural interactions including with Deaf students as a linguistic minority group. In the community, organizations provide services and advocate for civil rights for minority groups like the Deaf population. The National Association for the Deaf (NAD) is "the nation's premier civil rights organization of, by and for deaf and hard of hearing individuals in the United States of America" (www.nad.org), advocates for Deaf people's rights for communication access, equal services, and most states have their own associations to focus on access and equal rights.

Retention

Deaf students have roughly seventy percent drop-out rates (Boutin, 2008; Bowe, 2003; Lang, 1992). There are several reasons why graduation rates are low, and practitioners need to be aware so student affairs practitioners can improve programs and services to help Deaf students succeed. I discovered that a major factor contributing to a student's persistence is faculty aware-ness of the needs of Deaf students (Boutin, 2008). Awareness and action are powerful and greatly impact the success of Deaf students. Tinto (1993) says students develop social and intellectual coping skills to persist by socializing with faculty, students, and staff. In my classes, I found myself more comfort-able with Hearing people of color than Hearing white students and felt like I had to work harder to be accepted by white Hearing students. I felt comfort-able identifying myself with a 'minority group,' which included students of color. One time, a student of color and I discussed the graduation rates for our respective populations and how the issues were very similar. At the end of the last day of class, this student — my new colleague — and I parted with a hug; I felt that she understood my population in some ways. I will never forget that precious moment.

Woodcock et al. (2007) discussed fundamental barriers in getting qual-ifications. They examined Deaf students from undergraduate to doctoral level using ASL interpreters or CART (Court Aided Real Time) typed ser-vices, which provides speech to text format. Communication obstacles usu-ally increase from undergraduate to doctoral-level programs with the quality of interpreters or CART who are familiar with the context of the program in which Deaf students are enrolled. Students must also find practitio-ners who do not have negative attitudes toward deafness (Woodcock et al., 2007). Deaf students learn that it requires extra preparation time in graduate school in order to master the technical language and jargon of the field. I try to get the same interpreters for my classes because they are already familiar as the context builds up from class to class throughout the program. I often have to prepare my presentation with the interpreters to make sure we are on the same page how to say it from American Sign Language to English. It takes extra time and preparation.

When Deaf students overcome obstacles and graduate, usually more obstacles are in store for them when it comes to finding employment in their field. They must convince employers of their qualifications and their abil-ity to do the job (Woodcock et al., 2007). This indicates that Deaf students do experience fatigue, audism, and barriers not only in Hearing educational settings but in Hearing workplace settings. I experience fatigue, audism, and barriers in the work environment, and I have to educate employees to reduce them. I recall I had to remind my former boss (who knows how to sign) to actually *sign* when I was in the room. At times, it can be annoying. For jobs, I have had to explain to a prospective employer how to communicate with me and that I am quite capable of completing job-related tasks.

Deaf students who graduate with doctoral degrees and apply for faculty positions in departments other than ASL need to request ASL interpreters through the Human Resource office. Human Resource offices may or may not be aware of the cost of ASL interpreters and it is possible for employers not to provide accommodations if the cost is an "undue" or "unjustifiable" hardship (Woodcock et al., 2007). When Dr. I. King Jordan, the first deaf president of Gallaudet University, spoke to university presidents in an address, he received a compliment from his counterpart not on the content of his presentation but on how well he enunciated his words. Overall, institutions need to prepare Deaf students graduate for when they may face fatigue, audism, and barriers.

The more student affairs practitioners are familiar with ASL, the greater the impact to the campus diversity climate. Hurtado et al. (1998) and Loo and Rolison (1986) concluded that sufficient racial/ethnic enrollments can give potential recruits the impression that the campus is hospitable: "No matter how outstanding the academic institution, ethnic minority students can feel alienated if their ethnic representation on campus is small" (p. 72). Hurtado et al. (1998) mentioned that those institutions wanting to diversify the campus climate will aim at increasing ethnic and racial student ratios; similarly, campuses which increase Deaf student populations in primarily Hearing institutions will also help in diversification efforts. Student affairs practitioners who make campuses more Deaf-friendly environments will be helpful. They can do this by making an effort to have more people know ASL, or by creating a Deaf Studies program, adding more Deaf students on campus, creating deaf-friendly spaces, and conducting workshops about audism.

At primarily Hearing institutions, Nichols and Quaye posit that if someone has some type of disability that is visual, people really do not know how to approach or talk to the person (Harper et al., 2009). Accommodation(s) from a campus Center for Disability Services can help some of the communication barriers where an ASL/English interpreter can facilitate communication for both Deaf and Hearing students. However, at hearing institutions, it will not always be completely accessible for Deaf students, they have to request ASL interpreters, and ASL interpreters cannot be with Deaf students all day in every setting.

Lang (1992) says that factors of persistence are academic preparation, challenges of learning through support services, leave of absence, program lengths, difficulty in carrying full loads, dissatisfaction with social life, and changes in major, to which Boutin (2008) adds communication skills. "Support services" in this instance mean interpreters. Hearing students who do not have disabilities will not have to deal with support services, but it is an additional item on the plate of Deaf students during college.

For college settings, Senghas & Monaghan (2002) say that language barriers make it difficult for Deaf students to communicate when interacting with hearing students and professors. My support system was the key to persistence in the ELP program. I had to cope with and use what I had (ASL interpreters), even though I talked to them a lot before or after class. I would talk to a professor if I felt I needed to as long I was comfortable. I had a colleague who told me:

> Be persistent when there are things you don't understand, ask and keep asking until you get it. I know that might seem obnoxious but the reality of it is that this is your education and you have to take charge. Also, I'd say don't be overly critical of yourself. It's so easy to get down on yourself but resist that temptation—you're a superstar and don't let anybody tell you differently!

I printed out this advice and put it by my computer to look it at often. My colleagues would check on me to see how I was doing; I am thankful to my fellow students who shared their notes with me; as deaf students know, it is difficult to take notes and watch interpreters at the same time.

Weidman (1989) mentions that one factor for persistence is association with faculty members who can influence students' educational goals. I am thankful for my support system of faculty members in the ELP program who took the time to guide me through classes. I was able to persist and finish the program because of ELP program faculty who took the time to talk to me and advise me whenever I asked. I recall one faculty member told me, "Invite me to your graduation." It made me feel cared for because of the professional relationship that we fostered together.

ELP faculty members often are members of organization(s) that promote contined learning in their respective fields. Likewise, the Deaf Studies *Today!* conference at Utah Valley University focuses on the exchange of information about relevant issues in the Deaf community. The conference is also an important Deaf space where Deaf people meet to create, renew, and maintain relationships. Second, the Convention of American Instructors (CAI) of the Deaf is a conference for not just for teachers, educational interpreters, but counselors or other professionals who work with deaf and hard of hearing students. The Southwest College Institute for the Deaf (SWID) and the National Technical Institute for the Deaf (NTID) are two higher education institutions that sponsor the CAI conference. Third, the Center for ASL/English Bilingual Education and Research (CaSEBER) has a mission to provide a bilingual professional development service that fosters informed educational mentorship and leadership, as well as provide collaborative opportunities for educators that implement and administer ASL/English bilingual professional development utilizing school-based language planning strategies. Practitioners and faculties should take advantage and attend these conferences to learn more about the Deaf population.

On the other hand, the National Association of Student Personnel Administrators (NASPA) mission statement states, "To be the principal source for leadership, scholarship, professional development, and advocacy for student affairs." NASPA has 12,000 student affairs professionals who oversee knowledge communities — Asian Pacific Islander concerns, gay, lesbian, bisexual and transgender issues, disability, and others — but none for the Deaf population. NASPA groups Deaf students within the community of those with disabilities, but Deaf students should be considered separate in student development. Practitioners and higher education programs must recognize Deaf populations as a linguistic minority group with a distinct language and culture (Lane, 1992).

IMPLICATIONS FOR PRACTITIONERS

If the Educational, Leadership, and Policy program and professional associations discuss Deaf students and apply best practices, it could impact Deaf students' retention rates. Below are recommendations based on personal experience, classwork, and a review of relevant literature:

- There is a lack of discussion about Deaf Identity Development (Glickman, 1993) and Deaf space for Deaf students (Bowe, 2003, Lane, 1992) in the both ELP program and higher education. Students come from communities to higher education and they need to feel at home on campus; I suggest institutions set up Deaf spaces (Senghas and Monoghan, 2002) where Deaf students can socialize in ASL and Hearing people who are learning or know ASL are welcome to come. Deaf spaces show people that Deaf students are a linguistic minority group where they can share their Deaf culture with other people and not be viewed as a disability group. Deaf students will feel more confident about themselves and their identity as a group.
- The statistics of race and ethnicity from the American Council of Education and NASPA has no information regarding Deaf students. NASPA is mentioned earlier and the American Council on Education

(ACE), founded in 1918 as an organization that focuses on higher education should support Deaf student populations. ACE and its member institutions serve eighty percent of today's college students; while
it has some dated information about students with disabilities, Latino
students,and other race minority groups. Deaf students should be also
considered part of the 'minority groups.' ACE should add Deaf students as a linguistic minority group in their statistics.

- There is a need for student affairs graduate programs to examine how
  they prepare future practitioners to be aware of the best practices that
  meet the needs of Deaf students. Deaf Identity Development, American Sign Language, Deaf culture, Audism, Cultural capital, Deaf space,
  and retention rates should be also be discussed.

- Institutions should monitor Deaf student retention and graduation
  rates since their national level graduation and retention rates have been
  historically lower than their Hearing peers (Boutin, 2008, Bowe, 2003,
  Lang, 1992). Institutions need to identify issues impacting graduation
  and retention rates and then develop programs for more positive outcomes (Reason, 2009, Tinto, 1993). There is a need for research regarding the statistics of low graduation rates for Deaf students.

- Institutions need to consider the capital value of Deaf Studies programs (Fernades & Myers, 2010) to enhance their university's diversity
  climate (Milem, Chang and Antonio, 2005). The more people know
  ASL, the more of a welcoming environment is created for Deaf students. Academic and student affairs practitioners can work together
  to justify the need for Deaf Studies program on campus, just like any
  other ethnic studies programs.

- Student affairs practitioners need to prepare Deaf students to graduate.
  Career services practitioners need to be aware of Deaf students' needs
  by attending workshops like Deaf Studies *Today!* and by partnering
  with their campus disability offices.

CONCLUSION

Student affairs practitioners need to be aware of the needs of Deaf Students
in higher education. Deaf students should not be ignored. Deaf students are
a linguistic minority group and they need different types of cultural capital
on campuses because a feeling of belonging is the key to persistence (Weidman, 1989). Deaf students are at high risk for persistence, yet there is no
data regarding retention rates from mainstream institutions. Accountability
is needed. Student affairs practitioners must be aware of stages in relationship, Deaf students' identity development, communication barriers in social

and academic settings, audism, Deaf space, and create cultural wealth community on campuses for Deaf students which can impact their retention and graduation rates. Again, as a linguistic minority group, language is the primary difference between Hearing and Deaf students. In the meantime, organizations and conferences can serve as a tool for practitioners' in bettering the educational environment of Deaf students.

REFERENCES

African Proverb. (n.d.). Quotes.net. Retrieved February 26, 2012, from http://www.quotes.net/quote/6994.

American Council on Education. Retrieved February 26, 2012, www.acenet.edu.

American Sign Language Teacher Association. Retrieved March 8, 2012, www.aslta.org.

Association for the Study of Higher Education Reader. Retrieved February 26, 201, www.asher.org

Association on Higher Education and Disability. Retrieved February 26, 2012, www.ahead.org

Bauman H-Dirksen, L. (2004). Audism: Exploring the Metaphysics of Oppression. *Journal of Deaf Studies and Deaf Education*, 9(2):239–246 doi: 10.1093/deafed/enh025.

Boutin, D.L. (2008). Persistence in Postsecondary Environments of Students with Hearing Impairments. *Journal of Rehabilitation*, 74(1) 25–31.

Bowe, F. (2003). Transition for deaf and hard of hearing students: a blueprint for change. *Journal of Deaf Studies and Deaf Education*, 8(4), 485–493. doi: 10.1093/deafed/eng024

California State University of Northridge. Retrieved March 8, 2012, www.csun.edu.

Cooper, D. L., Saunders, S. L., Winston Jr., R. B., Hirt, J. B.;, Creamer, D. G., & Janosik, S. M. (2002). *Learning Through Supervised Practice in Student Affairs*. New York, NY: Taylor & Francis Group.

Delgado, R. & Stefancic, J. (2001). *Critical Race Theory: An introduction*. New York: New York University Press.

Evans, K. J., Forney, D. S., Guido, F. M., Patton, L. D., & Renn, K. A. A. (2009). *Student Development in College: Theory, Research, and Practice, 2nd edition*. San Francisco, CA: Jossey-Bass.

Fernandes, J. K. & Myers, S. S. (2010). Deaf studies: A critique of the predominant U.S. theoretical direction. *Journal of Deaf Studies and Deaf Education*, 15(1), 30–49.

Furman, N., Goldberg, D., & Lusin, N. (2010). Enrollments in Languages Other Than English in United States Institutions of Higher Education, Fall 2009. *The Modern Language Association of America*. Retrieved from http://www.mla.org.

Gallaudet University. Retrieved March 8, 2012, www.gallaudet.edu.

Glickman, Niel S. (1993). Deaf Identity Development: Construction and validation of a theoretical model. Unpublished doctoral dissertation, University of Massachusetts, Amherst.

Harper, S. R., Quaye, J. S., Bensimon, M. E., Kuh, D. G. (2009). *Student engagement in higher education: theoretical perspectives and practical approaches for diverse populations*. New York, NY: Taylor & Francis.

Hurtado, S., Milem, J. F., Clayton-Pedersen, A. R., and Allen, W. R. (1998). Enhancing campus climates for racial/ethnic diversity: Educational policy and practice. *The Review of Higher Education*, 21(3), 279–302.

Lane, H. (1992). *The mask of benevolence: Disabling the deaf community*. New York: Alfred Knopf.

Milem, J. F., Chang, M. J., & Antonio, A. L. (2005). *Making diversity work on campus: A research-based perspective*. Washington, DC: Association of American Colleges and Universities.

National Association for the Deaf. Retrieved February 26, 2012, www.nad.org.

National Technology Institute for the Deaf, Rochester Institute of Technology. Retrieved March 8, 2012, www.ntid.rit.edu

NASPA Student Affairs Professionals in Higher Education. Retrieved February 26, 2012, www.naspa.org

Nichols, A. H., & Quaye, S. J. (2009). Beyond accommodation: Removing barriers to academic and social engagement for students with disabilities. In S. R. Harper & S. J. Quaye (Eds.), *Student engagement in higher education: Theoretical perspectives and practical approaches for diverse populations* (pp. 39–60). New York, NY: Routledge.

Pope, R. L., Reynolds, A. L., Mueller, J. A., Cheatham, H.E . (2004). *Multicultural competence in student affairs*. San Francisco, CA: Wiley, John & Sons, Inc.

Postsecondary Education Programs Network. Retrieved February 26, 2012, www.pepnet.org.

Reason, R.D. (2009). An examination of persistence research through the lens of a comprehensive conceptual framework. *Journal of College Student Development*, 50(60), 659-682.

Rochester Institute of Technology: National Technical Institute for the Deaf. www.ntid.rit.edu.

Senghas, R. J. & Monaghan, L. (2002). Signs of their times: deaf communities andculture of language. *Annual Review of Anthropology*, (31) 69–97.

Smith, D. G. (2009). *In Diversity's promise for higher education: Making it work*. Baltimore: The John Hopkins University Press.

Smith, W.A., Yosso, T. J., & Solorzano, D.G. (2006). Challenging racial battle fatigue on historically white campuses: A critical race examination of race-related stress. In C. Stanley (Eds.), *Faculty of Color: Teaching in Predominately White Colleges and Universities* (pp. 299-327). Bolton, MA: Anker Publishing.

Solórzano, D., Ceja, M, & Yosso, T. (2000). Critical Race Theory, racial microaggressions, and campus racial climate: The Experiences of African American college students. *The Journal of Negro Education*, 69 (1/2), 60–73.

Solórzano, D. (1997). Images and words that wound: Critical race theory, racial stereotyping, and teacher education. *Teacher Education Quarterly*, 24(3), 5–19.

Solórzano, D. (1998). Critical race theory, racial and gender microaggressions, and the experiences of Chicana and Chicano scholars. *International Journal of Qualitative Studies in Education*, 11(1), 121–136.

Taylor, J. S. (2000, April, 4). Portrait in alienation: Native American Students on predominantly white campus. (Speeches/Meeting Papers). Retrieved from http://eric.ed.gov/ERICWebPortal/custom/portlets/recordDetails/detailmini.jsp?_nfpb=true&_&ERICExtSearch_SearchValue_0=ED478059&ERICExtSearch_SearchType_0=no&accno=ED478059

Tinto, V. (1993). *Leaving college: Rethinking the causes and cures of student attrition*. Chicago: University of Chicago.

Torres, V. (2010). Association of Higher Education Reader. www.asher.org.

University of Utah. (2012). Educational, Leadership, and Policy program. Retrieved from www.ed.utah.edu/elp/Programs/MED/HED/Student-Affairs-Program-Description2

Weidman, J.C. (1989). Undergraduate socialization: A conceptual approach. *Higher Education: A Handbook of Theory and Research*, (5) 289–322. New York: Agathon Press.

Woodcock, K., Rohan, M. J., & Cambell, L. (2007). Equitable representation of deaf students in mainstream academia. Why not? *Higher Education*. 53(3), 359–379.

Yosso, J. Tara. (2005). Whose culture has capital? A critical race theory discussion of community cultural wealth. *Race Ethnicity and Education*, 8(1), 69–91. doi: 10.1080/1361332052000341006.

A Case Study of Sign Language Endangerment: Ban Khor Sign Language

NOPPAWAN CHAINARONG, VEE YEE CHONG,
AND JENNIFER WITTEBORG

APPROXIMATELY EVERY TWO WEEKS A SPOKEN LANGUAGE DISAPPEARS (Nettle & Romaine, 2000) and in the twenty-first century, half of the current spoken language will have died out. What are the similarities for sign languages? Using Thailand's Ban Khor Sign Language (BKSL, ภาษามือ) as a case study, we will attempt to study what causes a sign language to fade out of recognition. While BKSL is not yet on the list of endangered sign languages, still the question remains who determines, and by what methods, a sign language to be endangered.

BISU

Bisu is a spoken language in Thailand that is fading out of use. It is an oral language with no written form and is on the list of endangered spoken languages. If a Bisu speaker marries someone who speaks Thai or if a group of people speaking Bisu is approached by a Thai speaker, everyone switches to Thai because of the higher social status of Thai. This status is detected because employment within the Bisu community is often not available. More jobs are found where Thai is used; the language policy of the Thai government requires schools, radio, and television to use Thai. The Bisu people, however, have developed a written system for Bisu. They wrote two books in 1998 and presented it to the royal family during a televised ceremony. More people then recognized the Bisu language and culture. The pride within the Bisu community for their language increased. Are there any similar increased awareness for signed languages? (Person 2005)

SIGN LANGUAGE ENDANGERMENT

Australian Sign Language (Auslan) and Danish Sign Language (DTS) are already in danger of dying out. The determining factors of these languages dying out will be discussed later in this paper. The World Federation of the Deaf-sponsored conference on endangered sign language in Norway in November 2011 opened discussions on this issue and other endangered sign languages (WFD, 2016) but there are no 'blueprints' for handling this issue.

VILLAGE SIGN LANGUAGE

"A village sign language arises in an existing, relatively insular community into which a number of deaf children are born" (Meir, Sandler, Padden & Aronoff, 2010). Because of the size and broad nature of their userbase, languages like American Sign language (ASL) are not considered village sign languages but in other smaller, insular communities, these languages arise from the need for and the subsequent invention of communication among Deaf and hearing people within a village. Village signs tend to last between seventy to hundreds of years. BKSL has been used in northeast rural Thailand for the last seventy years by both Deaf and hearing people who call it the "language of the mute" (Zeshan, 2007).

Zeshan and others continue to collect data on at least nine endangered or village sign languages: Adamorobe Sign Language (Adsal; Ghana), Algerian Jewish Sign Language (AJSL; Israel), Alipur Sign Language (APSL; India), Counory Signs/Konchri Sain (KS; Jamaica), Kata Kolok Signs (KK; Indonesia), Mardin Sign Language (MarSL; Turkey), signing varieties of Mali Sign Language (LaSIMa; Mali), Yolŋu/Yulgnu Sign Language (YSL; Australia), and Yucatec Mayan Sign Language (YMMSL; Mexico) (http://www.uclan.ac.uk/research/explore/projects/endangered_sign_languages_village_communities.php and http://www.uclan.ac.uk/research/explore/projects/sign_languages_in_unesco_atlas_of_world_languages_in_danger.php).

VERIFYING SOURCES OF INFORMATION

Our colleague, Mr. Chong, is familiar with Kata Kolok and disagrees with its inclusion on the list. So the questions "who decides what sign languages are endangered" and "how are these conclusions reached?" must be explored. Ethnologue.com also lists Malaysian Sign Language (BIM) as endangered, but Mr. Chong (from Malaysia) also definitely knows this is inaccurate.

THE SIGNED LANGUAGE USED BY DEAF THAI

Nonaka (2004), Hulburt (2009), and the National Association of the Deaf Thailand have identified that several regional areas in Thailand use different signed languages:

- Ban Khor: Ban Khor village in Nakorn Phanom Province in northeast Thailand has a large group of deaf and their hearing relatives who use this village sign language
- Pla Pak: Meaning "red fish," Pla Pak is a village with many deaf who have their own sign language.
- Bangkok: Old Bangkok Sign Language is also another older sign language of Thailand. American Sign Language also influences Bangkok sign language
- Hat Yai: in the southern region of Thailand
- Chiang Mai: older signers in this area were seen using Original Chiang Mai Sign Language. Today, there is no active use of Chiang Mai and Hat Yai sign languages

BACKGROUND OF BAN KHOR SIGN LANGUAGE

Although considered as a national sign language, BKSL is typically restricted to small village usage. The positive attitudes toward Deaf people and sign language influence the use of the local sign language among hearing people in the community and allos for full integration of Deaf people into the village society. BKSL developed approximately sixty to eighty years ago as a local sign language but survived after change in the population and as increasing occupational and educational differences among villagers elevated the status and influence of Thai Sign Language. Most people in government and schools did not know about BKSL because it was indigenous, endangered, and undocumented. Economically, the village struggles to make a living by farming and selling produce and handmade items. The estimated number of BKSL users is about 1,000 (Nanoka, 2004).

POSSIBLE FACTORS FOR THE DECLINE
OF VILLAGE SIGN LANGUAGES

The world has become increasingly accessible to travelers. Technology is becoming widely available and meetings between different cultures results in influencing people one way or the other. Sometimes languages haven't developed academic signs and so they are borrowed from other sign languages that meet these needs.

A BRIEF HISTORY OF SIGNED LANGUAGE OF THAILAND

In earlier histories of Thailand, of 300,000 all and late-deafened individuals, approximately 65,000 were identified as 'deaf' or 'pre-lingual deaf' (Nonaka, 2004). By the 1950s, American-trained Thai educators offered to mix American Sign Language (ASL) with two older signed languages into deaf schools. Thai Sign Language is related to American Sign Language, Old Bangkok Sign Language, and Old Chiang Mai Sign Language because of language contact and borrowing. By 1951 the Sethsian School for the Deaf was founded by Mrs. Krairerk, a Gallaudet College graduate, who had returned to Bangkok after graduation and began to teach a class of twelve deaf children.

The Sethsian School for the Deaf in Bangkok in 1953 (left) and 1955 (right).

THAI SIGN LANGUAGE (THSL)

Old Bangkok Sign Language and Old Chiang Mai Sign Language are now only used by few signers over the age of forty-five. Thai Sign Language (ThSL; ภาษามือไทย) developed in market towns and urban areas, places where deaf people had opportunity to meet and interact. A ThSL dictionary, published in 1990, gave it recognition as the native sign language and the primary means for communication and instruction among Deaf Thailanders, and in 1999, Thai government formally recognized ThSL as a national language.

THE INFLUENCE OF AMERICAN SIGN LANGUAGE

Many countries use elements or signs of ASL: Barbados, Benin, Bolivia, Burkina Faso, Canada, Central African Republic, Chad, China, Côte d'Ivoire, Democratic Republic of the Congo, Gabon, Ghana, Jamaica, Kenya, Madagascar, Mauritania, Nigeria, Philippines, Singapore, Togo, and Zimbabwe. While sharing of languages cannot be prohibited, care needs to be exercised that other indigenous languages — no matter how small their impact may be — are preserved. Prestige with ASL is increased because its distribution comes from a Deaf university with a Deaf president, whereas Deaf in many other countries in the world are not even allowed to drive.

FACTORS OF LANGUAGE ENDANGERMENT

Some governments encourage medical intervention policy of cochlear implantation (CI) to 'fix' Deaf people, claiming that it saves money and preserves a social phonocentric value.

WHY PRESERVE VILLAGE SIGN LANGUAGE?

"Language diversity is essential to the human heritage. Each and every language embodies the unique cultural wisdom of a people. The loss of any language is thus a loss for all humanity" (UNESCO, 2003). Languages enrich each other (sign borrowing), encourage cognitive science (help illuminate how the brain fuctions and how we learn), uncover sources of evidence for understanding human history, and promote an appreciation of other cultures and people. This study has generated additional questions:

- Who determines which language is endangered?
- Who is determining which language survives? Who chose ThSL over BKSL or Chang Mai Sign Language? Who should be involved?
- Does national government recognition always mean that language is secure?
- How does a language become revitalized? Is there a way to set up an international blueprint for preservation of village sign languages such as BKSL?

REFERENCES:

Christian, D. (1988). Language planning: The view from linguistics. In Frederick J. Newmeyer (ed.) *Linguistics: The Cambridge Survey: Vol. 4, Language: The socio-cultural context.* Cambridge: Cambridge University Press, pp. 193–209.

Crystal, D. (2000). *Language Death.* Cambridge: Cambridge University Press.

Hurlbut, H. M. (2009). *Thai signed languages survey: A rapid appraisal.* SIL International.

Nonaka, A.M. (2004). *The forgotten endangered language: Lessons on the importance of remembering from Thailand's Ban Khor Sign Language.* Los Angeles, University of California.

Mathur, G. & Napoli, D. J. (2011). *Deaf around the world: The impact of language.* New York, Oxford University Press.

Meir, I., Sandler, W., Padden, C., Aronoff, M., (2010). Emerging Sign Languages. In Marc Marschark and Patricia E. Spencer (eds.). *The Oxford Handbook of Deaf Studies, Language, and Education.* Vol. 2, p. 267–280.

Murray, J. J. (2016). Conference summary: Sign languages as endangered languages. Retrieved from https://wfdeaf.org/news/conference-summary-sign-languages-as-endangered-languages.

Nettle, D., Romaine, S. (2000). *Vanishing Voices: The Extinction of the World's Languages.* Cambridge: Oxford University Press.

Person, K. R. (2005). Language revitalization or dying gasp? Language preservation efforts among the Bisu of Northern Thailand. *International Journal of Social Languages* 173, pp. 117–141.

Vail, P. (2006). Can a language of a million speakers be endangered? Language shift and apathy among Northern Khmer speakers in Thailand. In Nancy C. Dorian Small Languages and Small Communities 50 (ed), *International Journal of Social Languages* 178, pp. 135–147.

UNESCO Ad Hoc Expert Group on Endangered Languages (2003). Document submitted to the International Expert Meeting on UNESCO Programme Safeguarding of Endangered Languages, Paris, 10–12 March 2003. Retrieved from http://www.unesco.org/new/fileadmin/MULTIMEDIA/HQ/CLT/pdf/Language_vitality_and_endangerment_EN.pdf

Zeshan, U. (2007). The Ethics of Documenting Sign Languages in Village Communities. In Peter K. Austin, Oliver Bond & David Nathan (eds.) *Proceedings of Conference on Language Documentation and Linguistic Theory.* London: SOAS. www.hrelp.org/eprint/Idlt_31.pdf

www.uclan.ac.uk/schools/journalism_media_communication/islands/villagesign/index.php

http://www.utexas.edu/cola/public-affairs/media/video.php

http://www.jdcc.org/jewish-deaf-tidbits/documentation-of-algerian-jewish-sign-language

http://www.handspeak.com/byte/a/index.php?byte=adamorobe

http://elar.soas.ac.uk/deposit/panda2012avsl

www.ingramcontent.com/pod-product-compliance
Lightning Source LLC
Chambersburg PA
CBHW072123270326
41931CB00010B/1652